CHINESE AND JI
ENCOUNTERS BETWEEN

CHINESE
AND
JEWS
ENCOUNTERS BETWEEN CULTURES

中
華
與
猶
太

IRENE EBER
Hebrew University of Jerusalem

VALLENTINE MITCHELL
LONDON • PORTLAND, OR

First published in 2008 by Vallentine Mitchell

Suite 314, Premier House,   920 NE 58th Avenue, Suite 300
112–114 Station Road,   Portland, Oregon,
Edgware, Middlesex HA8 7BJ   97213-3786

www.vmbooks.com

Copyright © 2008 Irene Eber

British Library Cataloguing in Publication Data:
A catalogue record for this book has been applied for

ISBN 978 0 85303 673 9 (cloth)
ISBN 978 0 85303 674 6 (paper)

Library of Congress Cataloging-in-Publication Data
A catalog record has been applied for

This book has been published with a financial subsidy from the European University Institute.

All rights reserved. No part of this publication may be reproduced, stored in or introduced into a retrieval system, or transmitted, in any form or by any means, electronic, mechanical, photocopying, recording or otherwise without the prior written permission of the publisher of this book.

Printed by Biddles Ltd, King's Lynn, Norfolk

*In Memory of Hyman Smith
who loved life*

Contents

Acknowledgments	ix
Introduction	xi

PART I: HISTORY

1.	Jewish Communities in China: A Brief Overview	3
2.	Kaifeng Jews: Sinification and the Persistence of Identity	22
3.	Destination Shanghai, Permits and Transit Visas, 1938–1941	39

PART II: OLD TESTAMENT

4.	Translating the Ancestors: S.I.J. Schereschewsky's 1875 Chinese Version of Genesis	67
5.	Several Psalms in Chinese Translation	89
6.	Notes on the Early Reception of the Old Testament	109

PART III: LITERATURE

7.	Translation Literature in Modern China: The Yiddish Author and his Tale	123
8.	Martin Buber and Daoism	148

Transliteration of Names and Terms	170
Select Bibliography	180
Index	182

Acknowledgements

Research for these essays, and their editing was partially supported by the Louis Frieberg Research Fund. I must also thank the Harry S. Truman Research Institute for the Advancement of Peace of the Hebrew University of Jerusalem for its partial support. The help of the staff of the libraries and archives I mainly used is gratefully acknowledged. They are: the Harvard-Yenching Library and the Judaica Division of the Widener Library, Harvard University; the National and University Library of the Hebrew University and the Buber and Ravitch Archives housed there; the Archives of the Episcopal Church USA in Austin, Texas.

Over the years, while writing these essays, I was hospitably welcomed as Visiting Scholar either during sabbatical leaves or summer breaks at the John K. Fairbank Center of East Asian Research and the Center for the Study of World Religions, both at Harvard University. Revision of the essays was begun in 1996–97, while I was Judson Visiting Professor at the Andover Newton Theological School. I am grateful for having had the opportunity to spend the year on the Theological School's beautiful and tranquil campus.

I owe a special debt of gratitude to friends and colleagues here and abroad. Professor Steven Kaplan of the Hebrew University was the one who suggested collecting these essays in book form and Professor Raphael Israeli and Dr. Salomon Wald suggested their publication in English in addition to the Hebrew version. Their comments on the unrevised text of these essays were invaluable. Professor Lauren Pfister of the Hong Kong Baptist University also read several unrevised essays and gave me his much appreciated comments. For Joan Hill's expert bibliographical research at various stages of writing I am no less grateful than for the friendship that grew with each visit to Cambridge. Special thanks are due Dr. Uri Melammed whose help with biblical materials was indispensable. Dr. Shalom Eilati read portions of the Hebrew manuscript and his thoughtful suggestions for improving the text were deeply appreciated. Professor Avraham Altman's wise counsel and minute attention to detail saved me from several careless errors. Dr. Lihy Yariv-Laor read the Hebrew text in its entirety. For her constructive comments and critical eye, in addition to her encouragement and support, I am more grateful than I can express. Orit Wertheim, friend of many years and tireless champion of matters Chinese for the Hebrew reader, has my deepest respect and admiration. Were it not for her support and constant effort, the Hebrew project would not have seen completion. Finally, I must thank Lisa Hyde, whose editorial judgement on many matters pertaining to these essays I deeply value.

IRENE EBER
August 2007

Introduction

Traces of the Jewish-Chinese encounter still remain from days bygone on China's physical and intellectual landscape. They remain on the inscribed stele in Kaifeng, as stars of David on buildings in Harbin, as buildings or synagogues, now converted to other uses, in Tianjin and Shanghai. The Central European refugees are long gone from Shanghai's section of Hongkou, but old-time residents can still point to this or that shop, this or that humble building, where the refugees once lived and tried to make a living. Nor have the grand edifices entirely vanished where Shanghai's wealthy Sephardim (the Baghdadi Jews) had made their homes.

In Chinese literary magazines, which have long since ceased publication, we find stories by Shalom Aleichem, I.L. Peretz, Sholem Asch, and many other writers, whose Yiddish works in Chinese translation were once avidly read by Chinese intellectuals. Traces of the Yiddish literary tradition continue in reprinted editions of Sholem Aleichem's works. The translation of the Old Testament from Hebrew into spoken Chinese was a major Jewish-Chinese encounter by introducing both religiously motivated or simply interested Chinese readers to the history of Israel. Once the Old Testament became widely available, literate Chinese began to ask questions about this curious people – the Jews – who, without a country of their own and dispersed among the nations, persecuted and maligned, clung nonetheless tenaciously to their faith and identity as a people.

The essays collected in this volume on the Jewish–Chinese encounter are not intended to be a coherent history.[1] Written over many years, they attempt to do no more than to illustrate several moments in Chinese and Jewish history when both peoples met one another, either physically or by means of a written text. Today, when we can freely travel to China, when we delight in greeting Chinese visitors here, when we have unlimited access to Chinese books and newspapers, these encounters seem perhaps unremarkable. Yet, sixty or more than one hundred years ago, the time that these essays deal with, neither were China journeys easily undertaken, nor was Chinese reading matter readily available. The first seven essays discuss the several kinds of imprint Jews have left in China. The eighth, however, deals with the reverse process: Martin Buber's interest in and response to the ideas of philosophical Daoism. The inclusion of this essay is meant to indicate, even if in a most fragmentary and minute way, that the Jewish–Chinese encounter was not only a one-way road. Let me briefly take up this topic in the following.

Europe's fascination with China and things Chinese slowly developed after Jesuit missionaries, active in China in the seventeenth and eighteenth centuries, began to convey information about the vast and fabled empire. Knowledge about China spawned the 'China fashion' in Europe, which included the fad of Chinese gardens and imitation Chinese art known as chinoiserie.[2] Fanciful literary accounts, often verging on the bizarre, entertained those who had a taste for the strange and exotic. Some of this 'China craze' also spilled over into works written for a Jewish audience, a topic that is still largely unexplored.[3]

In the early decades of the twentieth century, at the time when Buber first became interested in Chinese thought and literature, information about China, her history, people, and present state, was also made available to Yiddish audiences. Aimed at the casual reader, one early account is a booklet of 1910 in the 'home library' series. The author, Akiba Fleishman, freely mixed fact and fancy thereby managing to write a lively account of China and the Chinese. He credited China with 6000 years of history, 7000 years of Buddhism, and 5000 years of Confucian religion. He wrote admiringly about the empire's large population – fifty cities have one and a half million inhabitants – and Beijing was built, according to him, thousands of years ago. Chinese children begin to learn at the age of six, but the subjects taught in school have no practical value. Reading and writing is very difficult, stated Fleishman, the latter being done 'as if painting' (dort werd geshribn malendig).[4] Others attempted to convey something about Chinese religious life, beliefs and thought. About Laozi (according to the authors, the name means 'the old venerable child'), some curious legendary material was introduced by M. Birnboim and D. Kassel. His mother carried him in her womb for four years, and when born with a long grey beard, he immediately rose up in the air. On the day of his birth, together with thunder and lightning stars fell from the sky.[5] Confucius was also not neglected. Rather more prosaically, Confucius, with his nine daughters but no son (he had died at an early age), wanted to marry his friend's daughter. The friend was not eager, leaving the decision nonetheless to his daughters. The youngest consented, and she did bear Confucius a son. The philosopher Mencius was portrayed as a great patriot, who loved his people and his country. According to Western missionaries' views, the authors wrote that 'in spirit he was similar to the Jewish prophets.'[6]

Apparently such popular books did not satisfy more discriminating readers. In 1925, A. Almi (1892-1963, penname for Elihu-Haiim Sheps), who wrote for Yiddish newspapers in New York, published *Di Chinesishe Filozofje un Poesje* (Chinese philosophy and poetry). In his introduction he lamented Jewish narrow-mindedness, provincialism and disinterest in China:

> China with more than 400 million [population]... should be most certainly of the greatest interest to the genuinely cultured person. [Especially to the man who]... searches for himself or the world, or both; for the person who wants to find something.[7]

In the 1930s, travelers to Asia described the sights they had seen and among them, Meylekh Ravitch (1893–1976, pen name for Zaharia-Chone Bergner) was inspired to write a number of poems with Chinese content which appeared in his poetry collection, *Kontinentn un Okeanen* (Continents and oceans).[8] Ravitch wrote these poems after leaving China, and on the basis of his extensive travelogue, which he never published.[9] Yosel Lerner, on the other hand, though he was never in China, tried his hand at translating classical Chinese poetry into Yiddish. His book, *Bajm offenem Fenster* (At the open window), which includes thirty five poems by Chinese poets, was published in Tel Aviv in 1979. Obviously, Lerner was not able to translate directly from Chinese and had to depend on one or another translation into European languages.[10] Yet Lerner's and others' attempts to convey something about China to Yiddish readers – as far removed from the Chinese world as Chinese readers were from the several Jewish worlds – tells us something about ideas, knowledge and wisdom that know no barriers of time and place, belonging to all those who care to search for them.

* * *

The first three essays in this collection are concerned with Jews living among Chinese, and Jews trying to reach China as their haven from Nazi persecution. I am indebted to Professor H.Z. Schiffrin, who many years ago suggested that I study the Jewish communities in modern China. Despite his welcome suggestion, research on so narrow a topic yet so broadly linked to many others, could not be easily undertaken due to the near total lack of sources. There thus began two decades of patient collecting of data: documents, interviews, articles, letters, published and unpublished memoirs, newspapers, in short, anything relevant to nineteenth and twentieth century Jewish communities.[11] A picture about the lives of the people who lived in the Jewish communities eventually emerged, but it was not until recently that the essays based on the documentary record are ready for publication.[12] The general introduction to the subject is a considerably revised version of an introduction written for the 1992 exhibition catalogue of Chinese Judaica at Harvard University's Widener Library.[13]

Professor Ch'en Shou-yi, my teacher during my student years, had an abiding interest in Sino-Western relations. It was from him that we, his students, first learned about the existence of a Jewish community in Kaifeng. Even if not much can be added to the extensive work of other scholars, there are still many problems relevant to both Chinese and Jewish history that must be addressed. One intriguing question that presented itself early on was how Kaifeng Jews integrated (not assimilated) socially and religiously into Chinese society, while nonetheless preserving and remembering well into modern times their Jewish identity.[14] This may be but a small question, yet it must be raised if we are seriously concerned with how Jews have accommodated themselves to other cultures. The first Jewish community in China was established in Kaifeng and the last to constitute itself was in Shanghai when the Central European refugees arrived due to the Nazi regime's forced emigration policy. Although much has been written about this community (and there are a number of documentary films), many basic questions have neither been posed nor answered. In the present essay, written especially for this publication, a simple question required an answer: how did a Berlin, Hamburg, Viennese or Leipzig Jew manage to cover the formidable distance from Germany and Austria to Shanghai? What configuration of circumstances induced or forced him/her to embark on this journey to a country about which so very little was known?

Aside from actual contacts between Jews and Chinese, where the former came to live among the latter, there was still another encounter by means of written texts and the ideas and information contained in them. Here I was specifically interested in what the Old Testament (O.T.) in Chinese translation was like and how it was translated. True, the Biblical text was brought to China by Protestant missionaries in the second half of the nineteenth century as part of their larger efforts at converting Chinese to Christianity. But in the annals of translation, Samuel I.J. Schereschewsky's transposition of the Hebrew Old Testament into spoken Chinese holds a unique place. Never before (or thereafter) was the Hebrew masoretic text the actual source. Never again would a translator, thoroughly versed in the text and its Jewish commentary tradition, attempt to create (and recreate) the O.T. as a Chinese text. The article in this volume is the product of many years of research and an even longer interest in Schereschewsky for whom China became an actual and spiritual home.[15]

Yet, in order to determine how skillful a translator Schereschewsky, in fact, was I decided to take a close look at a number of Psalms in Chinese translation. Did Schereschewsky and his coworkers understand the poetic principles of the Psalms and was he and they able to cast them into Chinese? Can the Chinese Psalms be considered poetry? The essay in this volume was written for a conference in Taipei that, due to illness, I was unfortunately unable to attend.

To inquire into the motives of a translator and the techniques he used to accomplish his task is, however, only one part of the story. How the text was received and appropriated, the journey it embarked on in the receptor culture, all these were important in the continued encounter. The Chinese OT – and not necessarily only Schereschewsky's translation – provided a stimulus and a means for Chinese intellectuals to inquire about Jews and Jewish history. Not all of the Chinese O.T. readers were newly converted Christians. Some read the O.T. for its literary value, its poetry, as well as for its human drama. For others the O.T. provided potent symbols that they incorporated into works of prose and poetry. The brief article included here on the reception of the O.T. was presented as a paper in the international workshop on the Bible in modern China, held in 1996 at the Truman Research Institute of the Hebrew University.

As already indicated, interest in the Jewish–Chinese encounter began when, as an undergraduate student, I was initiated into the study of Chinese language and culture by Professor Ch'en Shou-yi. Our small band of aspiring China scholars met for classes in the basement of Carnegie Hall, not the famous New York concert hall, but to us a no less inspiring structure on the campus of the Claremont Colleges. Century by century, China's vast world unfolded before us in the confined space of Carnegie's subterranean classrooms, and on entering and leaving we were treated to the amazing beauty of a flowering camellia bush. Knowing that I was Jewish, Professor Ch'en remarked once that Yiddish literature was translated into Chinese in the 1920s. Although it would be some years before I could devote time to study that topic, thanks to my teacher's offhand remark I eventually published an article on Yiddish literature in Chinese translation.[16] The essay in these pages is, however, a much revised version of a later one which appeared in *Asian and African Studies* (Jerusalem), Vol. 8, no. 3 (1972), pp. 291–314.

Among these several encounters, the intellectual one is not included, though of course, it too exists.[17] However, instead of addressing the Chinese encounter with and reception of Jewish thought, the essay in this collection illustrates the reverse process: the reception of Chinese thought, specifically Daoism, by a Jewish thinker.[18] Martin Buber's interest in China occurred initially within the context of the larger German attraction which began toward the end of the nineteenth century. This interest took, however, a characteristic turn when Buber combined it with his specific religious and philosophical agenda. For Buber this was not apparently a passing phase; he continued to read and use the Daoist text (as well as other Chinese philosophical writings) even after he left Germany for Jerusalem and was occupied with entirely different matters. Unlike the brief and incidental literary encounters, when Yiddish writers were temporarily attracted to China or Chinese themes, Buber's sustained philosophical interest is a unique phenomenon in Jewish thought.

These essays were written mostly for the Sinological reader and would have come hardly to the notice of a broader audience. It is hoped that by bringing them to a wider readership, interested in intercultural relations and contacts between peoples, together with the transposition of ideas from one cultural context to another, some questions will be answered while new ones will be raised.

NOTES

1. The essays are lightly revised from the Hebrew version by the same title published in Jerusalem, Bialik Institute, 2002. Included here is an additional essay, 'Several Psalms in Chinese Translation'.
2. Among the several works on this subject, A. Reichwein, *China and Europe*, Taipei: Ch'engwen reprint, 1967, originally published in 1925, is still one of the best surveys.
3. Chang Shoou-Huey, 'China und Jiddisch, Jiddische Kultur in China – Chinesische Literatur und Jiddisch', in Roman Malek, ed., *Jews in China, From Kaifeng...to Shanghai*, Sankt Augustin: Monumenta Serica, 2000, pp. 479–95.
4. Akiba Fleishman, *Di Chineser, Seier Lebn, Emune un Sittn* (The Chinese, Their Life, Belief and Customs), Warsaw: Verlag Yiddishm Tageblatt, n.d. [1910], pp. 11, 18, 21, 29.
5. Mordechai Birnboim, D. Kassel. *Chine un Manchurien, Mongolien, Tibet, Korea, un andere*, Warsaw: Yiddish, 1918, p. 53. Part of the series "Voelker und Laender", this small book contains a number of illustrations, including an example of Chinese writing printed upside down.

6. Ibid, pp. 56–7, 63.
7. A. Almi, *Chinese Philosophy and Poetry*, New York, 1925, p. 6. Almi chose to write about the two topics together because, as he stated, for the Chinese both are similar in language, method and concept of life, p. 60. I am indebted to Dr. Chang's essay for introducing me to Almi and the Yiddish poets mentioned below.
8. *Continents and Oceans*, Warsaw: Literarishe Bletter, 1937. The section "Asian Poems" includes poems on Japan, Singapore, and on the Trans-Siberian railway, on which the poet traveled. See also, Chang, 'China und Jiddisch', p. 490.
9. The travelogue is in the Hebrew National and University Library Archive. My essay about the travelogue and several of the poems is 'Meylekh Ravitch in China, A Travelogue of 1935',in Monika Schmitz-Emans, ed., *Transkulturelle Rezeption und Konstruktion, Festschrift für Adrian Hsia*, Heidelberg: Synchron, 2004, pp. 103–17.
10. At the open window. Chang Shoou-Huey, "China Rezeption auf Jiddish. Zu den Li-Tai-po Uebersetzungen," *Jiddischistik Mitteilungen*, no. 18 (November 1997), pp. 1–16.
11. The archive that was eventually assembled from the contributions of people from Harbin, Tianjin and Shanghai is now housed in Yad Vashem, and includes written materials as well as artifacts and photographs. The newspaper files in five languages remain at the Hebrew University.
12. A brief essay which began my study of the Jewish communities was written for the *Encyclopedia Judaica Yearbook 1973*, pp. 183–4.
13. *China and the Jews*, A Sampling of Harvard Library Resources for the Study of Jewish Life in China and Chinese Jewish Relations, 1992.
14. The initial article on this topic was, 'The Jews of Kaifeng: The Persistence of Identity', *AJA Quarterly*, Vol. 16, no. 5 (1971), pp. 19–23. The present article is a much revised version of this earlier one, which appeared in *Monumenta Serica*, Vol. 41 (1993), pp. 231-247. This article has also appeared in Jonathan Goldstein, ed., *The Jews of China*, Armonk-London: M.E. Sharpe, 1999, pp. 22–35, Vol. I.
15. The original version was published in the *Bulletin of the School of Oriental and African Studies*, Vol. 56, Part 2 (1993), pp. 219–33. My biography of Schereschewsky together with a critical analysis of his O.T. text was published as *The Jewish Bishop and the Chinese Bible*, Leiden: Brill, 1999.
16. 'Yiddish Literature and the Literary Revolution in Modern China', *Judaism*, 16 (1967), pp. 42–59. The well-known author and poet Jacob Glatstein wrote two essays in Yiddish based on this article, which came to my attention only in Chang Shoou-Huey's essay. Glatstein's essays are in *In der Velt mit Yiddish Essayn* (In the world with Yiddish essays), New York, 1972.
17. The subject is discussed by Xun Zhou, *Chinese Perceptions of the 'Jews' and Judaism, A History of the Youtai*, Richmond: Curzon, 2001.
18. My earlier introduction for Martin Buber, Alex Page, trans., *Chinese Tales, Zhuangzi: Sayings and Parables and Chinese Ghost and Love Stories*, New Jersey-London, 1991, pp. ix-xxiii, deals only briefly with how Buber understood Daoist philosophical concepts. The present essay appeared in *Monumenta Serica*, Vol. 42 (1994), pp. 445–64.

PART I: HISTORY

1

Jewish Communities in China: A Brief Overview

Jews have encountered Chinese people for perhaps 1,000 years or more. They came to China for various reasons and in pursuit of diverse goals. Traders along the Silk Road in the ninth century were the first to arrive, although they have left only the scantiest of records of their presence and they never settled within China's borders for any length of time. Merchant groups arrived around 400 years later: no doubt, not all at once. They settled in China's south-eastern coastal cities as well as in the interior. Some 700 years thereafter came merchants, businessmen, and industrialists who made their homes in many parts of China, but primarily in the treaty ports and in the three north-eastern provinces, known as Manchuria.[1] These were followed in the twentieth century by refugees fleeing from the Bolshevik Revolution and the Civil War, and later from Nazi persecution. The final, and for the first time reciprocal, Chinese–Jewish encounter has been taking place in recent years with the establishment of diplomatic and trade relations between Israel and China, tourism, and academic exchanges.

Sporadic in nature until now, with no appreciable impression on either Jewish or Chinese life, these encounters nonetheless reflect crucial moments in both Chinese and Jewish history and raise questions about many aspects of this history. Still, only at the present time is there a genuine meeting of the two peoples in China, Israel, and elsewhere and they are at last beginning to explore more systematically each others' history, culture, and traditions.

THE JEWS OF KAIFENG

The romance of the Silk Road, the traders who came along it, Jews among them, continues to intrigue scholars and laymen alike. Who were these Jews who joined the great caravan trade, travelling from oasis to oasis, braving Central Asia's formidable deserts? What impelled them to leave home and kin, perhaps in Persia, perhaps farther West, in the eighth and ninth centuries, the heyday of the Tang dynasty (618–906)? Was it the lure of wealth only? Or was it also the spirit of adventure?

Are the Chinese Tang figurines of bearded men with high boots and backpack which we find displayed in museums indeed likenesses of Jews? And if so, what happened to their models? Did they remain in China and disappear in the course of time? Or did they return home, telling wondrous tales about the great Chinese empire? There are no clear answers to these questions. But attesting to the entrance or exit of, at least, one Jew, we have his anonymous calling card, as it were: a *Selihot* (penitential) prayer written on paper and left at Dunhuang, one of China's traditional gateways along the Silk Road.[2]

In spite of huge gaps, of centuries, for which there is no information, the history of the Jews who lived in Kaifeng from the early twelfth century is better known. They came probably from India and from Persia sometime before 1120 as groups of merchants, travelling overland and by sea. Kaifeng was then the capital of the Northern Song dynasty (960–1126), a metropolitan centre with a population of over one million. It was a commercial and industrial city, at the hub of an overland and river communications network. Their arrival must have taken place before the outbreak of full-scale hostilities in the 1120s between the Chinese and their Inner Asian neighbours, the Jurched.

By the time the Jews built their synagogue in 1163, the Jurched had established their own dynasty in the north, while Chinese rule was confined to the areas south of the Yangzi River. The subsequent Southern Song dynasty (1127–1279), however, also ended when the Mongols conquered both north and south China, establishing, in turn, their own, the Yuan, dynasty (1279–1368). Thus the first nearly 150 years of Jewish life in China did not take place under Chinese, but under foreign, rule. During this time and probably close to 100 years thereafter, contacts were most likely maintained with other Jewish communities outside of China. Jewish communities within China, aside from Kaifeng, also existed in Yangzhou and Ningbo on the southeastern coast as well as in distant north-western Ningxia, and contacts with these communities are on record until the early sixteenth century. But these communities vanish from view in the following centuries.[3]

From the time of their arrival in the early twelfth century to their first description by the seventeenth century Jesuit missionaries in the Ming dynasty (1368–1644), the community underwent a process of integration into Chinese society. Jews received Chinese surnames, organizing themselves into lineage families. Members of these lineages had careers in Chinese government service when they participated in the official examinations and acquired degrees. Jews were apparently active in all walks of life as merchants, artisans, government officials, and clerks. Being polygamous, they had secondary wives generally of Chinese parentage and, by the nineteenth century, when Protestant missionaries first encountered the Kaifeng Jews, they were in appearance indistinguishable from the Chinese population.[4]

Although most religious practices were retained until perhaps the early years of the nineteenth century, a gradual adjustment, both in Jewish self-perception and in Jewish observances, can be discerned. The synagogue, rebuilt several times after destruction by fire or flood, was in use until 1849, despite the demise of the last religious leader in 1810. Men prayed three times a day with a *minyan* (ten men); liturgy and prayers were in accordance with the rabbinical (Talmudic) tradition; *haphtarot* were read on Shabbat; the yearly cycle of Torah reading was observed; *kashrut*[5] and circumcision were practiced; seasonal festivals were celebrated. At the same time, however, knowledge of Hebrew was gradually lost; festival practices were joined to Chinese religious observances; burial and memorial observances were adjusted to the Chinese religious environment.

The self-perception that evolved in the course of time was of Jewish families associated with other such Jewish families whose identity was connected with a specific place, namely Kaifeng. Jewish identity was thus transformed from a people and community to lineage, place, and family. This family-related identity was strengthened by a transformation of religious identity. Increasingly, in the course of centuries, Kaifeng Jews had all the earmarks of a syncretic religous sect. They had a shrine, a religious leader, scriptures, dietary practices, all of which were characteristic (although always with significant variations) of other religious sects. Kaifeng Jews considered their own history part of Chinese history, but beginning in a different past. They perceived the transmission of Jewish tradition as an orderly process from one biblical personage to another, thus asserting the religion's legitimacy.[6]

After falling into disuse in the 1849 flood, the synagogue was dismantled sometime between 1851 and 1866.[7] Circumcision was probably discontinued by the beginning of the twentieth century. Some forms of *kashrut*, especially abstinence from pork (possibly as a result of Muslim influence), were apparently retained longest. Nonetheless, the memory of a Jewish past did not cease among a number of, although not all, families. Even if, according to Jewish law (*halakha*)[8], these families cannot be considered Jewish, the fact is that they continue to identify themselves as Chinese Jews, as Jews and as 'descendant[s] of the Yellow Emperor', as Shi Zhongyu described himself in 1982.[9]

THE JEWS OF SHANGHAI

Shanghai's Baghdadi Community

The years 1839–42 are a watershed in Chinese history, for they mark the infamous Opium Wars forced upon the Chinese by Great Britain. In their wake began the Western penetration of China, the opening of treaty ports along China's south-eastern coast, the establishment of foreign concessions and legations and, a half century later, the rise of Russian influence in Manchuria.

Unlike the Kaifeng families, the Jews who came to China's shores in the mid-nineteenth century from Iraq did not integrate into Chinese life. They remained Jews in China, that is, outsiders who founded their own communal institutions within the treaty port of Shanghai, and there created a vibrant community with a rich cultural life.[10]

Two factors, unique to the Chinese setting, were conducive to the community's growth. The Baghdadis became part of the privileged foreign population in Shanghai who had their homes and businesses in the International Settlement.[11] Chinese politics, nationalism, or the civil wars and rebellions that swept over China in the second half of the nineteenth and the first two decades of the twentieth century were of minor concern. In the treaty ports it was business as usual: what mattered was the international market. To all appearances, Jews were equal trading partners in this thriving business community. The second factor was the virtual absence of anti-Semitism. The Chinese did not distinguish between foreigner and Jew, and when it came to business, both Europeans and Americans apparently put their prejudices aside.

Prior to the arrival of the Westerners in the nineteenth century, Shanghai, the city that was to become the 'Paris of the Orient', was a busy centre for Chinese coastal and inland junk trade. When the British chose this site on the Huangbu jiang (Whangpoo River) for their international port, they were well aware of its potential. So, apparently, were members of the Sassoon family, who came shortly after the Opium Wars.[12]

The Sassoons, like most of the families who eventually settled in Shanghai prior to the First World War, were of Baghdadi origin. They had come to Bombay in the early-nineteenth century, founding successful business enterprises there, and from their Bombay base joined the British China trade after 1840.[13] The Sassoons and other families prospered rapidly as a result of lucrative land speculations on the China coast, large-scale investments in the Yangzi Valley, as import and export merchants and brokers, and as insurance and shipping agents of the opium trade.[14] The Sassoons were founding members of the Hongkong and Shanghai Banking Corporation, one of the major banks in the Far East, and members of the various Sassoon family enterprises served for many decades on the Bank's board. In the first decade of the twentieth century, not only the Sassoons but also the Hardoon and Kadoorie families made considerable fortunes in banking, transportation, and construction. Their activities contributed greatly to the growth and development of both Shanghai and Hong Kong. British in outlook and taste, the Baghdadis (also referred to as the Sephardim)[15] created the first institutions of Jewish life in Shanghai and in Hong Kong. In 1909, Shanghai's Shearith Israel Synagogue was located on Seward Road, and the Beth El Synagogue, its congregation dating from 1887, on Peking Road. In the 1920s two magnificent synagogues were constructed in Shanghai: Ohel Rachel in 1920, financed by Sir Jacob Sassoon, and Beit Aharon on Museum Road in 1927 (torn down in 1985), financed by Silas A. Hardoon. Members of prominent families – the Somekhs, Ezras, or Solomons – were active in communal affairs in the synagogues as well as in the Shanghai Jewish School founded in 1900. The Ellis Kadoorie School was a unique institution, being supported by Chinese and foreign firms, as well as private patrons. In 1910, the Baghdadi community officially constituted itself as the Shanghai Jewish Communal Association. Its president for more than three decades was D.E.J. Abraham.

Although influential Jews were members in treaty port clubs, the Shanghai Jewish Club was the centre of social activities. Despite their thriving social and religious life, Zionism as a Jewish political movement did not have large numbers of adherents among the Baghdadis. Still, it was a Baghdadi, Nissim Ezra Benjamin Ezra, who edited the Anglo-Jewish paper, *Israel's Messenger*, the official organ of the Shanghai Zionist Association, for more than three decades from its inception in 1904.[16]

Aside from Silas A. Hardoon and his wife, the Baghdadis were seemingly little involved in Chinese affairs. Hardoon, on the other hand, is said to have supported the Buddhist revival in the Yangzi Valley, and his wife (Luo Jialing, d. 1941), backed the Women's Chinese and Western Medical School in Shanghai. On their magnificent estate on Bubbling Well Road the Hardoon couple also maintained a 'college' where the well-known scholar, Wang Guowei (1877–1927), wrote some of his important works.[17] Upon his death in 1931, Hardoon was interred in an impressive marble mausoleum in the estate's park. The funeral was attended by his many Chinese friends; the prominent scholar Zhang Binglin (1867–1936) gave the funeral eulogy.[18]

The Baghdadi community was never very large and is estimated to have been less than 1,000 souls. It retained its exclusive character into the second and third decades of the twentieth century. However, the 1930s were already troubled times for Shanghai's business and financial establishments. The Japanese presence in the Shanghai area from the beginning of 1932 did not yet threaten the foreigners' lives or livelihood, and neither the International Settlement nor the French Concession were under Japanese control. For the time being, only the Chinese bore the brunt of the invader's oppressive measures. But the outbreak of the Sino-Japanese War in July 1937 produced major disruptions in Shanghai's business world after the Japanese increasingly encroached on foreign commercial interests.[19] An era was drawing to a close and, indeed, ended when the Pacific War broke out in December 1941.

Shanghai's Russian Community
The tiny Jewish community of Russian origin which was in Shanghai in the first decade of the twentieth century was augmented at two different times. First, when, as a result of the Bolshevik Revolution, numerous Jews fled to Shanghai, and second, when worsening economic conditions in Manchuria around 1930 caused Russian and a small number of Polish Jews to gradually move south. Many of these newcomers, who were of lower socio-economic status, made their homes in the Hongkou district, part of the International Settlement, which, since the end of the nineteenth century, also had a growing Japanese population. After the outbreak of the Sino-Japanese War, some of the fiercest battles took place in the Hongkou area, depriving these Jews of their homes and livelihood. In addition, there was, however, also a fairly well-off middle class, of which many made their homes in the French Concession where they developed their own distinctive cultural and religious life. Similarly to the Sephardim, population figures are hard to come by and vary significantly, depending on the source. A 1937 estimate gives 4,500 Jews affiliated with the 'Kehila Ha'Ivrit Ha'Ashkenazit' (The Hebrew Ashkenazi Congregation). But there must have been more unaffiliated Jews, so that perhaps a 1940 estimate of 6,000 is closer to the actual number.[20]

The Russian Jews with their admixture of Polish and Siberian Jews were Ashkenazi Jews.[21] But as in Europe, this did not lead to sectarian divisiveness, and their congregation, constituted as Ohel Moshe, was for many years on the same premises as the Baghdadis' Shearith Israel on Seward Road. Seemingly unmindful of the gathering storm, the community finally built an impressive structure in 1941, the New Synagogue, which was located in the French Concession and also included new club facilities. Concerts, poetry readings, and theatrical performances in Russian were regularly featured. A weekly newspaper, *Nasha Zhizn* (Our Life), which had a remarkably capable journalistic and editorial staff, kept the Russian-speaking community informed of events in Shanghai and abroad. After the outbreak of the Second World War, access to the Tass news agency was especially important since it was the source of information from German-occupied Central and Eastern European areas. As it was a Zionist paper, Palestine figured prominently in *Nasha Zhizn's* pages.

The community took special pride in the Jewish Company, formed in 1932, which was part of the Shanghai Volunteer Corps. The latter came into existence in the 1850s when rebels and Chinese imperial soldiers threatened the International Settlement. The 120 or so members of the Jewish Company and their Jewish officers were an independent national military unit within the Corps, similar to other such units. Wearing the Star of David on their uniforms, the Jewish Company consisted mainly of Russians 'with a permanent job and spotless reputation', according to 'Our Life' (the English page of *Nasha Zhizn*), although by the 1940s several Sephardi Jews and newly arrived Central Europeans had also joined up.[22]

Ever-growing numbers of Central European Jewish refugees in Shanghai together with pressure from the Japanese military, led Russian Jewish community leaders by 1941 to search for ways of accommodation with the new power. For their part, the Japanese authorities, were pursuing policies designed to exert control over the many national and ethnic groups, among them the several Jewish groups. However, only after Pearl Harbor in 1942 did Russian Jewish leaders openly acknowledge steps toward unifying and consolidating Jewish activities in accordance with Japanese aims.

Like the Sephardi Jews, the Russians came to China to make their homes there. Also like the former, the Russians constituted themselves as a community among Shanghai's foreign population. Like most foreigners, their day-to-day contact with the Chinese was in their businesses and with their Chinese servants at home. China's troubled politics of the 1930s, the Guomindang government, Japan's invasion of Manchuria – none of these events really impinged upon their lives. The outbreak of the Sino-Japanese war in 1937 affected the poorer members of the Russian Jewish community who had been domiciled in Hongkou, where heavy fighting took place between Chinese and Japanese forces, more so than others. But whether poor or well-off, China and the Chinese, their history and traditions, did not seem to arouse more than their passing curiosity. Isolated (and insulated) from the country's affairs, their immediate concern was the flood of refugees in the late 1930s, and how these, for the most part German-speaking, newcomers affected their political status and personal well-being.

Shanghai's Refugee Community
Unlike the previous two groups of Jews who had come to Shanghai in search of homes and livelihood, the refugees from Central Europe regarded Shanghai as a temporary way station to elsewhere, preferably the United States. Their adjustment to life in Shanghai was, therefore, painful and slow, and was exacerbated by the fact that most landed penniless in the teeming city. German Jews, mostly professionals, had begun to trickle into Shanghai shortly after the establishment of the Third Reich in 1933, principally because of the ease of obtaining a Chinese visa.[23] After *Kristallnacht*, in November 1938, the trickle turned into a flood of mostly German and Austrian Jews. Among these were many who came directly from the concentration camps of Dachau and Buchenwald, their release having been made contingent on their leaving Germany at once. Numbering perhaps 18,000–20,000, most of the refugees had landed by autumn 1939. Some Jews from Poland, Lithuania, and the Baltic states still managed to reach Shanghai in 1940 and in 1941 via Japan, among these a large group of several hundred Yeshiva students and their teachers. But both the war in Europe and the restrictions on immigration into Shanghai, which took effect in October 1939, effectively limited access to this last place of refuge.

The German-speaking refugees constituted the third and by far largest Jewish community in Shanghai. However, the community throughout its existence remained dependent on outside help and never achieved economic integration either before or after the war. The majority settled in Hongkou where rents were cheaper but which had a considerable Japanese population. Relief organizations, hastily constituted by the Sephardi and Russian communities, offered aid together with the American Joint Distribution Committee, which carried the major burden of the relief work. But, in spite of free meals, loans, medical care, and education for children, many refugees (an estimated 5,000 in 1941) existed in desperate conditions in overcrowded shelters, called *Heime*, where poor nourishment and disease took their toll. Dependence on the relief organizations with their proliferating committees led to an uneasy and often resentful relationship between the providers and recipients of charity. The refugees, for the most part of well-to-do middle class background, were not given a voice in the administration of aid.[24]

Yet many made the best of a difficult situation. When the opportunity presented itself, they relocated to the International Settlement or French Concession where they opened small enterprises, food stores, cafés, factories, and even engineering enterprises. ORT (the Society for the Encouragement of Handicraft) played an important role by providing training in a variety of skills to these former students, businessmen, and housewives. Journalistic enterprises flourished in particular (even if most of the newspapers were shortlived) and they established almost immediately a network of communication in German. Similarly significant were radio broadcasts in German which, aside from their entertainment programmes, also relayed valuable information on practical matters of Shanghai life. The refugees' ability to improvise, to find or create work in order to have an income, was remarkable. Their determination, even under adverse circumstances, to fashion a semblance of their own cultural life (song recitals, actors' workshops, dramatic performances, and lectures) stands as a triumph of the spirit.[25]

The outbreak of the Pacific War in December 1941 put an end to all hopes for an early departure from Shanghai. Worse than that, however, was the fact that those refugees who had found employment with British and American firms were within a year out of work when the firms came under Japanese management and when their former employers were interned. Sources of income dried up and many Jews became once more dependent on aid, by then rapidly dwindling. After Pearl Harbor, all of Shanghai, including the International Settlement, came under Japanese control. At the same time, increasing pressure was brought on the Russian community leaders to unify all Jewish organizational work and refugee aid.

THE HONG KONG JEWISH COMMUNITY

Today, Hong Kong is again part of China. The story of the Jews of Hong Kong belongs, therefore, to that of the other communities, especially since, at the start of this century, it is the only one left carrying on a lively Jewish tradition. In the mid-nineteenth century, Hong Kong, unlike Shanghai, was a Crown Colony, and the Sephardi Jewish families who settled there were closely related and connected to those in Shanghai. Ohel Leah synagogue is the oldest in Hong Kong and was, as in Shanghai, Sir Jacob Sassoon's contribution to the community in 1902. The Jewish Recreation Club was a gift of Sir Elly Kadoorie in 1909. The initial community of only a few families was Sephardi, and, as in Shanghai, identified its interests with those of the British. Although in the course of time Ashkenazi Jews also settled in Hong Kong, the congregation remained a small one until more recent decades. Between the wars the colony may have had no more than around 75 families.

Hong Kong's increasingly important place in international commerce has been, undoubtedly, responsible for the growth of the Jewish community in recent years. However, a large percentage consists of transients. Today there are around 3,000 Jews in Hong Kong; there are Orthodox, Conservative, and Reform congregations, as well as a Habad Lubavitch congregation; a day school; and kosher restaurants. The nineteenth-century Jewish Recreation Club is now the fashionable Jewish Community Centre, and has a membership of over 700 families. Hong Kong's Jewish bankers, businessmen, and lawyers have come from many countries – the United States, South Africa, Australia – and Israel; only a few were born and raised in Hong Kong. English is their common language, and not many know Chinese. Some will remain in Hong Kong for the duration of their contracts; others will stay as long as business continues to be profitable. The community might shrink or grow but, at this juncture, in addition to the Hong Kong properties it owns, the Jewish community is probably among the wealthiest in the world.

THE HARBIN AND TIANJIN COMMUNITIES

Located in present Heilongjiang province, on the Sungari River (Songhuajiang), Harbin was at the turn of the century an insignificant outpost in China's frontier region. Jews began to arrive in Harbin shortly after 1898, when Russia obtained land concessions from the Qing dynasty (1644–1912) government, which included the right to build the Chinese Eastern Railway as a short-cut across Manchuria to Vladivostok. The railway brought to Harbin a large European (mostly Russian) population, which transformed Harbin into a commercial and transportation centre, and endowed the city with an unmistakable

European-Russian character that has remained its hallmark ever since.

The first group of Jews came from Siberia, where they had engaged in profitable mining enterprises, cattle raising, dairy production, and commerce. Some remained in the north-east; others moved on to Tianjin to found the Jewish community there. The Manchurian Jewish population grew rapidly after the Russo-Japanese War (1904–05), when Jewish soldiers either deserted from the Russian army, or decided not to return home after the end of hostilities. By 1908, there were some 8,000 Jews in Harbin, and in 1907 they had built their first synagogue. Border crossings in these sparsely populated areas were apparently easy, and were probably aided by long-established trading patterns across both sides of the frontier. Thus the influx from Russia continued over the next decade, reaching a peak after the Bolshevik Revolution and Civil War, when both Russian and Polish refugees arrived. Although Jews settled in other Manchurian cities – Mukden (Shenyang), Dairen (Dalian), and smaller towns along the Chinese Eastern Railway – the Harbin community was the largest, with 12,000 to 13,000 souls by 1920.

The end of the Qing dynasty and the establishment of the Chinese Republic in 1912 ushered in a period of warlord rule which, however, did not adversely affect the Jewish community. In the first decades of the twentieth century, Heilongjiang continued to be a sparsely populated region, and its rich mineral resources were virtually unexploited. In this vast, open frontier area, co-existence with Chinese warlords and local strongmen was fairly easy, and Jewish enterprise in timber, coal mining, soybean processing, and pelts flourished. There were several banking firms, including the more modest Jewish People's Bank, and Jews were active as officers of the Harbin Stock Exchange. Jewish capital contributed in some measure toward the transformation of Harbin into a thriving urban centre.

Unlike Shanghai's Jews, the Harbin community was more homogeneous, consisting primarily of Russian Jews with a sprinkling from Poland. Communal institutions, designed to care for the aged, needy, and orphaned, developed rapidly, especially after 1918, when aid for fleeing refugees was urgently needed. Harbin boasted a Jewish hospital, a library, a Jewish school and, for a time, a Jewish high school. As in Shanghai, the community's cultural activities were extremely important, as were its Russian journals. *Evreiskaya Zhizn* (Hebrew Life) appeared uninterruptedly for more than 20 years, from 1920 to 1943, and *Gadegel* (The Flag) was published from 1932 to 1942.

Like Shanghai, Harbin had a considerable White Russian population, and in both cities the two communities kept aloof from each other. But, in distinction to Shanghai, Harbin's Jewish young people attended the Russian high school, while those in search of higher degrees – such as law – studied at academic institutions connected with the Chinese Eastern Railway. Therefore, and despite anti-Semitic undercurrents, forms of contact existed between the two Russian-speaking communities.

Zionism played an important role both in the Jewish community's cultural activities and in its politics. Seats on the Community Council, for which elections were held for the first time in 1919, were apportioned according to party affiliation, both Zionist and non-Zionist, with the majority of the seats allocated to the Zionist parties' representatives. Dr Abraham I. Kaufman (1885–1971) provided vigorous leadership as Zionist and community head before as well as after the Japanese invasion of Manchuria in 1931.

The Harbin community was more vulnerable to economic change than its Shanghai counterpart. Changes in the management of the Chinese Eastern Railway in the mid-1920s affected Jewish business enterprises by bringing increased Chinese participation into the Manchurian economy. Moreover, after 1929, the worsening world market had an impact on those wealthier Jewish families whose enterprises reached beyond Manchuria and Asia. The economic difficulties were exacerbated by the Japanese invasion of Manchuria and the establishment of the Japanese puppet state of Manchukuo in 1932. Chinese government control in Manchuria, whether by a warlord or by the Nationalist government after 1928, had never been firm. This changed once the Japanese took over and attempted to create a strong government with a tightly controlled economy. The Jewish community which, in fact, rarely had to deal with the Chinese authorities, was now confronted with a changed situation. When the Japanese acquired the railway, tens of thousands of Russians left the railway zone and Harbin, depriving many Jewish shopkeepers and artisans of their economic base. Subsequently, numerous Jewish families left for Tianjin and Shanghai. For those who remained, the Community Council and Dr. Kaufman spared no effort to enlist the goodwill of the new authorities.

Although Manchukuo was accessible to refugees fleeing Nazi persecution via the overland route – by way of Russia and the Trans-Siberian Railway – only a few professionals (mainly physicians) actually received permission to remain in the puppet state. Manchukuo transit visas, sporadically available in 1940 and the first half of 1941, enabled some refugees to reach Shanghai, and the Harbin community extended whatever help it could to those passing through.

Japanese strategies of gaining control through co-operation (later applied in Shanghai, as noted above) were largely successful, and led to the creation of the National Council of Far Eastern Jews which, as a unified body, was to act on behalf of all Manchurian communities. The Council held three conferences in Harbin in 1937, 1938, and 1939 with the participation of delegations from Jewish communities in Manchuria and China. The conferences were also attended by representatives of the Japanese authorities. In return for co-operation with and loyalty to Manchukuo, Jews were granted the right to maintain self-governing religious and cultural institutions.[26]

Compared to Shanghai and Harbin, the Tianjin community was small, never numbering more than around 2,500 persons. It consisted mostly of Russian Jews, with a small number from Poland and Germany. Some Jews might have settled in Tianjin as early as 1860 or 1870, when north China was opened to Western penetration, but it was not until 1904 that Jews purchased land for a cemetery and established a community within the foreign concession, registering it with the Russian Imperial Consulate. The initial Jewish population, having drifted south from Manchuria, was not well-to-do. Hence the first communal institution, the Hebrew Association of Tientsin, had as its primary function the extending of interest-free loans.

Tianjin's Jewish population grew rapidly after 1917, and under the able leadership of Lev I. Gershevich (1878–1950) various communal institutions, such as the Tientsin Jewish School, a high school, and the 'Kunst'(Art) club, were founded in 1925 and 1928 respectively. The school, well known in Jewish circles, served both Tianjin and other communities in north China. Its medium of instruction was English, and the curriculum, aside from including Jewish subjects, was geared toward gaining students entrance to European and American universities. As elsewhere, the club, with its auditorium for theatrical performances, was the centre of Jewish life. It housed a library, and its reading room stocked newspapers in Russian, English, and Hebrew. A handsome synagogue was constructed in 1939. Recently renovated, its premises were turned into an entertainment spot in the 1990s. Similar to Russian communities elsewhere, Zionist activities were important and reinforced the Jewish identity of the younger generation.[27]

Tianjin's British Concession was the hub of commercial life, and the majority of the Jews had their businesses and homes there. Until the onset of the world depression in 1929, the most lucrative enterprise by far was the fur trade. Furs were obtained in Manchuria in periodic purchasing forays by the firms' compradors, sorted and processed on

Tianjin premises, and shipped to American and European markets from the city's port. More than 100 firms engaged in the fur trade. In spite of suffering the effects of the worldwide decline in the demand for furs in the 1930s, many establishments managed to diversify. Bristles, for example, for brush manufacture became a lucrative product. In contrast to Harbin, therefore, the Tianjin community did not experience disastrous economic setbacks in the 1930s. After the start of the Sino-Japanese war in July 1937, Tianjin came under Japanese control, as did most of north China. Similarly to Harbin, only a handful of refugees received permission from the Japanese authorities to resettle in Tianjin, as the Japanese preferred to concentrate them in the Shanghai area.[28] Thus, the Tianjin Jewish community saw no marked increase in numbers due to the refugee influx.

The Jewish population of the Manchurian communities as well as of Tianjin seemed to have been little aware of the growing Chinese nationalism in the 1930s. Japan's gradual military expansion into north China following the Manchurian conquest was seemingly ignored. To be sure, the Chinese political scene was extraordinarily complex, if not chaotic, in the 1930s. Chiang Kai-shek (Jiang Jieshi), head of the Nationalist government in Nanjing, tried to stir a cautious course between the Japanese military threat and warlords of dubious loyalty, while attempting to wipe out the fledgling Communist armies in south central China. Firmly, and for the most part, comfortably settled in the foreign enclaves, Jews regarded Chinese national aspirations as remote, with little impact on their own lives.

THE WAR AND ITS AFTERMATH

The war years between December 1941 and August 1945 affected each Shanghai Jewish community differently. Despite their close identification with the British, not all Sephardi Jews were British passport holders. Those who were 'friendly' nationals by virtue of their documents escaped internment in 1942. Others suffered internment together with several thousand British and American citizens who were held in a number of camps throughout Shanghai and in Yangzhou. Not every enemy alien was imprisoned, however, and some were spared incarceration for health reasons. As Soviet Russia was not at war with Japan, the Russian community was not affected. Still, community leaders took no chances and *Nasha Zhizn* in its editorial of 12 December 1941 exhorted 'all the Jews of Shanghai' to remain quiet and to obey the instructions of the authorities. Throughout December various Jewish leaders called on the Japanese military authorities, and by the end of the month the effort to unify Shanghai's Jewish communities was made public.[29] Subsequently, Russian community leaders were charged with the increasingly unpleasant tasks of implementing Japanese policies concerning the refugees. But neither the Shanghai Russian community nor the Tianjin and Harbin communities were adversely affected by the war. Except for worsening economic conditions and Japanese efforts at control and surveillance (not directed exclusively against the Jews, but at all foreigners), the Russian communities were not endangered.

German and Austrian refugees (the latter were considered German after the March 1938 *Anschluss*), after having had to surrender their citizenship in November 1941, were designated 'stateless' persons. Not all refugees from German-occupied territories were deprived of citizenship. Polish passport holders, for example, with a government in exile until diplomatic relations were terminated, were still Polish citizens. In spite of proposals emanating from various quarters over the years to resettle the refugees in localities other than Shanghai, nothing came of these.[30] Then, in February 1943, the Japanese ordered all stateless refugees, that is, those who had arrived since 1937, into the 'designated area' of Hongkou by 18 May. Precisely which events in Asia or in Europe, or which pressures, prompted the Japanese military to act at this time is not clear. Obviously, however, the proclamation imposed new and unforeseen hardships on the Central Europeans. Whereas most refugees had remained in Hongkou from the time of their arrival, others lived and worked in different parts of Shanghai. These were now forced to move into the already overcrowded district.

The ghetto, as it came to be called, was a closed area; to-come-and-go passes had to be obtained from the Japanese authorities. Confinement, in addition to restrictive methods of Japanese surveillance, poor diet and sanitation, and sky-rocketing inflation, especially from 1944, led to real suffering and hardship. Vitamin deficiencies, lowered immunity to disease and, above all, real hunger, were commonly experienced by many refugees until the end of war. By mid-1944, even black market rice became scarce and prohibitively expensive when the refugees, lacking wheat flour for bread, attempted to supplement their diet with rice.

As early as 1942, the Japanese instituted self-policing when the Jewish *Baojia* (militia system) was organized, with men between the ages of 20 to 45 serving on a rotating basis. Their tasks, deeply resented by many refugees, included also the guarding of exits to prevent persons without valid passes from leaving the area. The *Baojia*'s role in the war years is a controversial one, and much remains to be learned about individual members' ability to either sabotage Japanese efforts or to exploit their positions for personal gain.

The end of war did not bring peace to China. Civil war erupted in 1946 between Mao Zedong's and Chiang Kai-shek's armed forces. Three years later, the People's Republic of China was established under Mao's leadership. But in the summer of 1945, the events that brought Mao Zedong to power were still in the future. Some of Shanghai's Jews considered remaining in China since, for the Russians and, particularly, for the Baghdadis, Shanghai had been home for a generation or more. Members of the Hardoon family, for example, intended to resume the family's business activities in Shanghai. But their hopes were shortlived. By 1947, the Nationalist government introduced measures restricting trade by foreigners and, by 1948, the Communist armies were massing for the conquest of south China.

The Harbin Jews had other problems. The Soviet government declared war on Japan in August 1945, and almost at once the Soviet army occupied Manchuria. Although the area was returned to China in 1946, it soon came under Chinese Communist control. While emigration from Shanghai got under way in April 1946, the Civil War, which divided north from south, effectively stopped Manchuria's Jews from leaving until the beginning of 1950.

The enormous enterprise of shipping thousands of persons out of Shanghai was undertaken by the American Joint Distribution Committee with the occasional co-operation of the International Refugee Organization. The majority of the Jews came to Israel, especially after the establishment of the state in 1948; others went to Australia and the United States. They carried with them their possessions as well as their memories, which they increasingly treasured as the years went by. The exodus lasted three years, ending in 1950 with the departure of a hospital ship from Tianjin that carried over 700 sick and disabled people to Israel. When the offices of the 'Joint' closed down in June 1951, about 800 Jews remained in Shanghai and several hundred more were still scattered throughout north China, Manchuria, and even as far away as Xinjiang province. Meanwhile, however, the Hong Kong community had reconstituted itself, numbering then around 200 persons.

Jewish communal structures did not cease to exist all at once. In the autumn of 1955, the Tientsin Hebrew Association continued to function for its 130 Jews, but the synagogue had been sold earlier that year. Harbin's 319 Jews were still able to maintain communal institutions without outside financial assistance. In Shanghai, the Council of the Jewish Community supported a shelter for the disabled and looked after the interests of its 679 Jews. The Jewish Club was still in existence, and services continued in the Russian community's New Synagogue until the end of 1955, or perhaps 1956, when the synagogue was sold.

Neither suddenly nor violently, but gradually, China's modern Jewish communities faded away. Of those men and women who were still in China in 1955, some eventually also left. But others, perhaps feeling too old to start a new life elsewhere, chose to live and die in the land they called home. The new government extended them this privilege. By 1985, the sole survivor on the Chinese mainland was probably a women named Hanna Agre, who lived in Harbin.

The history of Jews in China, broadly outlined here, is more complex than may appear at first glance. To fully understand it – the long history of the Jews in Kaifeng, the short history of the modern communities – various contexts and relationships should eventually be considered. Kaifeng's Jews need be seen within Chinese social and religious history. Shanghai's Sephardi and Russian communities assume new dimensions when viewed as part of Asian colonial history. The several Jewish communities in China's north-eastern provinces, more specifically part of Russian colonial aspirations, should be viewed also within the context of one of China's economically developing regions and its intricate local politics. Finally, for more than a decade Japan's role in China and Japanese political attitudes and policies toward non-Chinese foreigners, including Jews, were major factors in the several communities' functioning and safety, especially in the 1940s. Thus, unresolved and challenging questions still remain now that a new chapter of a very different encounter between Jews and Chinese is about to be written and a kind of Jewish communal life is beginning to be once more part of Chinese life.

NOTES

1. The treaty port system came into being with the signing of the so-called 'unequal treaties' after the conclusion of the Opium War in 1842. The first of these, signed between Great Britain and China, opened five ports of the south-eastern coast to foreign trade and residence. As a result of subsequent concessions forced on China, especially that of extraterritoriality, the treaty ports were effectively removed from Chinese control and jurisdiction.
2. The document, discovered by the eminent French sinologist, Paul Pelliot, is described by Phillipe Berger and M. Schwab, 'Le plus ancien manuscrit hebreau', *Journal Asiatique*, 11th ser., Vol. 2 (July–August 1913), pp. 139–75.

3. Among the large literature on Kaifeng Jews, three important works are: Donald D. Leslie, *The Survival of the Chinese Jews, The Jewish Community of Kaifeng*, Leiden: E.J. Brill, 1972; Michael Pollak, *Mandarins, Jews, and Missionaries*, Philadelphia: The Jewish Publication Society of America, 1980; William C. White, *Chinese Jews*, Toronto: University of Toronto Press, 1942, 3 Vols. The essay by Chen Yuan, 'Kaifeng Yiciloye jiao' (Kaifeng's Jewish religion), *Dongfang Zazhi*, Vol. 17, no. 5 (1920), pp. 117–22; no. 6, pp. 119–26; no. 7, pp. 103–7, can still be read to good benefit.
4. W.A.P. Martin, 'Affairs in China', *The New York Times*, 29 August 1866, p. 2. Martin seemed to see a Jewish likeness in some Jews, but it is hard to know just what he meant by this.
5. *Haphtarot* (Hebrew 'conclusion') refers to selections from the prophetic books read at special times after the reading of the Torah. *Kashrut* (Hebrew, from *kasher*, fit) refers to regulations concerning Jewish dietary laws.
6. For a more detailed description of this process, see below, pp.33–4
7. A more exact date cannot be supplied. Two Chinese Christians dispatched to Kaifeng at the end of 1850 by George Smith, Bishop of Victoria, still found the synagogue standing. But when the missionary, W.A.P. Martin, next travelled to Kaifeng in 1866, the building had been completely dismantled.
8. *Halakha* (Hebrew 'law') refers to the legal portions of Talmudic literature.
9. Shi quoted by Michael Weisskopf, 'Judaism only a Dim Memory to Chinese Descendants', *The Washington Post*, 9 April 1982.
10. The history of the Shanghai Sephardi community is discussed in the informative volume by Maisie J. Meyer, *From the Rivers of Babylon to the Whangpoo – A Century of Sephardi Jewish Life in Shanghai*, New York: University Press of America, Inc., 2003. See also Chiara Betta, 'S.A. Hardoon (1851–1931): Marginality and Adaptation in Shanghai', Ph.D. Dissertation, University of London, School of Oriental and African Studies, 1997.
11. The International Settlement developed gradually in the mid-nineteeth century outside walled Shanghai as a combined British-American area. The Settlement also included a large Chinese population and had its own administration, the Shanghai Municipal Council, consisting of elected representatives.
12. On the history of the Sassoon family, see Stanley Jackson, *The Sassoons*, New York: E.P. Dutton and Co., 1968.
13. The enterprises of the several Sassoon family members are described in some detail in Arnold Wright, ed., *Twentieth Century Impressions of Hong Kong, Shanghai, and Other Treaty Ports of China: Their History, People, Commerce, Industries and Resources*, London: Lloyd's Greater Britain Publishing Co., Ltd., 1908, pp. 224–6.
14. The various Jewish enterprises in the early years of the treaty port are listed in C.W. Rosenstock, comp., *Rosenstock's Directory of China and Manila, July 1 to December 31, 1909*, Vol. 15, Manila: The Rosenstock Publishing Co., n.d., pp. 160, 208–9, 297.
15. This designation is also generally applied to Spanish Jews and after 1492 to Jews along the North African coast, the Balkans, the Turkish empire, and other non-European countries.
16. 'First Annual Report of the Shanghai Zionist Association, Shanghai, 1904'. The first general meeting was held 27 March 1904.
17. Jiang Junzhang, 'Cangsheng mingzhi daxue di huiyi' (Reminiscences of the college to propagate the sage Cang Jie's wisdom), *Chuanji wenxue*, Vol. 9, no. 6 (December 1966), pp. 12–16.
18. A colourful figure in the treaty port setting, Hardoon has inspired a largely anecdotal biography. See Xu Zhucheng, *Hatong waichuan* (Hardoon's unofficial biography), Hong Kong: Wenyi Shuwu, 1982. See also Chiara Betta, 'Myth and Memory, Chinese Portrayal of Silas Aaron Hardoon, Luo Jialing and the Aili Garden Between 1924 and 1995', in Roman Malek, ed., *Jews in China, From Kaifeng...to Shanghai*, Sankt Augustin: Monumenta Serica Institute, 2000, pp. 375–400.
19. See Robert W. Barnett, *Economic Shanghai: Hostage to Politics, 1937–1941*, New York: Institute of Pacific Relations, 1941.
20. *The Shanghai Evening Post and Mercury*, October 28, 1940, p. 2.
21. This designation is usually applied to Central and Eastern European Jews.
22. *Nasha Zhizn*, 6 June 1941, p. 9.
23. Officials of the Chinese Nationalist government were in charge of Shanghai passport control until the outbreak of the Sino-Japanese War in July 1937. Since the Chinese, however, had no jurisdiction over extraterritorial foreigners, they were also not empowered to prevent the entry of foreigners. This topic is discussed in greater detail below, pp. 46–7

24. David Kranzler, *Japanese, Nazis, and Jews, The Jewish Refugee Community of Shanghai, 1937–1945*, New York: Yeshiva University Press, 1976, provides a good survey of the relief efforts. A number of memoirs by former refugees have appeared in recent years. Among these, Ernest G. Heppner, *Shanghai Refuge, A Memoir of the World War II Jewish Ghetto*, Lincoln-London: University of Nebraska Press, 1993.
25. A collection of posters, announcing dramatic performances, Judaica Collection, Harvard College Library, attests to the variety of the theatrical fare.
26. A fully documented study of the Manchurian Jewish communities is still lacking. A brief survey is, Boris Bressler, 'Harbin's Jewish Community, 1898–1958: Politics, Prosperity, and Adversity', in Jonathan Goldstein, ed., *The Jews of China*, Armonk-London: M.E. Sharpe, 1999, Vol. I, pp. 200–15. For a study of Jewish–Japanese interaction in the 1930s, see Avraham Altman, 'Controlling the Jews: Manchukuo Style', in R. Malek, ed., *Jews in China, From Kaifeng... to Shanghai*, Sankt Augustin:Monumenta Serica Institute, 2000, pp. 279–317.
27. A recent memoir of Tianjin life is by Isabelle Maynard, *China Dreams, Growing Up Jewish in Tientsin*, Iowa City: University of Iowa Press, 1996.
28. Some exceptional cases are on record, however, where the Chinese puppet administration in Shanghai granted permits to reside in Tianjin.
29. *Nasha Zhizn*, 2 January 1942.
30. At one time the Philippines were considered, at other times a scheme for resettling the Jewish refugees in Yunnan was proposed. On the former, see *The North China Daily News*, October 17, 1939, p. 8. On the latter, see John Ahlers, 'The Proposal to Send 100,000 German Jewish Refugees to Yunnan Province', *China Weekly Review*, 22 July 1939, pp. 226–7; 'Berglas Publishes Plan for Settling 100,000 Jewish Refugees in China', *China Weekly Review*, 5 August 1939, p. 305.

2

Kaifeng Jews:
Sinification and the Persistence of Identity

The origin, history, and condition of the Jews of Kaifeng has been discussed in scholarly and popular writings by Jews and Christians alike ever since news of a Jewish community in Kaifeng first reached Europe in the seventeenth century.[1] In the 1920s and more recently in the last ten years Chinese scholars too have taken up this topic and a number of books and articles dealing with the Kaifeng Jews have appeared. Except for Chen Yuan's important early article,[2] however, no new information has emerged in China to supplement the well-known facts contained in the compilation by William Charles White of 1942 and the excellent study by Donald D. Leslie of 1972. This essay will address one aspect in the life of the Kaifeng Jews that has so far not received much attention, namely the process of sinification. By sinification I mean the gradual adaptation of customs from the Chinese environment which led, not to assimilation and disappearance, but to the strengthening, at least, among some Jews of their Jewish identity. Rather than remaining strangers, a transformation of Jewish identity took place that allowed Jews to integrate into Chinese society. Sinification permitted their survival as part of the Chinese environment.

The history of the community has been preserved in fragments. Whatever information exists is derived from several kinds of sources: (1) Five inscriptions on stones or stelae which date from 1489, 1512, 1663 (1663a and 1663b, one on each side of the stele), and 1679.[3] The stones were erected to commemorate special occasions in communal life such as the rebuilding of the synagogue after a fire or flood or, as in the case of the 1679 stone, the erecting of a memorial archway. The inscriptions are useful for supplying names and historical data as well as for conveying the leading families' (the composers of the inscriptions or their sponsors) perception of their early history and integration into Chinese society. They are especially useful for indicating how they understood their Judaism, and how they wanted their Judaism to be seen by others.[4] (2) 'The Memorial Book of the Dead', which is a register of all seven lineages (men and women) together with prayers for the dead. It was apparently composed in the seventeenth century and there are no entries after 1670.[5] (3) Jesuit accounts of Kaifeng in the seventeenth and eighteenth centuries, of which the eighteenth-century information by Jean-Paul Gozani (published in 1707) and Jean Domenge, who visited Kaifeng in 1721 and 1722, is especially important. (4) Apparently no visitors came to Kaifeng between 1725 and 1850, but after that date accounts by both Protestant missionaries and other travellers provide fragmentary and only partially useful information.

Due to the limited source material the process of sinification cannot be recaptured in detail. The general pattern over a period of roughly 700 years can, however, be outlined as follows: (1) From the time of their arrival early in the twelfth century until the mid-fifteenth century, Kaifeng Jewry was apparently strengthened and reinforced by contacts with other Jewish communities within and without China. Its numbers may also have been augmented by new arrivals. In the course of this 300-year period, kinship organization in accordance with the Chinese style lineage system was adopted. (2) Contacts with communities outside of China probably ceased by the mid-fifteenth century. Moreover, sometime around the beginning of the seventeenth century the Jewish presence in Chinese cities other than Kaifeng disappeared, and the community continued in complete isolation. Despite ongoing sinification (its lifestyle, included the taking of Chinese secondary wives and concubines, and the successful integration of members into Chinese society) its Jewish identity persisted. Neither in these nor in later centuries is there evidence of discrimination against the Jews. (3) In the eighteenth century and thereafter, the Kaifeng Jews were identified and, in turn, identified themselves as a religious sect, not dissimilar from other popular syncretic sects that were present in Chinese society. This sectarian identity persisted into the twentieth century and, instead of obliterating Jewish identity, served to reinforce it. To this day a number of Kaifeng families still refer to themselves as Jews, even if they are in no sense practicing Jews.[6] In what follows I will first briefly outline the history of the Kaifeng Jews, then offer some thoughts on how to understand the process of sinification together with the persistence of Jewish identity resulting from kinship and sectarian identity.

HISTORY

Jewish traders probably first came to China in the late eighth or early ninth century. Having arrived by sea, Jews as well as Arabs traded together in the south, at Guangzhou (Canton) and, no doubt, also in the north, in the Chinese capital of Chang'an. By the ninth century the capital was a cosmopolitan city with two large markets. Among peoples from Central Asia who flocked to Chang'an, there were Persians and others from further west as well as Jews. A *Selihot* (penitential) prayer written on paper which was recovered in Dunhuang, one of the traditional gateways to China, attests to Jews having arrived and/or left by that route.[7] However, there is no evidence that a permanent community was established at this time.

Some two centuries later, but probably before 1120, Jews began to arrive in Kaifeng, the capital of the Northern Song dynasty (960–1126). They may have come in small groups both overland and by sea. Some may possibly have originated in both Yemen and Persia for, as R.J. Zwi Werblowsky has argued persuasively, the Kaifeng Jews' liturgy is related to the Yemenite as well as the old Persian rite.[8] But according to their own account (the 1489 inscription)[9], they came from India as cotton merchants. Whatever their origin, they must have arrived before war engulfed northern China in the early twelfth century. In the 1120s northern China was threatened by invasion from China's inner Asian neighbours, the Jurchen, and it is highly unlikely that overland caravans could have reached the capital after the start of full-scale hostilities. It is moreover unlikely that groups of strangers would have tried to travel to the inland capital from the sea coast during the disturbances. Hence it should be assumed that the Jews came not much later than 1120 and that some years of settling in passed before they built a synagogue.[10] According to the 1489 account, the synagogue was built in 1163. By that date northern China was ruled by the foreign Jurchen (Jin) dynasty, while Chinese rule was confined to the area south of the Yangzi River.

Jewish merchants came to Kaifeng for several obvious reasons. During the Northern Song dynasty Kaifeng was a multi-functional metropolitan centre of more than one million people. It was a commercial and industrial city, at the hub of an overland and river communications network. A vigorous import-export trade connected Kaifeng to the eastern seaboard and to the Yangzi delta with its flourishing port cities.[11] Therefore, Jewish traders arriving in, say, Yangzhou or Ningbo on the south-eastern coast might have found it desirable to have permanent business representatives in the capital, especially since Jewish communities were quite likely also established in the twelfth century in Yangzhou and Ningbo[12].

Between the Jews' arrival early in the twelfth century and the first notice about a Jewish presence in Kaifeng by Matteo Ricci (1551–1610) in 1605 – the date of Ricci's meeting with the Jew Ai Tian in Peking – the community underwent a process of integration into Chinese society. Jews received Chinese surnames and were apparently organized into lineage families. Members of these lineages had careers in Chinese official life as military men, or in the civil service. When individuals participated in the official examinations, acquired degrees, and were assigned positions, their families also benefited and rose in status. In addition, Jews were apparently active in all walks of life as merchants, artisans, and government clerks.

The synagogue, built in 1163, was in use until around 1849 when it was severely damaged by floods. Until 1810 there was a community leader, or head of the religious sect (*zhangjiao*).[13] Men prayed three times a day with a *minyan* (ten men); liturgy and prayers were in accordance with the rabbinical (Talmudic) tradition; *haphtarot* (prophetic portions) were read on the Sabbath; the yearly cycle of Torah reading was observed; *kashrut* and circumcision were practiced. The Jews celebrated seasonal festivals, even if there seems to have been a gradual sinification of festival practices by including ancestor worship and seasonal foods common to Chinese festivals, as is indicated by the 1663a inscription.[14] Polygamy and concubinage were practiced. The first wife, at least, until the end of the seventeenth century, was Jewish; secondary wives and concubines were Chinese.

Sometime between 1851 and 1866 the synagogue was dismantled. Whatever Jewish practices still remained came gradually into disuse, although some form of *kashrut* continued as late as the beginning of the twentieth century. Abstinence from pork (possibly as a result of Muslim influence) is a persistent memory to the present day.[15] Circumcision was probably discontinued around the turn of the century, and knowledge of Hebrew, which had been reported as weak already by the eighteenth-century Jesuits, apparently disappeared altogether after the demise of the last *zhangjiao* in 1810. Nonetheless, today as well as in previous decades, visitors to Kaifeng, when meeting members of the Shi, Zhao, or Ai families, are invariably told that these families are Jewish. Numerically the community was never very large. At its peak in the eighteenth century it consisted of perhaps 2,000 individuals. Prior to the Second World War there may still have been between 200–300 families. It is hard to tell how many families today identify themselves as Jewish.[16]

JEWISH IDENTITY AND KINSHIP ORGANIZATION

By what means was this identity retained? Is not, we are inclined to say, Jewish identity in part connected to Jewish practices? Have not Jews, dispersed in Western culture, ceased to be Jews within a generation or two when they were no longer practicing Jews? Is it the strength of a particular group's Judaism, something within Judaism, that allows Kaifeng families to cling to their Jewish memory? Or should the answer be sought more specifically in Chinese culture and society as well as in the Kaifeng setting on the North China Plain?

It is of no small significance that early in the fifteenth century the surname Zhao was bestowed by imperial decree on one An San (Hassan?)[17] and that other Jewish families probably acquired their Chinese surnames at about the same time. The use of Chinese family names by the Jews of Kaifeng suggests that more or less contemporaneously they adopted the Chinese lineage family organization. Chinese lineages generally trace their origin to one ancestor, go by one surname, are domiciled in one locality, and hold some properties, such as burial grounds, in common. The following evidence can be cited to support the assumption of a lineage family organization in Kaifeng. First there are the various terms used for family on the five stone inscriptions. In the 1489 inscription the term *shi* is used for families, indicating surnames, rather than individual families.[18] (The 1512 inscription discusses individuals rather than families and, therefore, furnishes no further evidence.) The 1663a inscription mentions for the first time the 'seven names' (*qi xing*), clearly indicating that lineages are referred to.[19] The most obvious example is found in the 1679 inscription when 73 names (*xing*) are said to consist of 500 families (*jia*).[20] The 1663b inscription further distinguishes blood relations (*zu*) or immediate family from more remote family.[21]

Further evidence may be adduced from burial customs. According to Wang Yisha, the Jews date the use of family cemeteries variously to the late nineteenth century or after the 1642 flood. The latter is a more likely date and, furthermore, reaffirms the increasing adoption of lineage and agnatic forms of family organization, according to which burial, particularly in north China, customarily took place in family cemeteries. He lists a number of sites in Kaifeng's suburbs or in adjoining hamlets and notes that Jin Ziru's family cemetery and Li Enshou's family cemetery have each a 'foremost' grave marked 'Old Ancestor's Grave'.[22]

The importance of the ancestor in the lives of lineage families can also be seen in the keeping of ancestor portraits. Sixty year old Shi Zhongyu remembered in 1982 that his mother owned several ancestor portraits.[23] Mrs Phyllis Horal visited Kaifeng and actually saw one such portrait. It is painted in the manner of conventional Chinese ancestor portraits and shows a distinguished man in official robes.[24] However, none of the nineteenth and twentieth-century visitors mentions family ancestral halls, although apparently an ancestral hall (*citang*) was part of the synagogue. According to the Anglican missionaries, the Jews did use ancestral tablets.[25]

Finally, Bishop White, writing in 1919, makes reference to a family register (*jiapu*) which was kept by the Shi family.[26] This was most certainly a lineage register customarily kept by large Chinese lineages and thus quite different from the genealogy register of the dead (now in Cincinnati) in which all seven lineages appear. Apparently the Zhao family too had such a register, which presumably was taken away by an Englishman.[27]

The transformation of a community of families, or even clans, into a group of lineages has significant implications for the question of identity. When Jews acquired Chinese surnames and began to adjust family and community organization to lineage and family organization, identification with the larger and amorphous community became less important than identification with the lineage and agnatic group. Thus individuals identified first with the family and second with the lineage. As long as lineages remained Jewish, individual Jews were unlikely to abandon their Jewish identity. Although Jewishness could be forgotten and abandoned by an entire family, especially if that family left Kaifeng, Jewishness would continue within the lineage as long as the lineage remained intact and was domiciled in the same locality What then bound Kaifeng Jews together was not community, but family identity.

This is not to negate the importance of the synagogue in Kaifeng Jewish life. As long as the synagogue was in existence, it was a centre for housing the all-important scriptures and for meeting in worship. Jews met in the synagogue, however, as members of Jewish families and not as members of a Jewish community. But it was not the building that determined or even sustained the identity of the congregants. Indeed, because of the kin-centred identity which evolved, Jews could identify as Jewish even after there was no longer a synagogue.

The gradual weakening of Jewish practices in the late eighteenth and nineteenth centuries, and especially the loss of Jewish learning that accompanied the general intellectual decline among Kaifeng Jewish families, did not, however, lead to a weakening of Jewish identity among all the families. The intellectual decline among, what were, no doubt, élite families, was, however, a serious problem. Men like Zhao Yingcheng (1619–57?), or his younger brother, Zhao Yingdou, were actively engaged in the maintenance of Judaism in Kaifeng,[28] but they were also degree holders and served in provinces other than their native Henan.[29] Although they periodically returned to Kaifeng, either at the conclusion of their tour of duty or to observe mourning periods, their working lives and their Jewish lives did not coincide. While this is not exactly a brain drain, it nonetheless indicates that those most versed and most vitally interested in the maintenance of Jewish practices in Kaifeng were men whose status and position required them to be elsewhere. They could not be counted on to maintain Jewish learning in Kaifeng in a sustained fashion.

JEWISH IDENTITY AND SECTARIAN IDENTITY

Whereas Jewish identity was eroded on one level, on another it was reinforced because Jewish religious practices came to be regarded as similar to those of a popular religious sect. Like other sects, the Jews were called a *jiao*; they had a shrine, a religious leader, and they engaged in certain practices which differentiated them from other sectarians. Their Judaism, as can be partially gleaned from the stelae inscriptions, was evolving into a Judeo-Confucian syncretism. As a popular sect, Judaism did not have to be regarded by others as the religion of strangers, but could be seen to fit into a mosaic of syncretic sectarian groups which characterized Chinese religious life in the north as well as in other parts of China. Identifying with a sect together with family identity, rather than undermining or obliterating Jewish identity, served to maintain it even after the synagogue fell into complete ruin and was dismantled in the mid-nineteenth century. To understand this sectarian identity it will be useful first to take a look at how the Jews were referred to and how they referred to themselves. As was noted above, between the seventeenth and the twentieth centuries Kaifeng Jews were referred to and identified themselves as a *jiao*, which can be translated variously as religion, religious sect, or teaching. Two different names were in use, one was *Tiaojin jiao* (sinew plucking sect – a reference to meat preparation where animal blood is carefully avoided), the other was *Jiao jing jiao* (scripture teaching sect). According to the Jesuit Jean Domenge (1666–1735), the Jews were also called *Lanmao huihui* (blue cap Muslims).³⁰ These designations do not appear on the stone inscriptions. Nor does the term Israel (*Yici luoye*) appear as the name of the people. In the 1489, 1512, and 1663a inscriptions, Israel is used only in reference to the founding or the establishment of the teaching (*jiao*).³¹ Thus the 1489 inscription opens with the statement, 'The founder (*zushi*) who established the teaching [religion] of Israel was Abraham...' The term *zushi* is generally used for founders of religious sects. When the adherents of this religion, that is the Jews, are referred to, the term Israel is not used and they are simply called the followers of the teaching (*jiaozhong* or *jiaoren*).³² Quite probably 'sinew plucking sect' and 'scripture teaching sect' were popularly used by their Chinese neighbours and, although accepted by the Jews, were avoided in official statements, which these stones represent. The Jesuit Jean-Paul Gozani (1647–1732) seems to imply just this when he wrote in 1704 that the '...idolators first gave them this name [*Tiaojin jiao*].'³³

Whether called 'sinew plucking' or 'scripture teaching', the Jews considered themselves and were considered by others a *jiao*. In this particular context, *jiao* is probably best translated as religious sect, for their Chinese neighbours may very well have thought of them as one of the many popular sects whom they in part resembled. By the nineteenth century, place and religion were linked and the alley in the vicinity of the synagogue where they lived was called the 'sinew plucking sect' alley. This was changed to the 'scripture teaching sect' alley and may have changed again. The term *Youtai ren* or Jew is of more recent usage and Kaifeng families refered to themselves as *Youtai ren* only in the twentieth century.

To understand the significance of this designation as a sect, the prevalence of popular sectarianism in Chinese society requires some explanation. Sectarian religions, consisting of mixtures of Buddhist, Daoist, Confucian, and folk elements had appeared for the first time in the fourteenth century. Generally considered 'unorthodox' by the official establishment, syncretic sectarianism came to be both localized and highly fragmented and the sects were known by many different names. Depending on local conditions, sectarian religious groups often developed millenarian and political aims. At such times local officials took notice of their activities and when they reached a militant stage the rebellious sectarians were suppressed. Several of the great popular rebellions of the last 700 years – beginning with the rebellion that led to the overthrow of the Mongol (Yuan) dynasty in 1368 – had their origin in religious sectarianism turned politically militant. However, as long as these sects pursued purely religious goals, gathering adherents, meeting in prayer, and observing ceremonials in their meeting houses and shrines, they generally escaped the notice of local officials. Hence the paucity of information about their more quiescent phases.[34]

In spite of the widely varying syncretic combinations among the sectarian groups, there were nonetheless several characteristics which most shared. A sect had a leader or sect master (*jiao zhu*), a set of sacred writings or scriptures, generally referred to as 'precious books' (*bao juan*) or 'holy books' (*jing*) and a meeting place for worship and prayer. A set of distinct doctrines differentiated one sect from another and membership was conferred in acts of initiation.[35] Many sects also had dietary practices, including vegetarianism. Members of sects were usually recruited from among the lower strata of the population (peasants, small-town artisans, and merchants), although lower grade officials, clerks, and military men were also known to be members of religious sects.

Susan Naquin describes White Lotus sects in which hereditary transmission of sectarianism within families assured the sect's longevity as well as cohesiveness. She writes, 'There, sect patriarchs were simultaneously lineage ancestors (both termed *zu* parent-children relationships reinforced those between teachers and pupils, and the intimate and double-stranded connection between generations slowed the dilution of religious doctrine and the loss of organizational control.'[36] However, even when sect adherence was not hereditary, sects generally were not merely associations of individuals. Those who joined tended to bring in other members of their households. Sect membership frequently was family membership.[37]

In the eighteenth century and at the beginning of the nineteenth, sects were widely dispersed throughout China, in the Yangzi Valley, along the south-eastern coast, as well as on the North China Plain. Prior to the great Eight Trigrams Uprising of 1813, popular religious sects flourished in the vicinity of Kaifeng within a circumference of 100 to 200 kilometres.[38] Popular religious sects on the North China Plain, in parts of Henan and Hebei, existed well before 1813. They were a part of the rural as well as the urban scene.

City and countryside were not rigidly isolated from one another, people travelled to and fro in pursuit of livelihood, and people met in day-to-day activities. F. W. Mote has pointed out that even if townsman and countryman differed, in China the city and country were of the same fabric. Cities were not islands in a rude and crude countryside, and they bore no resemblance to the semi-autonomous city-states in Europe. He writes, 'The rural component of Chinese civilization was more or less uniform, and it extended everywhere.... It was like a net in which the cities and towns of China were suspended.'[39] However, to establish a clear connection between sectarianism and Kaifeng Jews is not easy. As long as a religious sect did not develop political aims, thereby becoming a real or imagined threat to the established order, it was considered harmless and escaped official attention. Throughout its history, the 'sinew plucking sect' apparently had no political ambitions.

By the eighteenth and nineteenth centuries the Jews had so completely blended into their environment that they were indistinguishable from their Chinese neighbours. Their religious practices also were not too dissimilar. If their Chinese neighbours assumed that the Jews belonged to a harmless religious sect, they would consider the 'sinew pluckers' not much different from other sects with which they were familiar. Like other syncretic sects, the 'sinew plucking sect' had a meeting place; it had a set of sacred writings shared only by those who participated in sectarian worship; it had a leader who was the keeper of the scriptures; and it had dietary and other practices. In all likelihood, this sectarian identity suited the Jews and they perpetuated it as a remembered identity, even after the synagogue disappeared, the scriptures were sold, and Jewish practices were discontinued.[40]

When the Jews were identified as well as accepted, the identification of a *jiao* of scripture teaching or sinew plucking they severed, on the one hand, the connection to a foreign and universal religion, and forged, on the other, a link to the native and local religion. Identifying as Jewish in eighteenth, nineteenth, and even twentieth-century Kaifeng meant not underscoring difference or outsider status; rather, it meant emphasizing particularity within universality, being a particular group among any number of other groups who were also particular. Shi Zhongyu described himself in 1982 as a Jew and as a 'descendant of the Yellow Emperor',[41] thus expressing quite accurately both his forebears' and his own identity.

Sectarian identity, both conferred and accepted, seems more important than the fact that sometimes Jews were considered Muslims because of obvious but superficial similarities. In any event, the acceptance of Muslim identity appears to be a relatively recent phenomenon, related to the weakening of kin and sectarian identity and the severing of links to their native place, Kaifeng. In the periodic rebellions, wars, and conquests of the twentieth century, families dispersed and moved to various parts of China, thus losing their connection to place which figures importantly in maintaining family identity.

The Jin family is a case in point. At some time, early in the twentieth century, Jin family members came to identify themselves as Muslims, without apparently also being practicing Muslims. Jin Xiaojing, now of Beijing, accidentally rediscovered her Jewish origins when she traced her family background to Kaifeng, where Muslim Jins were not known, but Jewish Jins certainly were.[42] Not mistaken ascription, but the weakening of both native place ties and family identity contributed to some Kaifeng Jewish families eventually becoming or being considered Muslim.

Sectarian identity was, furthermore, affirmed in those portions of the stelae inscriptions which discuss the Jews' religious and historical beginnings. These, though unfortunately sparse, statements show, however, that Kaifeng Jews saw themselves as part of the broad stream of Chinese tradition and culture, with merely some divergent developments in the past.[43]

ADAM, ABRAHAM, AND PAN GU

The three inscriptions, those from 1489, 1512, and 1663a, reveal interesting variations. According to the first, 'The Patriarch (*zushi*) Abraham, who established the religion (*jiao*) of Israel, was the nineteenth generation descendant of Pan Gu Adam'. The 1663a inscription has it somewhat differently, 'The establishment of the Israel religion is in the distant past. It began with Adam, the nineteenth descendant of Pan Gu, and continued through Noah and Abraham'. The 1512 inscription does not mention Pan Gu, but distinguishes between the first ancestor (*shizu*) of the Israel religion, Adam, 'who originally came from the West country of India in the Zhou period' (traditional dates, 1122–221 BC), and Abraham who founded the religion and is, therefore, the religion's ancestor (*jiaozu*).[44]

The joining of Adam and Pan Gu, and in the 1489 inscription even Abraham, is quite amazing, for the Pan Gu myth bears absolutely no similarity to the Adam or Abraham stories. Pan Gu was a giant whose body after he died became the created world and everything within it. The Pan Gu myth is thus a creation story and presents creation as transformation, made possible by the act of dying, whereas in the biblical Genesis story, Adam was created after the creation of the world. In the 1489 inscription, Pan Gu and Adam are, so to speak, contemporaries, although having the two names side by side could also mean that Pan Gu and Adam are one and the same person. Whatever the case may be, Abraham is a descendant of both, and here and elsewhere in the inscriptions the succession is patrilineal, in accordance with Chinese usage, in which women do not figure.

The several terms which are used for Adam and Abraham indicate how their functions are perceived. Both the 1489 and 1663a inscriptions place Abraham's name in close relationship with the development of the religion, and he is, therefore, referred to variously as the Patriarch of the religion or its ancestor. Among the characteristics ascribed to Abraham that allow him to occupy this exalted position are understanding the correct teaching (*zheng jiao*) and understanding the true heaven (*zhen tian*).[45] Adam as the first ancestor has no contact with religious developments and is, therefore, not given the title of Patriarch (*zushi*) which is reserved for those who have contributed to the transmission of the teaching. The inscription assigns a pivotal role to transmitters like Moses, who is called the 'master of the law' (*shifa*) and to Ezra, under whom it shone with renewed brightness (*fuming*).[46]

Finally, mention should be made of the fact that in addition to Pan Gu, the 1489 inscription also refers to the 'creation (*kaipi*) of heaven and earth', following which the Patriarchs transmitted the teaching.[47] The term *kaipi* has, however, none of the Genesis implications. It means literally 'separation [of heaven and earth]' and thus conforms to the Chinese view that the world began as an 'opening up', when heaven ascended and earth descended. Given this context and the terminology used, creation, therefore, did not indicate to either the Jewish or the Chinese reader of the inscription that God created the world. Nonetheless, it is also stated that the 'great origin comes from Heaven' (*dayuan chu yu Tian*).[48]

HEAVEN, GOD, THE WAY

None of the five inscriptions introduce a new and strange god,[49] or a new term for God. When referring to the Jewish God, in most cases Heaven (*Tian*) occurs and occasionally *di*, perhaps best translated with deity. This, however, presents a problem. We cannot be certain whether the Jews had actually come to consider Heaven as synonymous with the biblical God, or if they were simply using a convenient term known to all for the purpose of the inscriptions. The latter may be the case. Reference to Heaven is made in various contexts and is frequently coupled with the important term for respect or reverence (*jing*), admonishing believers to revere Heaven or show reverence for Heaven.[50] Both the 1489 and 1663a inscriptions sometimes join reverence for Heaven with honouring ancestors (*cun*). According to the 1489 inscription, sacrifices cannot be offered to the ancients if Heaven only is revered without also honouring ancestors. The 1663a inscription stresses revering Heaven and observing the regulations (*fa*) of the ancestors. Belief in Heaven was, therefore, shown as an integral part of filial piety and ancestor worship. Might this indicate perhaps that belief in the One God was considered a private, or sectarian, matter not meant for public display?

Heaven is also sometimes referred to in conjunction with the Way (*Dao*), that is, Heaven's Way. Although it might seem occasionally that *Dao* and Heaven are used synonymously, this is not in fact the case. Revere *Dao*, admonishes the 1489 inscription, but do not forget Heaven; or, in another place, *Dao* has no form similar to the Way of Heaven above. Yet the 1489 inscription, when using *Dao*, seems also sometimes to refer to God. In the 1663a inscription, Abraham is said to have known that the Way of Heaven has neither sound nor smell. Heaven is thus not awesome, inspiring fear and dread. Only the 1512 inscription mentions fear of Heaven's decree (*wei Tianming*), which is, however, not the same as fearing Heaven.

Obviously in these inscriptions Jewish and Chinese beliefs about beginnings, creation, and what happened thereafter are intertwined in a useful syncretism. It is useful because the inscriptions reveal a compatible accommodation that allowed Jews to be Chinese without ceasing to be Jews. Centre stage is occupied by the men (not women) – Adam, Abraham, Moses – who make the history that eventually brings the Jews to Kaifeng. According to the inscriptions, this might have been during the Zhou or during the Han dynasty (206 BCE-AD 220). There is no divine guidance, no God who punishes or makes promises, but there is also no backsliding and no complications. What matters then in those portions which deal with the history prior to the building of the synagogue in Kaifeng is the account of the handing down of the tradition. As seems to be the case in some other sectarian traditions,[51] these inscriptions attempt to show legitimate succession and transmission.

In this essay I have argued that the Kaifeng Jews' process of integration into Chinese society – their sinification – has not led to assimilation and extinction of all Kaifeng Jews. In fact, because of its rather unusual features, this process led to the maintenance of Jewish identity and to the persistence of Jewish memory. After a patrilineal kinship organization of lineages evolved among Kaifeng Jews, Jewish identity was shifted from a people and community to lineage and family. Jewish identity was linked to Kaifeng since Chinese lineages are always associated with specific localities. When individual Jewish families dispersed, as has been the case especially in the twentieth century, the tie to both lineage and place was severed, leading to the cessation of Jewish identity. On the other hand, families who remained in Kaifeng and who may have had also stronger and longer lasting kinship associations, like the Shi and Zhao families, continue to identify themselves as Jewish to the present day.

Being Jewish in Kaifeng was not an individual matter. It meant belonging to a family and to a group that identified itself as Jewish and was identified as such by others. Chinese society was (and still is to a large extent) composed of overlapping social groupings, including occupational, kinship, religious, and similar associations in which membership might be by birth, marriage, or adoption. A person had to be a member of an identifiable group, and Kaifeng Jews were no exception to this.

To account for the persistence of Jewish memory, religious identity was also considered in this essay. Jewish practices in Kaifeng, no matter how much was lost or forgotten in the course of time, had most of the earmarks of Chinese sectarian religion. Like other sectarians, the 'sinew pluckers' had a shrine, scriptures, and practices that distinguished them from other sects. Acts of initiation conferred membership; a set of distinct doctrines, not shared by others, distinguished the 'sinew pluckers' in the eyes of their Chinese neighbours. Whether the sectarian identity was conferred and then adopted, or first adopted and then conferred, is not the issue, nor can the question be satisfactorily answered. What is significant, however, is the transformation of religious identity from a foreign universal religion to a syncretic sectarian religion which was no longer foreign.

The syncretism consisted in combining, or in fusing, Confucian and Jewish concepts, as pointed out by Andrew Plaks. It also consisted in establishing a history that was commensurate with Chinese history, and a transmission of the tradition that verified the religion's legitimacy. Without having to bother themselves (and others) about matters such as sin, punishment, or divine intervention Jews affirmed that their history began with a first ancestor, and continued through worthy men thereafter. These men knew the correct religion, or teaching (*zheng jiao*), were benevolent (*ren*) and righteous (*yi*), and, as in Abraham's case, were not misled by ghosts and spirits (*gui shen*).[52]

The combination of family and sectarian identity, I suggest, was so durable that even if successive generations increasingly forgot after the synagogue disappeared, the memory of a Jewish past did not cease.

Because of a unique process of acculturation and transformation, which began probably some 200 years after their arrival in Kaifeng, the identity of the Kaifeng Jews was strengthened rather than destroyed, allowing for its persistence into the twentieth century.

NOTES

1. Michael Pollak, *Mandarins, Jews and Missionaries, The Jewish Experience in the Chinese Empire*, Philadelphia: The Jewish Publication Society of America, 1980, is an exhaustive summary and analysis of all accounts about Kaifeng Jews that were available to both Jews and Christians.
2. Chen Yuan, 'Kaifeng Yiciluoye jiao' (Kaifeng Jewish religion), *Dongfang Zazhi*, Vol.17, no.5 (1920), pp. 117–22; no. 6, pp. 119–26; no. 7, pp. 103-107.
3. William C. White, *Chinese Jews, A Compilation of Matters Relating to the Jews of K'aifeng Fu*, Toronto: University of Toronto Press, 1966, 2nd ed., Part II, pp. 35–9, 51–4, 80–5, 94–5, 104–7. Two stelae are preserved in the twentieth century, the stone with the 1489 and 1512 inscriptions and the nearly illegible 1679 stone. The stone with the two 1663 inscriptions has disappeared. The 1489–1512 stele is today in the Kaifeng museum. In addition to White's English translation of the inscriptions, there is a German translation of the 1512 inscription by Willy Tonn, 'Eine jüdische Inschrift der Synagoge in K'aifeng Fu aus dem Jahre 1512', *Gemeindeblatt der jüdischen Gemeinde zu Berlin*, Vol. 20, no. 8 (August 1930), pp. 360–4. A Hebrew translation of the 1489 inscription was prepared as an appendix by Andrew H. Plaks, "Matsevet zikaron le'hanukat beit-hakneset 'ha'Emet ha'Tehorah' be'Kaifeng laregel beniyato mehadash (1489)' (The memorial stone at the renovation of the synagogue 'Truth and Purity' in Kaifeng (1489), *Pe'amim*, no. 4 (1989), pp. 83–8.
4. See Andrew H. Plaks, 'The Confucianization of Chinese Jews: Interpretation of the K'aifeng Stelae Inscriptions', unpublished paper on how the inscriptions interpret Jewish concepts in reference to Confucian thought.
5. Donald D. Leslie, *The Chinese-Hebrew Memorial Book of the Jewish Community of K'aifeng*, Belconnen: Canberra College of Advanced Education,1984.
6. However, a recent Chinese convert to orthodox Judaism in Israel from the Jin family will most certainly practice the commandments (*mitzvoth*), see Michael Freund, 'How Wen-Jing Became "Shalva"', *The Jerusalem Post*, 22 June 2004, p. 5.
7. White, *Chinese Jews*, Part I, p. 140.
8. R.J. Zwi Werblowsky, 'A Note on the Jewish Community in Kaifeng. A Liturgical Perspective', in Holger Preissler and Hubert Seiwert, eds, *Gnosisforschung und Religionsgeschichte, Festschrift fuer Kurt Rudolph zum 65. Geburtstag*, Marburg: Diagonal-Verlag, 1994, pp. 587–95.
9. White, *Chinese Jews*, Part II, p. 37. White's Chinese text for the stone inscriptions is used throughout this essay.
10. On the other hand, the Jews may have remained in Kaifeng precisely because they were unable to return home due to the unsettled conditions in the north. I am grateful to Professor Steven Kaplan for this suggestion.
11. The high degree of commercial and industrial development in the Northern Song dynasty is discussed by Robert Hartwell, 'Markets, Technology, and the Structure of Enterprise in the Development of the Eleventh-Century Chinese Iron and Steel Industry', *Journal of Economic History*, Vol. 26, no. 1 (March 1966), pp. 29–58.
12. The existence of a Jewish community in Ningbo in the fifteenth century is well established. Sometime between 1457 and 1465 (following the 1461 flood?), several Kaifeng Jews obtained a Torah scroll there, which they brought back to Kaifeng. Another scroll also from Ningbo was brought to Kaifeng by Zhao Ying. Early in the sixteenth century a certain Jin Pu from Yangzhou obtained an additional scroll for the Kaifeng community. The Yangzhou and Ningbo Jewish communities disappeared from view sometime in the seventeenth century. Donald D. Leslie, *The Survival of the Chinese Jews: The Jewish Community of Kaifeng*. Leiden: Brill, 1972, pp. 29, 146.

13. It might be misleading to translate *zhangjiao* with rabbi, since wider responsibilities are implied by the Chinese term. A more accurate translation of the Chinese term would be head of the teaching or head of the sect.
14. White, *Chinese Jews*, Part II, pp. 81-82. The 1663a inscription speaks of filial piety (*xiao*) as being the subject of the scriptures; sacrifices to ancestors take place in summer and winter with seasonal foods; the foods at the mid-autumn sacrifice are without seasoning.
15. Qu Yinan, for example, remembers her grandfather's refusal to eat pork. Quoted by Mathis Chazanov, 'Chinese Jew Traces her Heritage', *Los Angeles Times*, 8 December 1985.
16. See Wang Yisha, 'The Descendants of the Kaifeng Jews', in Sidney Shapiro, ed., *Jews in Old China, Studies by Chinese Scholars*, New York: Hyppocrene Books, 1984, pp. 167–87, and Leslie, *The Chinese-Hebrew Memorial Book*, pp. 293–300, which provides a breakdown on the basis of the Memorial Book.
17. Leslie, *Survival of the Chinese Jews*, p. 26.
18. White, *Chinese Jews*, Part II, p. 38.
19. Ibid., p. 94.
20. Ibid., pp. 104–5.
21. Ibid., p. 95.
22. Wang, 'The Descendants of the Kaifeng Jews', pp. 183-4; Myron L. Cohen, 'Lineage Organization in North China', *The Journal of Asian Studies*, 49 (August 1990), p. 513. See also White, *Chinese Jews*, Part I, p. 16: burial in family cemeteries was practiced after the 1642 flood.
23. Michael Weisskopf, 'Judaism Only a Dim Memory to Chinese Descendants', *The Washington Post*, 9 April 1982.
24. Mrs Horal kindly made a photograph of the portrait available to the Department of East Asian Studies at the Hebrew University of Jerusalem.
25. 'Missionary News', *The Chinese Recorder*, 50 (November 1919), pp. 780–8
26. Ibid. According to the Anglican missionaries in Kaifeng, only the Shi family kept a register, which was discovered in 1919. See also Wang, 'The Descendants of the Kaifeng Jews', p. 186, according to which the register cannot be located. However, in *Zhongguo Youtai chunqiu* (Spring and Autumn of Chinese Jews), Beijing: Haiyang Publishers, 1992, p. 197, Wang mentions a family register for both the Shi and Zhao families.
27. Zhao Yunzhong's account to Mikami Teicho, who visited Kaifeng in October 1940. Mikami Teicho, 'Kaifeng yudakyoto no Genjo hokoku' (Report on the present day status of Kaifeng Jews), *Shina kukkyo Shingaku*, 5, no. 1 (June 1941), pp. 76–7.
28. After the disastrous 1642 flood when most of Kaifeng was inundated and the synagogue was completely destroyed, the Zhaos were, according to the 1663b inscription, prime movers in the rebuilding of the synagogue and in the restoration of the water-damaged scrolls. It is regrettable that the two books, one by Zhao Yingcheng, *Sheng jing ji bian* (A Record of the Disaster of the Holy Scriptures), the other by Zhao Yingdou, *Mingdao xu* (Preface to the Illustrious Way), are no longer extant. White, *Chinese Jews*, Part II, p. 84. Personal statements, in addition to the official inscriptions, might have thrown light on the problem of literati status and Jewish identity.
29. Leslie, *Chinese-Hebrew Memorial Book*, pp. 227–30.
30. Leslie, *Survival of the Chinese Jews*, p.108.
31. White, *Chinese Jews*, Part II, pp. 35, 52, 80.
32. Ibid., for example, pp. 83, 94, 104, in the 1663a and b and 1679 inscriptions.
33. Leslie, *Survival of the Chinese Jews*, p. 49.
34. Two useful accounts on popular sectarian religions are by Daniel L. Overmyer, *Folk Buddhist Religion, Dissenting Sects in Late Traditional China*, Cambridge: Harvard University Press, 1976, and Susan Naquin, *Millenarian Rebellion in China: The Eight Trigrams Uprising in 1813*, New Haven: Yale University Press, 1976.
35. Steven Harrell and Elisabeth J. Perry, 'Syncretic Sects in Chinese Society: An Introduction', *Modern China*, 8, no. 3 (July 1982), p. 286. The authors point out that all sectarians met the latter two criteria.
36. Susan Naquin, 'Connections Between Rebellions: Sect Family Networks in Qing China', *Modern China*, 8, no. 3 (July 1982), p. 339.
37. Susan Naquin, 'Millinarian Rebellion in China: The Eight Trigrams Uprising in 1813', Ph.D. Dissertation, Yale University, 1974, p. 128, n. 101, p. 427.
38. Sects were reported in Shangqiu county, approximately 200 km south-east of Kaifeng; in Hua county, approximately 100 km north-east, and in Jun (Yu) county, approximately 200 km. south-west. Naquin, 'Millinarian Rebellion', maps, pp. 132, 149, 257.

39. Frederick W. Mote, 'The Transformation of Nanking, 1350–1400', in G. William Skinner, ed., *The City in Late Imperial China*, Stanford: Stanford University Press, 1977, p. 105.
40. In 1940 Zhao Yunzhong, having adopted twentieth-century nomenclature, referred to Judaism as *Youtai jiao* and to himself as *hui chang*. See Mikami, 'Report', p. 76.
41. Shi quoted by Weisskopf, 'Judaism Only a Dim Memory'.
42. Jin Xiaojing, 'Woshi Zhongguo Youtai ren' (I am a Chinese Jew), *Shehui Kexue Zhanxian*, no. 4 (1981), pp. 35–7.
43. The 1489 inscription was composed by a Kaifeng Jew, Jin Zhong. White, *Chinese Jews*, Part III, p. 124. Zuo Tang, who composed the 1512 inscription, may have been a Yangzhou Jew, according to White, Part II, note, p. 47. Leslie, *Survival of the Chinese Jews*, p. 29, however, writes that he was 'almost certainly not a Jew'. Leslie, furthermore, suggests that the inscription was not written in Kaifeng, and that the inscribed stone was brought to the city by a group of non-Kaifeng Jews. The 1663a inscription was composed by Liu Chang, a non-Jewish scholar and court minister.
44. White, *Chinese Jews*, Part II, pp. 35, 80, 52.
45. Ibid., p. 35.
46. Ibid., pp. 52–3. However, the 1512 inscription in another place takes up the topic of transmission with Adam as the first Patriarch who transmitted the teaching to Noah.
47. Ibid., p. 35.
48. Ibid., p. 38.
49. I am grateful to Professor Lauren Pfister for repeatedly raising the question of the term used for God in the inscriptions. Apparently the Jews were not troubled by which Chinese term to use, as would be the nineteenth-century Protestant missionaries. On this topic, see I. Eber, 'The Interminable Term Question', in I. Eber, S.K. Wan, K. Walf, with R. Malek, eds., *Bible in Modern China, The Literary and Intellectual Impact*, Sankt Augustin: Monumenta Serica Institute, 1999, pp. 135–61.
50. See, for example, the comments on *jing* by Julia Ching, 'What is Confucian Spirituality?', and Wm. Theodore de Bary, 'Human Rites: An Essay on Confucianism and Human Rights', in I. Eber, ed., *Confucianism: The Dynamics of Tradition*, New York: Macmillan, 1986, pp. 63–80, 109–32.
51. Daniel L. Overmyer, 'Attitudes Toward the Ruler and State in Popular Religious Literature: Sixteenth and Seventeenth Century Pao-chuan', *Harvard Journal of Asiatic Studies*, 44, no. 2 (1984), p. 369.
52. The reference may be to witchcraft, perhaps to such activities as spirit calling or spirit writing, which were not condoned by elite Confucians. But the reference may be also to Confucius' statement about keeping one's distance from the spirits. *Analects*, XI:11.

3

Destination Shanghai, Permits and Transit Visas, 1938–1941

Following the November 1938 pogroms against Jews in Germany and Austria, known as *Kristallnacht* (Night of the Broken Glass), the Nazis initiated a major reorganization of the existing Jewish organizational framework. The aim was to achieve a tighter organization and, together with this, firmer Nazi control over all aspects of what remained of Jewish life. A foremost goal of the Nazis, however, was also to have the new Jewish organization, Reich Association of Jews in Germany (Reichsvereinigung der Juden in Deutschland), put its major effort behind forcing Jewish emigration. Toward this end, the Reich Central Office for Jewish Emigration (Reichszentrale für Jüdische Auswanderung) was set up under Reinhard Heydrich, who appointed the head of the Gestapo, Heinrich Müller, as its chief. Thus Jewish emigration came to be both controlled and forced, similar to what was developed earlier in Austria after the annexation (*Anschluss*) in March 1938.

These changes, and especially *Kristallnacht*, led to the sudden mass emigration to Shanghai which, within a brief eight months – from November 1938 to September 1939 – brought around 20,000 refugees to China's shores. Most of the refugees arrived by sea on German, Italian, French, and Japanese vessels, although Scandinavian and British ships also carried some of the involuntary immigrants. The start of the Second World War in Europe ended German shipping participation in the exodus and, when Italy entered the war in June 1940, Italian ships too no longer sailed to Shanghai. For a little over one year, French vessels, sailing from Marseilles, would carry refugees to Saigon, from where they made their way to Shanghai. But increasingly, until June 1941, when Germany attacked Soviet Russia, refugees, now much reduced in numbers, used the overland route mostly via Harbin and Dalian (Dairen) to reach Shanghai.

Shanghai, between 1939 and the outbreak of the Pacific War in December 1941, was far from a comfortable haven. The city was divided between the International Settlement, run by the Shanghai Municipal Council (SMC), the French Concession, and the Chinese portions, controlled by a Japanese dominated Chinese puppet municipal administration. The outbreak of the Sino-Japanese War in July 1937 had caused vast numbers of Chinese from the countryside to flee in search of shelter to Shanghai's foreign enclaves. Now, a year later, in addition to the Chinese refugees, came the Central European refugees. Most of them settled in partially destroyed Hongkou (Honkew), actually a portion of the International Settlement, but in fact under Japanese jurisdiction.

This essay will address two interrelated issues. One is the Nazi pressure brought to bear on the Jewish population and the voluntary and involuntary choice of Shanghai as destination by a considerable number of Jews. The second concerns the means set in motion by the SMC and the Japanese in 1939 and 1940 to keep the refugees out of Shanghai.

THE POLICY OF JEWISH EMIGRATION

After the Nazis came to power, the major thrust of their anti-Jewish policies was to effectively separate and isolate Jews from German society. However, an SS (Security Service) memorandum of May 1934, addressed to Heydrich, already then opened with the statement that 'the aim of the Jewish policy must be the complete emigration of the Jews'.[1] Perhaps because 1933–36 was a time for creating, above all, economic stability in Germany, Hitler stipulated for the time being other priorities which included forging political and economic relationships in the international arena. Thus emigration as an actual policy, first mentioned in September 1936,[2] became within the next two years a policy of forced emigration of German, including Austrian, Jews. Herbert Hagen, head of the Security Service, had proposed a number of concrete steps that would be eventually implemented, first in Austria after the annexation of March 1938, and then in Germany. Among Hagen's proposals were eliminating Jews from the economy; bringing political and legal pressure on them to force emigration; increasing the technical means of emigration. Naming possible destinations for Jewish emigration, Hagen had also mentioned China.[3] Two major reasons were undoubtedly responsible for the near two-year delay in implementing Hagen's proposals. One was the thorough reshuffling of the Nazi leadership in the course of which Party men assumed increasing power in all areas of German life. Another, more specifically related to this topic, was the change from a pro-China to a pro-Japan foreign policy under the direction of Joachim von Ribbentrop, who headed the Foreign Office from February 1938.

Economic pressures on the German Jewish population multiplied in 1937. But the test of Hagen's proposals came only after the Austrian annexation. Hagen arrived in Vienna on 12 March together with the Wehrmacht's first units. He was followed a few days later by Adolf Eichmann who, as adviser on Jewish affairs to the Security Service, set immediately to work devising the apparatus that would include the liquidation of Jewish property and the Jews' forced emigration.[4] So successful was Eichmann and the Vienna Central Office for Jewish Emigration (Zentralstelle für jüdische Auswanderung), established on 20 August 1938, that his operation became the 'model' for the Berlin Office, the establishment of which began after *Kristallnacht* and was complete by 4 July 1939.[5]

Nonetheless, Jews were not departing in sufficiently large numbers even in 1938. The Évian Conference, which met on 6–13 July 1938 to discuss the refugee question, was clear indication for Hitler and the Nazis that most countries were unwilling to open their gates to untold thousands of pauperized refugees. A report on Évian circulated by the German Foreign Office succinctly stated, 'Nearly all countries characterized Jewish immigration as a burden and rejected raising their quotas.'[6] This included the United States. Despite increasingly fewer destinations, compelling Jews to leave Germany and the now annexed Austria continued to be the central policy of the Nazi regime. Thus a Foreign Ministry circular of 25 January 1939 reiterated that the aim of Germany's Jewish policy was emigration.[7]

DESTINATION SHANGHAI

By would-be immigrants Shanghai was regarded differently before and after *Kristallnacht*. Although few would have elected to go to Shanghai before November 1938, a group of 26 families, among them at least five well-known physicians, reached Shanghai as early as the beginning of November 1933.[8] And a German embassy letter of March 1934 even warned of a 'stream of Jewish physicians into China'.[9] Yet, most, like Inge Deutschkron, would not have considered going to China about which they knew nothing except that it was a country always at war and a place of 'indescribable poverty'.[10]

H. (Peter) Eisfelder in his informative memoir writes that, when after exhausting all other possibilities, the family decided on Shanghai in October 1938, they were unable to obtain any kind of information. Nor did they have a clear idea where in China Shanghai actually was.[11] Yet, like the Eisfelders, there were others who were not deterred by lack of information, or by China's disturbed conditions. In October 1938, for example, China was the leading destination for Austrian refugees.[12] Wilhelm Deman recapitulates a warning by a lady who came to his thriving office in Vienna where he and his wife prepared translations. She said, according to Deman:

> Don't be misled by this whirlwind of work. Read the handwriting on the wall! Don't believe that a Jew will be allowed to remain in Vienna and work! Try with all your might to leave this hell! I have managed to get a ticket to Shanghai…[and] hope to leave for Shanghai next week.[13]

Ultimately, however, it was *Kristallnacht* that left people no choice but to depart as quickly as possible, especially men who had been arrested and incarcerated in concentration camps. Grete Deman, attempting to get her husband Wilhelm released from Dachau, sent a copy of one second-class steamship ticket to the Vienna police as evidence that he would indeed emigrate.[14]

Howard (Horst) Levin, a teenager, was arrested on 10 November in Berlin by the Gestapo when he sought to rescue his father, who had been arrested earlier in the day. Howard was taken to Sachsenhausen, but was released two months later when his sister showed the Gestapo a paid-up booking for Shanghai on the Conte Biancamano. As told by Levin, 'I then had to check in at the Police station a few days later and received a passport with the exit visa and the "J" stamp, and I had ten days to leave the country with all of ten Marks.'[15]

The release of Jews from camps if they were in possession of emigration papers, had been ordered by Heydrich in January 1939,[16] and 'papers' could be both ship passage or a visa to another country. The engineer, Hugo Dubsky, incarcerated in Dachau, for example, had managed to obtain a visa from the Chinese consulate in Amsterdam, and Siegfried Cohen claimed to have visas for his two sons, also in Dachau, from the Chinese Consulate General.[17] But matters were not always easily arranged. Ships did not depart daily, and the bureaucratic machinery did not always grind on as it was supposed to do in accordance with the Nazi timetable. Hence, even if the necessary papers were ready, the person might still not have been released from the concentration camp.

A letter from the Vienna physicians' advisory section indicates both the predicament and despair (as well as the need for discreet wording):

> ...a number of colleagues, due to circumstances beyond their control, have been put in a position where they cannot commence their journey [to China]. Despite this we cannot remove these gentlemen [from the list] because we still hope daily that they will be able to depart, in which case [their departure] will be very urgent.[18]

Heydrich's January directive also included communists who had already been the victims of Nazi terror in 1933. Communist party members Günter and Genia Nobel were arrested in a Gestapo sweep in 1936 and jailed for three years. When released on 1 August 1939, they were given the option of leaving Germany within four weeks or being taken to a concentration camp. But with a criminal record, their only choices were Palestine or Shanghai. According to the Nobels' account, they decided on Shanghai for ideological reasons, as they opposed the establishment of a Jewish state at the expense of the Palestinian people.[19] Although Eisfelder remembers his family being unable to obtain much information about Shanghai, among party members emigration possibilities may have been more widely disseminated. Alfred Dreyfuss, also a communist, was told by a fellow Buchenwald prisoner that a Vienna branch of a Dutch organization was managing Shanghai emigration.[20]

Pressure to emigrate began in Austria shortly after the *Anschluss*; in Germany, as mentioned earlier, the turning point was after *Kristallnacht*. Starting in February 1939, Herbert Hagen, Kurt Lischka, Eichmann, and others began to make concerted efforts to send Jews to Shanghai. Heinrich Schlie, head of the Hanseatic Travel Office in Vienna and Berlin, was entrusted with the task of exploring Japanese and Chinese reactions to a large-scale arrival of Jewish refugees.[21] Schlie was also to find the means – ship space or ships for charter – to get the Jews under way, which in the course of spring and summer he accomplished with exemplary efficiency, not to mention financially profitable results for himself.[22]

Although the bulk of the refugees arrived on Italian liners, German vessels were also doing a brisk business in refugees throughout spring and summer 1939. To name but a few: in January the *Potsdam* docked with 120 refugees aboard; the specially chartered *Usaramo* landed 459 in June; the *Gneisenau* arrived with 116 in July; the *Scharnhorst* had 154 aboard in August.[23] After the success with the *Usaramo*, Schlie was eager to charter more ships, declaring his readiness to send another transport of 1,000 to 1,500 Jews. The major problem, however, was that he wanted to use German ships, but these, as transatlantic carriers, were equipped with oil fuel engines. Oil, wrote Schlie, had to be purchased abroad with foreign currency,[24] and in 1939, foreign currency was not what Germany had in abundance, or wanted to use on behalf of Jews.

Like the Italian ocean liners, German ships were lavishly appointed luxury vessels, most of them with first and second-class accommodations and outside cabins only. The *Gneisenau* (Germany's largest passenger ship aside from the *Scharnhorst*), for example, accommodated 295 passengers in both classes and 281 ship personnel.[25] Its 116 Jewish passengers in July 1939 were thus about one-third of its non-Jewish passengers. At a time when Jews were increasingly excluded from contact with Germans in public places,[26] ship space was apparently not considered a problem, and discriminatory practices against Jewish passengers seem not to have occurred. Ernest Heppner sailed on the *Potsdam* on 3 March 1939. He recalls in his memoir that '...no sooner would I pick a deck chair to sit in for a moment than a steward would be at my side, offering hors d'oeuvres and drinks.'[27] Mrs Annie Witting, sailing on the *Conte Verde*, reported at length from on board ship:

> Our ship is... many storeys high. The director of the ship received us and led us to our cabins, where he handed us over to the cabin steward. We are in a luxury cabin with private bath, and a first class cabin with shower for our children.... Our cabin has wall-to-wall carpeting and white wood walls; beds, closets... all are white lacquer, there is direct and indirect lighting, two windows, a large mirror.... After a bath, we were taken to a wonderfully appointed dining room, where we had our welcoming dinner.... We have our own table steward who served us especially attentively, we have our room steward and stewardess, and a Chinese boy.[28]

The Shanghai destination was, however, not welcome in several quarters, both Jewish and Nazi. Dr Julius Seligsohn, member of the governing body of the Reich Representation of Jews in Germany (Reichsvertretung der Juden in Deutschland), is quoted as saying, 'It is more honorable to suffer a martyr's death in Central Europe than to perish in Shanghai.' He and others tried to resist German pressure to transport Jews on 'Jewships'.[29] Nor did the Council for German Jewry in London favour the Shanghai destination, being strangely oblivious to the desperate situation that had developed after *Kristallnacht*. In retrospect, these reactions seem especially bizarre, since most German Jewish leaders tried to explain that they had no control over the Shanghai emigration and that, moreover, colonization schemes being studied in London 'might come too late for a very great part of German Jewry.' 'Please trust us,' stated a letter in February 1939, 'when we tell you that we are unable to diminish the emigration from Germany....'[30]

The German Jewish leadership's desperation was, no doubt, exacerbated by the apparent inability abroad to comprehend the catastrophe both German as well as Austrian Jews were facing. More telling even than the letter just quoted is the report of a secret conference Pell[31] had with Berlin's Jewish leaders:

> They are, of course, very nervous and jumpy.... They are quite frank about the ship loads of their co-religionists which they are heading in various directions such as Shanghai.... They said that they had to get their people out, whether there was an easing of tension or not. At any moment an incident might occur which would endanger the very lives of their people. They could not afford to take chances, with the consequence that they were ready to yield to the pressure of the secret police and enticements of the shipping companies.... I pleaded with them that they were doing more harm than good... that they were defeating our efforts to open up places... but they laughed in my face. After six years of dealing with the problem they are very hard. They do not believe in promises.[32]

The decision to ship Jews to Shanghai did not meet with unanimous approval from the Nazi establishment either. In 1939, the German Foreign Office also had misgivings about Jewish immigration to China, fearing that it might endanger trade relations. Indeed, Germany's trade with China had increased significantly since 1936, and was an important source of foreign currency as well as wolfram, from which tungsten was obtained. The Foreign Office under Constantin Freiherr von Neurath, together with German industrialists, had been vitally interested in both continuing and expanding trade relations.[33] However, once Joachim von Ribbentrop assumed power in foreign affairs, political considerations took precedence even over economic interests. A lengthy memorandum of January 1939, received by the Qingdao consulate, indicated beyond a shadow of doubt that the Jewish question was a major factor in Germany's foreign policy and consisted in the removal of all Jews living in the area of the Reich. Far from damaging Germany's reputation abroad was the argument that wherever Jews are, anti-Semitism will rise. Supporting anti-Semitism is the object of German foreign policy, for it is the best advertisement for Germany's Jewish politics.[34] In view of this, it seems odd that in May 1939 Kurt Lischka, of the Reich Central Office for Jewish Emigration, received a note from the Foreign Office with the request to decide between Jewish emigration and China trade. 'It must be decided', stated the note, 'if Jewish emigration to China is to continue or if [to incur], according to the view of the Foreign Office, the loss of German commercial relations with China.'[35] Did this note reflect differences within the Foreign Office, or between some officials in the Foreign Office and the Reich Central Office? Whatever the case may have been, the note was taken seriously, as indicated by the appended comments of subsection II 112 (Jews), which refer to a possible closure of China to Jewish mass emigration. A closure of sorts did, in fact, occur several months later when in Shanghai it was decided to institute the 'permit system'. But before then the China-bound exodus was slowed down, not by the Shanghai authorities, but by Germany's invasion of Poland and the start of the Second World War.

THE PERMIT SYSTEM

In November 1938 there were approximately 500 refugees in Shanghai; by August 1939 their number had risen to 17,000, despite scarce ship accommodations since the beginning of the year.[36] But why were refugees able to come to Shanghai at a time when most countries limited their entry? What made Shanghai and China different? Shanghai's peculiar situation is usually described as the absence of visa requirements, which is not entirely accurate. Until the outbreak of the Sino-Japanese War in July 1937, passport control at the port was carried out by officials of the Nationalist (Guomindang) government, with its seat in Nanjing. Foreigners travelling to Shanghai were advised to obtain visas at Nationalist embassies and consulates abroad. Due to Shanghai's status as an extraterritorial treaty port,[37] Chinese officials could not deny entry to foreigners, however, and those who had no visas could obtain them at the port of entry for a fee.

After the July 1937 outbreak of the Sino-Japanese War, the Nationalist government continued to be internationally recognized, and its European consulates continued to issue visas, which British and probably other shipping lines required for accepting bookings.[38] But meanwhile, in Shanghai, neither the SMC nor anyone else was legally empowered to exercise passport control. Thus, it was not the absence of visa requirements but the absence of passport control that enabled thousands of refugees to land in Shanghai.[39]

Shanghai, a metropolis of between four to five million people, of whom the majority were Chinese, was also in other ways peculiar. Instead of one municipal government there were three: the Chinese municipal administration which, after 1937, was a puppet of the Japanese occupation; the administration of the French Concession under the jurisdiction of the French Consul General; and the SMC, which administered the International Settlement. The International Settlement was, however, not sovereign territory, and the SMC was not an independent authority. Consisting of 14 elected members – five Chinese, five British, two Japanese, and two Americans – the SMC was merely empowered to carry out the directives of the Consular body whose Consuls General represented their countries. In addition there was the Japanese Special Naval Landing Party, which also wielded political power. Its territory was Hongkou, actually a part of the International Settlement across Suzhou Creek, where most of Shanghai's Japanese population had come to live. The Japanese claimed jurisdiction over this and adjacent areas 'by right of conquest', which the SMC did not recognize but which, in fact, it had no way of challenging.

Concern in Shanghai over the refugee influx became evident soon after the arrival of the first large contingent of refugees on 24 November 1938, on the Italian liner, the *Conte Verde*. Unable to deny entry to Europeans with and especially without means of support, the SMC was at first primarily intent on letting it be known that it was not about to assume the burden of housing and feeding the new arrivals. But after the refugee influx was obviously assuming ever increasing proportions, diplomatic efforts as well were set in motion in Europe to prevent by various means the refugees from leaving.[40] (The pressure, mentioned earlier, on German Jewish leaders not to send refugees to Shanghai was part of these efforts.) As long as the Nazi regime, however, forced Jewish emigration and shipping companies were raking in large profits, no amount of diplomatic manoeuvring could halt the Jewish traffic. Throughout spring and summer, the Consular body in Shanghai and the SMC were similarly powerless. Michel Speelman, Chairman of the Committee for the Assistance of European Jewish Refugees in Shanghai (CAEJRS) summarized the dilemma:

...there is no authority at present in Shanghai who could interfere with the landing of refugees, except the Japanese military authorities, who could only do it at the unanimous request of the whole Consular body. Such a request is entirely out of the question.[41]

Although the record does not show that the Shanghai Jewish leaders, charged with refugee maintenance, ever proposed closing the gates of Shanghai, how to house, feed, and care for an unlimited influx of destitute refugees was a major concern. No doubt, they would have liked to see the imposition of some limitations. Men like Michel Speelman, Ellis Hayim or Eduard Kann were businessmen, stock, and insurance brokers; relief work was not exactly their line of business. Yet, under the circumstances, they had no choice but to take charge of a situation for which they lacked experience.

The British, on the other hand, did want to see the refugee stream halted. In their view, still another destabilizing element had been added to an already unstable situation since the fighting in and around Shanghai a year earlier. Diplomatic efforts had brought no results, and the SMC was not legally empowered to close Shanghai as long as the Consular body did not decide on that course. Neither the German nor the Italian consuls would have supported such a move in spring and summer 1939.

The Japanese, too, wanted to end the refugee influx, but their dilemma was even greater. They did not want to risk the charge of discrimination, and Tokyo did not want to antagonize its German ally; Tokyo, furthermore, did not want to endanger its relationship with the United States, where Jews were considered both powerful and influential. The Japanese position was published under three points in the *Asahi Shimbun* newspaper even before the real influx began: (1) Jews will be treated the same as the rest of the population, (2) immigration laws valid for other foreigners in North China will be applied to Jews, (3) 'Red' Jews will not be allowed into North China.[42]

The third point is of considerable interest. I mentioned earlier that in accordance with Heydrich's directive, communists incarcerated in concentration camps were released when they were able to show evidence of emigration. Apparently, not many communists managed to get to Shanghai, but those who did seem not to have escaped the attention of the Shanghai Municipal Police[43] or that of the Japanese authorities. The reaction of the latter, whose paranoia about communist and Soviet designs in Asia rivalled that of the Nazis in Europe, was to suspect Jewish refugees of harbouring communists in their midst. Whether the Japanese were actually aware of the existence of an active communist group within the refugee community, as the Nobels claimed existed,[44] is not certain. That they, however, feared attempts at communist infiltration and possible friction between communists and the large White Russian community is clear.[45] Hence, the third point of not allowing communist Jews, even if Japan would not discriminate against Jews, into areas under its control.

It may have been the frustrating impotence in Shanghai, together with Germany's double-dealing negotiations that resulted in the German-Soviet Pact of 23 August 1939, which finally forced a Japanese decision to close the Japanese controlled portions of Shanghai to the refugees. The decision to do so may have been further reinforced by the so-called Nomonhan Incident, that is, the armed clashes between Soviet and Japanese armies on the Manchukuo-Mongol border in summer 1939. Whatever the confluence of circumstances, the permit system – the requirement to obtain a permit for entering Shanghai – had its beginnings in the Japanese memorandum of 9 August 1939, which called for a 'temporary' closure of Hongkou to refugees.[46] The SMC's immediate reaction was to 'forbid any further entry into International Settlement of refugees from Europe'.[47] The move was quite certainly triggered by fears of being swamped by refugee masses who, no longer able to settle in Hongkou (north of Suzhou Creek), would now come to the International Settlement (south of Suzhou Creek). Thus, while the conflagration in Europe was only three weeks away, preparations got under way in Shanghai to limit refugee entry.

But agreement among the three parties, the Japanese, SMC, and the French, was not easily reached about conditions of entry for refugees and who, in the first place, a refugee was. Negotiations dragged on past the outbreak of the Second World War, when German ships ceased to sail to Shanghai, and into October, by which time each of the three decided to stipulate its own conditions.[48] As published in the *Municipal Gazette* on 27 October 1939, the permit regulations valid for the International Settlement required that a person be in possession of $400 'show money' (*Vorzeigegeld*), children under the age of 13 had to have $100, or a permit from the SMC which was granted on the basis of immediate family in Shanghai, an employment contract, or marriage to a Shanghai resident.[49] There were some differences in the French and Japanese requirements: French permits did not have an expiration date and the Japanese did not require 'show money'.[50] But what was important was that the number of permits issued was at the discretion of each of the three authorities, who could issue as few or as many as they chose.

The permit system as devised had, however, several unforeseen consequences.[51] It did not actually work to the detriment of those refugees who still managed to arrive by sea, at least until July 1940, although thereafter the consequences were dire. Secondly, it was open to political manipulation, especially by the Japanese. Thirdly, for a brief duration in summer 1940 counterfeit and/or purchased permits appeared. Some, but apparently not all, such permits were caught by the authorities. Let us take a closer look at these to see how each worked.

Between October 1939 and July 1940, many refugees apparently found it easier to obtain 'show money' rather than permits. Among the 90 refugees who arrived on 4 April 1940 on the *Conte Verde*, only 18 had SMC permits, while 72 landed with 'show money'.[52] According to the police report of 23 May 1940, of the 213 refugees arriving on the *Conte Rosso* on 2 May only 47 had permits. The October regulations, stated the report, are not stopping the influx; enforcing possession of permits together with money alone will 'act as a brake'.[53] And according to Meir Birman, if a person can show the required sum of money, permits are easily obtained on arrival.[54] Some refugees used their own money, whereas others resorted to a revolving HICEM fund.[55]

As far as the SMC was concerned, possession of either a permit *or* 'show money' had not been a satisfactory solution. Therefore, in May 1940, renewed efforts were made to stop the influx, which led to the issuing of revised regulations, effective as of 1 July 1940.[56] According to these, both a permit from one of the three authorities *and* 'show money' were required. Procedures of application for permits and evidence of funds were more tightly regulated, and permits were now issued by the SMP. As previously, arrivals had to be immediate relatives of financially competent Shanghai residents, or had to have an employment contract, or intend to marry a Shanghai resident.[57]

Did the permit system in its revised form stop refugees from arriving? A clear answer cannot easily be given, principally because by summer 1940 several events coincided to inhibit refugees from reaching Shanghai. The first permit regulations were issued at the outbreak of war in Europe and the cessation of German shipping to Shanghai; the second permit regulations coincided with Italy's entry into the war. The two major carriers, German and Italian, were, therefore, eliminated. To be sure, this still left Japanese vessels as well as other smaller shipping lines; however, the only ports of origin between mid-summer 1940 and late autumn 1941 were now Lisbon,[58] Marseilles, and quite likely Odessa.[59] According to a report of the Shanghai German Consulate

General of February 1941, approximately 4,000 persons received permits, and immigrants continued to arrive (for the most part overland now) until October 1940. Thereafter there was a steep decline: only 97 arrived in November and 66 in December. The report attributes the decline to the new requirement of having to pay for the journey in foreign currency.[60] However, there is no way of knowing how accurate, or how all-inclusive, these figures, in fact, are. In March 1941, for example, there were, according to Birman, still 2,000 relatives with SMC permits in Germany.[61] Whatever the actual numbers, obviously permits were made available, but fewer persons were able to use them in 1940 and 1941.

In addition to reduced shipping and currency problems, there were still other reasons why, though permits were issued, they were in the end not used. For example 37 permits for close to 100 people, including the families of Sonnenfeld, Goldman, Szmulewicz, Grynszpan, and Jakubowski, arrived at the Warsaw HIAS (Hebrew Sheltering and Immigrant Aid Society JEAS) office in May and June 1940. But crossing from German-occupied to Russian-occupied Poland was impossible, and by mid-June the Italian border was no longer open.[62] On 6 September 1940, Dr. J. Morgenstern informed Birman, 'All emigration from the General Government has been stopped since April 1 of this year....'[63] What Birman and others in Shanghai could not have known, when they sent the permits to Warsaw, was that the Germans prevented Jews from leaving Poland, assuming that their departure would be at the expense of Jewish emigration from Germany, Austria, and the Protectorate. Although the closure was presumably still informal policy in May, by October it had been officially ordered.[64] Timing was, therefore, of the essence. Grasping opportunities or missing them were questions of life and death. Had the permits arrived before April, lives might have been saved; as it was, the permits were wasted and the people for whom they were earmarked most likely perished.

Did 14-year old Judith and 10-year old Michael Spitzer survive, or did they perish because of the delays in obtaining permits and funds for the crossing from France? Dr Franz Spitzer and his wife Louise arrived in Shanghai in 1939. Their children had been left in children's homes in France. When the Germans invaded France, Michael ended up in occupied France, whereas Judith was in Vichy territory. Although the parents were eventually able to obtain permits for the children (mailed to a relative in Limoges), they were unable to raise the funds for the childrens' passage.[65] By the time American relatives were contacted, it was already too late. The start of the Pacific War on 8

December 1941 ended all sea travel from Europe, and Birman returned the partial funds intended for the childrens' passage to the Spitzers.[66]

Time lost and opportunity vanished forever were at work in Howard Levin's case. While beginning to make arrangements for permits for his mother and sister (his father had died in May 1939), he was taken seriously ill in October 1939. Howard was not on his feet until early summer 1940, when neither German nor Italian ships docked any longer in Shanghai. He had nearly collected the documents for the overland route, when Germany attacked Russia in June 1941. Howard Levin never saw his mother and sister again.[67]

Let us now turn to how the permit system was exploited in Japanese Shanghai politics. Elections for the Municipal Council were scheduled for 10-11 April 1940. Traditionally, the Japanese were represented by two members, but in 1940 they put up five, hoping to increase their representation by means of a larger vote. Voting eligibility was based on the so-called ratepayers' principle, that is, on paid-up taxes, and both property owners and tenants who paid an assessed value were entitled to a franchise. Hongkou's large refugee population, among whom a number met the ratepayer requirement, thus became a valuable pool of voters for the Japanese candidates. Although refugees had been advised to abstain from political activities,[68] several busily wooed potential voters in the canvassing office set up by the Japanese.[69] Shanghai's foreign community realized that their future might very well be decided by these transient newcomers. Under the screaming headline, 'Emigres Deciding S'hai Fate, British-American Bloc Votes Equal Japanese; Jewish Holding Balance', the article went on to say, 'Leaving their homelands within only the past year or so, German and Austrian Jewish refugees today hold the destiny of the International Settlement... in their hands.' The article repeated the charge that the Japanese are bribing the refugees with permits for their relatives when, in fact, the refugees 'know nothing of the history of Shanghai' and its foreign investments.[70]

The charges were not unfounded. Ever since instituting the permit system, the Japanese Consul General had issued far fewer permits than the SMC. Calling it 'a special occasion', Meir Birman had noticed the sudden and dramatic increase in Japanese permits, which by June he estimated at 900.[71] (The permits, as we shall see below, were accompanied by the equally sudden issuance of transit visas.) Having constructed and put in place a careful method whereby the CAEJRS and the SMP controlled the refugee influx, both must have realized now how easily it could be circumvented. Eduard Kann's angry letter to

Consul Ishiguro expressed not only his own but also the SMC's frustration. He strongly objected to the issuing of '1,000 immigration permits for Hongkew residence' when applications:

> ....were submitted without the intermediary of our Committee, so that the latter was not enabled to investigate the bona fides of the applicants, nor could we examine the prospects of the new arrivals to make a living in Shanghai.

And he pointedly added, 'Recently the Electioneering Association, consisting of refugees, a body without judicial standing, has inaugurated a campaign for the issue of immigration permits.' Therefore, he wanted it on record that the CAEJRS cannot be responsible for persons whose background was not examined, nor can it guarantee their livelihood.[72]

Nonetheless, despite Japanese efforts, a political take-over by means of refugee votes in this 'most momentous municipal election that the city has seen', was not to be. As in previous years, two Japanese, two Americans, and five British were elected to the Council. As it turned out, overwhelmingly large numbers of refugees did not vote for the Japanese candidates. According to a newspaper report, many were seen voting not at the Hongkou market, where there would have been greater Japanese surveillance, but at the Shanghai Volunteer Corps Drill Hall in the International Settlement.[73]

Some months later Captain Inuzuka Koreshige, in charge of Jewish affairs at the Shanghai Naval Headquarters, wrote a rather threatening letter to the CAEJRS, prompted, one may surmise, by the failure to get the Japanese candidates elected. He reminded Speelman that a country admits aliens provided they exert themselves 'to enlarge the prosperity of the country'. Japan has admitted refugees into that portion of Shanghai which is under occupation, therefore:

> ...in view of the sweeping anti-Semitism which it is feared might spread and be aggravated in the Far East, it would appear to be to their [the refugees'] own best interest... to endeavor at all times to make the best possible impression upon... [the Japanese authorities].[74]

Whether it was the failure to capture political power, or for other reasons, by September 1940 the Japanese Consulate General no longer issued permits, waiting ostensibly for new directives from Tokyo. The

French Concession stopped issuing permits on 4 June 1940,[75] thus leaving only the SMC, which continued to issue them until summer 1941. However, since it was impossible to obtain Manchukuo (the former Manchuria) transit visas on SMC permits, and since Italy's entry into the war had turned the overland route into the major road to China, the latter were quite useless.

The permit story does not end here, for in the summer of 1940 several 'middlemen' and counterfeiters appeared who either promised or actually produced permits. Some were presumably issued by the Special Naval Landing Party, others by the Japanese Consulate General. A Shanghai attorney, Dr Herbert Frank, claimed to be able to get Japanese permits, which was vigorously denied by Birman, who wrote that permits were not available through 'middlemen'.[76] He did concede later, however, that there had been 'shady characters' who sold permits and that some refugees, in fact, succeeded in coming with these to Shanghai.[77] In August 1940 a ring of five currency counterfeiters was arrested, two of whom, Heinz Abronheim and Erich Schrangenheim, claimed to be able to procure Special Naval Landing Party permits.[78] Whether it was with their or others' permits, according to Birman, some people actually arrived in Shanghai with forged permits,[79] or with Japanese permits obtained from 'middlemen'.[80] But not everyone was that lucky and the Japanese consul in Hamburg reported catching one counterfeit permit in July and two in August.[81]

More interesting are the permits which suddenly appeared in September 1940 and which were issued by the 'Bureau of Social Affairs, City Government of Great [sic] Shanghai' (*Shanghai tebie shi shehuijiu*...), signed by one Yao Keming. According to David Braun of the Reich Association, the permits were honoured by the Berlin Japanese consulate.[82] But in Shanghai, Eduard Kann was doubtful, and he consulted the Japanese consul who could not very well deny their validity to Kann, but who hinted that the permits emanate from 'untrustworthy' places.[83]

Despite the Japanese consul's veiled suggestion that something unsavoury was afoot, Meir Birman expressed cautious optimism about these new Chinese permits. In his view, 'Although the issuing of permits of Greater Shanghai is not sufficiently organized and therefore not as significant... meanwhile the Nanking regime, to which the Greater Shanghai authorities are subordinate, was recognized by both Manchukuo and Japan.' Recognition of Wang Jingwei's puppet government in Nanjing,[84] Birman indicated, might make these permits more legitimate and even change the Japanese consulate's views about issuing transit visas.[85] But Birman's optimism was premature, for the Japanese consul was not at all certain who was behind these permits, and in the end named two forgers, Hugo Deutsch and Heinrich Haas.[86]

TRANSIT VISAS

The permit system was especially pernicious when refugees, coming to Shanghai via Soviet Russia, Manchukuo, or Japan, required transit visas for those countries.[87] Without permits, transit visas were not issued. However, having a permit did not guarantee a transit visa. Although more research is required to fully understand the political implications and context of transit visa problems, I want to cite several examples here in order to demonstrate how permits and transit visas were manipulated, again by the Japanese.

To reach the Trans-Siberian Railway for the journey to the Manchukuo border, refugees had to, first of all, cross from German-occupied to Soviet-occupied areas of Poland. They had to be in possession of Soviet and Manchukuo transit visas obtained on the basis of the Shanghai permit. At the beginning of January 1940, it seems that the road from Germany to the USSR was open,[88] but in June 1940, Soviet transit visas could apparently not be obtained.[89] Then, in September, although transit visas had again become available, a large backlog developed because the Soviet consulate in Berlin issued only a few visas each day.[90] Some refugees who opted for air travel to Moscow encountered yet another difficulty, when it turned out that their transit visas were not valid for air travel.[91] The Soviets, furthermore, did not issue transit visas to stateless persons,[92] with the unfortunate consequence that even a young child, who by an accident of fate had been made stateless, could not be reunited with his mother.[93] On the whole, however, Soviet transit visas seem to have been more readily obtainable than Manchukuo transit visas. The brief chronology below will show the often doubtful information that was available and the arbitrary manner with which the coveted document was issued.[94]

12 December 1938   Transit visas can be obtained at the Manzhouli border.
22 December 1938   Soviet authorities notify Berlin Intourist that Jews on the way to East Asia are prevented from crossing the Polish-Russian border.
27 October 1939   The president of the Harbin National Council

	[Kaufmann] will go to the Manchukuo capital Hsinking to find a solution for transit visas.
23 November 1939	Manchukuo transit visas are not available.
26 January 1940	Hsinking will issue transit visas, if (1) the person has a permit from the Shanghai Japanese Consul General, (2) the person has a transit visa from a Japanese representative in Europe for travel to Dalian (to continue from there to Shanghai).
26 January 1940	According to American Express, Manchukuo transit visas must be requested in Harbin.
20 February 1940	Manchukuo transit visas can be obtained only with Japanese permits from Shanghai.
4 March 1940	The Manchukuo consulate in Hamburg demands 'in some cases' names of prominent Manchukuo citizens as guarantors for transit visas.
18 March 1940	Manchukuo consuls in Berlin and Hamburg refuse to issue transit visas without express permission from the Shanghai Japanese consul.
6 May 1940	Manchukuo and Japanese consuls are issuing transit visas on SMC permits since 4 May.
16 May 1940	Manchukuo transit visa problem has been solved.
24 May 1940	Manchukuo transit visas were issued until 15 May with SMC, French and Japanese permits. Since then there are again difficulties.
1 June 1940	No Manchukuo transit visas.
20 June 1940	No Manchukuo transit visas are issued on SMC and French permits.
28 October 1940	Still no Manchukuo transit visas with SMC permits.
2 November 1940	100 Manchukuo transit visas were issued in Berlin against Japanese permits.
20 March 1941	94 people are stranded in Manzhouli with mostly SMC permits, but no Manchukuo transit visas.

Let us try and take a closer look at some of the dates. By 12 December 1938, the exodus, mostly by sea, was just getting under way, and the Japanese decision not to discriminate against Jews had been taken only some days earlier, as mentioned above. That problems about securing transit visas developed in 1939 explains Kaufmann's planned journey from Harbin to Hsinking in October. However, what precisely these problems were due to is not at all clear. The armed conflict on the Mongolian People's Republic border between Soviet and Japanese armed forces was an unlikely cause, being some 200 miles south of the Manzhouli border crossing. The American Express information of 26 January 1940 is not repeated elsewhere and seems to be erroneous. The 20 February 1940 letter probably indicates Japan's desire for as complete control as possible over refugee transit visas and attempts to limit the influx. Thus, even before the revised permit system came into use, the decision had obviously been taken to firmly control the Manchukuo border.

The sudden reversal of this policy between 4 May and 15 May 1940, when transit visas were issued not only on Japanese but also on SMC and French permits, according to the letters of 6 May and 16 May, no doubt reflects Japanese attempts in Shanghai to exploit the permit system for political purposes, discussed above. At the time, nearly 1,000 Japanese permits were issued in Shanghai. When the Japanese failed to have their candidates elected, the transit visas ceased. Nonetheless, David Braun still managed to obtain 100 transit visas in November.

The 20 March 1941 date reveals what may have been a bureaucratic blunder, or perhaps even a case of bribery. A group of mostly Viennese refugees with SMC permits, but without transit visas, had somehow managed to buy tickets to Moscow and from Moscow to Manzhouli. How, asks Birman in Shanghai, did they do it? The information could be useful to others, he thought.

One final question concerning transit visas must be raised. If refugees were in possession of Shanghai permits and Soviet transit visas, might they not have travelled via Vladivostok to Shanghai, thus avoiding the Manchukuo trap? This was, indeed, considered in Shanghai and Berlin, but the Vladivostok option had several insurmountable problems. No organized Jewish community existed in the city and, according to Meir Birman, living expenses were extremely high in this far flung Soviet outpost.[95] Therefore, in comparison with Dalian (the Manchukuo port from which refugees sailed for Shanghai), where Jewish community leaders helped care for the refugees while they waited for passage, in Vladivostok the refugees would have to fend for themselves, or board the ship immediately upon arrival. For the German-speaking refugees the language barrier was, moreover, a formidable obstacle.

There was no passenger traffic between Vladivostok and Shanghai, and only once did refugees arrive on a Soviet freighter.[96] There was, however, a regular passenger service between Vladivostok and Tsuruga on the Japan coast, with three steamers per month. But this route obviously required a Japanese transit visa.[97] Aware of all these problems, Birman, nonetheless, explored in spring and summer 1940 a direct Vladivostok-Shanghai sea connection, especially since both SMC and French permits could then be used.[98] At first glance it had seemed that a charter ship might be the best solution. But the catch was that several hundred people had to arrive just before the ship sailed, it had to fly a neutral flag, and all provisions, including eating utensils, had to be brought on board for the voyage.[99] To have several hundred people arrive in Vladivostok at sailing time presented the greatest difficulty. David Braun in Berlin thought that a special train on the Trans-Siberian Railway might be chartered if a Soviet ship became available.[100]

Undaunted by these and other difficulties in Shanghai, Birman began to negotiate with the French Messageries Maritimes, which in October had two freighters in French Indo-China, and which, he thought, might be able to sail to Vladivostok in November and December. Yet, to make such plans under the tense circumstances in Shanghai seemed almost foolhardy, according to Birman:

> The only thing that worries us is the completely unclear situation... everyone is nervous, and no one knows what will happen here. Today French steamers can still come to Vladivostok; they can also dock in Settlement and French Concession ports. But what will happen in the next weeks or months no one knows, of course, in the present situation.[101]

Still, Birman continued to negotiate with shipping companies, only to discover in November 1940 that the remaining ships under a neutral flag were Panamanian. Greece had entered the war and US ships were needed for evacuation.[102] By spring 1941, nearly one year after he had begun efforts to charter a ship, Birman concluded that it was impossible to arrange for a Vladivostok-Shanghai steamer.[103] Fanning the sparks of false hopes, in May 1941, Intourist in Kovno was registering Vladivostok-Shanghai passage for persons with SMC permits.[104] Meanwhile, the German army stood poised to invade Russia one month hence.

The purpose of the permit and transit visa system was both to limit and control the refugee influx. However, it must be emphasized that the requirement was aimed at German and Austrian Jewish refugees – by far the largest number – with the damning red 'J' in their passports.

Others, Jewish or non-Jewish, without the 'J' (Poles, Hungarians, etc.) had no problem landing in Shanghai and readily received transit visas. As long as the sea routes remained open between 1939 and 1940, when large numbers of refugees could still arrive on Italian vessels, the permit system was largely ineffective. The situation changed drastically between 1940 and 1941, when most of the refugees had to make their way to Shanghai via the land route. During that time the Japanese cynically exploited the Manchukuo transit visa requirement by refusing transit visas on SMC and French permits, except for several brief weeks in 1940. Since far fewer Japanese than SMC permits had been issued, the number of refugees able to cross the Manchukuo border was, therefore, correspondingly limited.

Many questions remain. Many may never be answered. Among them I would ask why the Shanghai destination was not taken advantage of before *Kristallnacht*, but especially thereafter, in the eight brief months between November 1938 and September 1939. To be sure, ship accommodations became sparse and were sold out many months in advance once the exodus began. But when Schlie, Eichmann and others began making concerted efforts to despatch Jews to Shanghai – even sending the chartered *Usaramo* – might it not have signalled to responsible men in the Jewish establishment abroad that the Shanghai destination should be more forcefully pursued?

The Eisfelders grasped the opportunity even before *Kristallnacht* and, on their own initiative, left for Shanghai. They managed better than most and, together with relatives who had joined them, the Eisfelders opened the Café Louis some months after their arrival. In May 1947, they left China for Australia. Their son, Peter, who had grown in Shanghai from a teenager into a young adult, wrote in 1972:

> Whatever its shortcomings, its corruption, its filth, its often difficult to bear climate, Shanghai and China had enabled us to survive the most horrendous period in history and saved our lives. And that was all that really mattered in the end.[105]

Despite leaving Vienna after *Kristallnacht*, the Demans were able to bring some of their office equipment to Shanghai. Like the Eisfelders, they too, therefore, managed quite well throughout the most difficult years of the war by running the Gregg Business College. Their major problem occurred after 1945 when, due to the extremely small Austrian quota for the US, they were able to leave Shanghai only in

February 1949 – not for America as they had hoped (this would not happen until 1951), but for Austria. Both Demans were already in their fifties when they left Shanghai, but Grete was thankful, 'We escaped the gas chambers. Others were not so fortunate. True, we lost ten years of our lives. But certainly, we did not waste them.'[106]

Howard Levin came to Shanghai alone and penniless. Drawing on resources he did not know he had, young Howard earned his living by doing radio broadcasts, newspaper reporting, and by eventually becoming a middleman in transacting business deals with Chinese. He married and left China in May 1948 for the United States, where he became a successful businessman. Forty years later, Howard had no regrets:

> Looking back at the years I spent in China, I feel that I would not want to miss them out of my life. But although there were many difficult and dangerous periods, they did develop a sense of toughness and resiliency which has helped me a great deal....[107]

Gudao, Solitary Island, as Shanghai's International Settlement was sometimes called, was not a hospitable place. The Central European refugees, coming in the wake of the Chinese ones, were received apprehensively and reluctantly by all the players on the Shanghai scene. Having reached Shanghai's shores, however, they were not turned away, even if the motives for not doing so were political and not humanitarian. Still, the permit system was one more obstruction for Jews attempting to survive.

NOTES

1. Quoted in Saul Friedlaender, *Nazi Germany and the Jews, The Years of Persecution, 1933–1939*, New York: HarperCollins, 1997, Vol. I, p. 200.
2. Ibid., p. 224. At a high level meeting of several ministries of 29 September 1936 it was agreed that complete emigration was the goal.
3. 'Report by SS Oberscharfführer Hagen on Jewish Emigration', 13 September 1936, in John Mendelsohn, ed., *The Holocaust: Selected Documents in Eighteen Volumes*, New York-London: Garland Publishing Inc., 1982, Vol. I, pp. 40–57.
4. Yitzhak Arad, et al., eds *Documents on the Holocaust, Selected Sources on the Destruction of the Jews of Germany, Austria, Poland, and the Soviet Union*, Oxford-New York: The Pergamon Press, 1981, Eichmann letter to Hagen, 8 May 1938, pp. 93–5.
5. Friedlaender, *Nazi Germany and the Jews*, pp. 244–5, suggests that it may have been Josef Löwenherz, the new head of the Jewish community in Vienna, who proposed the establishment of the Central Office, as existing community services were inadequate for handling the onslaught of emigration applicants.
6. Yad Vashem Archives (henceforth YVA), JM/4857, 13 August 1938, signature illegible.
7. Arad et al., eds *Documents on the Holocaust*, pp. 126–31.
8. Shanghai Municipal Police Investigation Files, 1894–1944, Records of the Central Intelligence Agency, Record Group 263 (henceforth SMP), D5422, Police report dated 7

November 1933. The five were the doctors Rosenthal, Löwenberg, Hess, Elchengrün, and Keinwald.
9. YVA, JM/4857, Trautman to Foreign Office, 17 March 1934.
10. Inge Deutschkron, *Ich trug den gelben Stern*, Cologne: Verlag Wissenschaft und Politik, 1978, p. 51.
11. YVA, 078/21, H. (Peter) Eisfelder, 'Chinese Exile, My Years in Shanghai and Nanking, 1938–1947', as recollected by H. (Peter) Eisfelder, July 1972, p. 5.
12. Central Archive for the History of the Jewish People (henceforth CAHJP), A/W2532. This is a list, dated 16 to 22 October 1938, of persons leaving Austria. 132 went to China, 15 to Bolivia, 15 to Argentina, 7 to Panama, 25 to Palestine.
13. YVA, 078/56A, Wilhelm Deman, 'Ein Verlorenes Jahrzehnt, Shanghai 1939–1949, Tagebuchblätter eines Heimatvertriebenen', p. 15.
14. Ibid., p. 63, copy of her letter, dated 23 December 1938.
15. YVA, 078/72, Eber interview with Howard Levin, Jerusalem, 14 October 1988, pp. 1–8. The Germans had agreed to stamp Jewish passports with a red 'J' on the Swiss authorities' urging, as they did not want to shelter large numbers of Jews after the Austrian annexation. The red 'J' allowed Swiss border police to tell an Aryan from a Jew.
16. Mendelsohn, *The Holocaust*, Vol. 6, pp. 202–3.
17. CAHJP, A/W 2689, 4, letter to the Vienna Kultusgemeinde, 16 February 1939; A/W 2689, 3, letter to the Vienna Kultusgemeinde, 3 February 1939.
18. CAHJP, DAL 76, Israelitische Kultusgemeinde Wien, Auswanderungsabteilung, Ärzteberatung to DALJEWCIB, Harbin, 26 December 1938. Signature illegible.
19. Günter and Genia Nobel, 'Erinnerungen, als politische Emigranten in Schanghai', *Beiträge zur Geschichte der Arbeiterbewegung*, Vol. 21, no. 6 (June 1979), pp. 882–94.
20. Alfred Dreyfuss, 'Schanghai – eine Emigration am Rande', in Eike Middell, *Exil in den USA*, Leipzig: Verlag Philipp Reclam Jr, 1983, pp. 555–6.
21. YVA, 051/OSO/41, Schlie to Hagen, 17 February 939, reporting on what appears to be the first of his visits to the Japanese embassy.
22. These efforts are discussed in considerable detail in A. Altman and I. Eber, 'Flight to Shanghai, 1938–1940: The Larger Setting', *Yad Vashem Studies*, 28 (2000), pp. 51–86. Schlie's name appears on the list of Swiss bank accounts. *The Jerusalem Post*, 25 July 1997.
23. *The China Press*, 1 January 1939, p. 1; SMP, D5422 (c), 'Reports about Ship Arrivals from January 1939 to September 1939'.
24. YVA, 051/OSO/41, Schlie to Hagen, 7 July 1939.
25. For descriptions of these liners, see Arnold Kludas, *Die Geschichte der Deutschen Passagierschiffahrt*, Hamburg: Ernst Kabel Verlag, 1990, Vol. 5, pp. 83–94; Claus Rothke, *Deutsche Ozean Passagierschiffe, 1919 bis 1985*, Berlin: Steiger, 1987, pp. 47, 140, 281.
26. Friedlaender, *Nazi Germany and the Jews*, pp. 282–3.
27. Ernest G. Heppner, *Shanghai Refuge, A Memoir of the World War II Jewish Ghetto*, Lincoln-London: University of Nebraska Press, 1993, p. 32.
28. YVA, 078/1, Annie Witting's letter to all her friends, May 1939.
29. Abraham Margaliot, 'Emigration – Planung und Wirklichkeit', in Arnold Pauker, ed., *Die Juden im National Sozialistischen Deutschland, 1933–1943*, Tübingen: J.C.B. Mohr, 1986, pp. 303–16.
30. Joint Distribution Committee (henceforth JDC), RG 33/44, file 457, from Hilfsverein der Juden in Deutschland to JDC, Paris (forwarded to JDC, New York by Morris Troper), 10 February 1939, signed A. Prinz, F. Bischofswerder, V. Löwenstein. Copy in CAHJP, DAL 76.1, sent to HICEM, Harbin.
31. This is, no doubt, Robert T. Pell, who handled State Department issues connected with the Intergovernmental Committee on Refugees, established after the Évian Conference in 1938. See David S. Wyman, *The Abandonment of the Jews: America and the Holocaust 1941–1945*, New York: Pantheon Books, 1984, p. 137.
32. JDC, RG 33/44, file 457, letter from Theodore C. Achilles, Chairman, Departmental Committee on Political Refugees, Department of State, to George L. Warren, 31 March 1939. Pell's letter is dated 8 March.
33. For a summary of German trade in China and its implications for Jewish emigration, see Eber, 'Flight to Shanghai 1938–1939 and its Larger Context', in Roman Malek, ed., *Jews in China, From Kaifeng.... to Shanghai*, Sankt Augustin: Monumenta Serica Institute, 2000, pp. 417–32. For example, *The China Yearbook, 1938*, Shanghai, n.d., p. 44, shows an increase of

German imports from $105,385,294 in 1935 to $150,238,093 in 1936.
34. YVA, JM4857, Foreign Office, 25 January 1939, signature illegible, 14 pp.
35. YVA, 051/0S0/41, note, 31 May 1939, signature illegible.
36. *The China Press*, November 26, 1938, p. 3; SMP, D5422 (c), 12 August 1939; CAHJP, DAL 76, Dr Triger, Auswanderungsabteilung, Ärzteberatung, Kultusgemeinde Vienna, to DALJEWCIB, Harbin, 15 February 1939.
37. After China's defeat in the Opium War (1839–41), the foreign powers opened a number of ports by treaty on the China coast where foreigners were not subject to Chinese law but to that of their home countries. Extraterritoriality refers to the areas as well as the status of foreigners living there.
38. Public Record Office (hereafter PRO), FO 371/24079, minutes. The first page of this document is missing. The contents indicates that the date is sometime in early January 1939. Quite likely, other nationals followed the British example.
39. YVA, 078/85, 'Consular Body Unable to Halt Refugee Flow from Europe to Sh'hai,' *The Shanghai Times*, 5 February 1939.
40. The diplomatic steps undertaken are described in greater detail in A. Altman and I. Eber, 'Escape to Shanghai, 1938–1940: The Larger Setting'.
41. JDC, RG 33/44, file 457, M. Speelman, 'Report on Jewish Refugee Problem in Shanghai', 21 June 1939.
42. CAHJP, DAL 76, German translation of a Dutch translation from Japanese which appeared in *Algemmeen Handelsblad*, 11 December 1938. The German translation is entitled 'No Discrimination of Jews in North China'.
43. SMP, D 5422 (c), a Russian informer, D.S.I. Gigarson, watched and reported on Jewish gatherings.
44. Nobel, 'Erinnerungen'.
45. 'Chise Youtai ren lai Huhou, Bai E shangji beiduo (After Red Jews come to Shanghai, White Russians are deprived of livelihood)', *Xin Shenbao*, 18 December 1938, p. 2.
46. YVA, 078/86, Shanghai Municipal Archives, memorandum received by the SMC Secretariat August 11, 1939. This document is an unsigned copy of the memorandum.
47. PRO, FO 371/24079, W14479, addressed to the British Ambassador, Shanghai, 15 August 1939.
48. For the several drafts on conditions, see YVA, 078/86, Shanghai Municipal Archives. There is Eduard Kann's draft of 23 August 1939; E.T. Nash's (Assistant Secretary to the SMC) of August 1939; Consul Ishiguro's of 15 September 1939.
49. The text is in YVA, 078/88, Shanghai Municipal Archive.
50. CAHJP, DAL 87, Meir Birman to HICEM, Paris, 5 June 1940. The relatives in Shanghai had to prove possession of money.
51. It also seems to have led to confusion in Chinese consulates abroad. Mr. Rene Unterman, Honorary Consul for Rumania in Antwerp, obtained a Chinese visa in Lisbon when he fled to Johannesburg, and from where he tried to book passage to Shanghai. Upon being refused, he turned to the Chinese Consulate General in Johannesburg for help, where it was assumed that permits were a mere formality and could be simply requested from the SMC. YVA, 078/88, Shanghai Municipal Archive, from Consul General, F.T. Song, to SMC, 19 November 1940.
52. CAHJP, 86.4, CAEJRS to DALJEWCIB, 8 April 1940.
53. YVA, 078/88, Shanghai Municipal Archives, police report sent to the SMC Secretary and Commissioner General, 24 May 1940.
54. CAHJP, DAL 86, Birman to South African Fund for German Jewry, 30 May 1940.
55. CAHJP, 86.2. List of immigrants prepared by CAEJRS. HICEM was an emigration association set up in 1927 by three organisations. Their initials form HICEM.
56. CAHJP, 86.3, Birman to Reich Association, 6 June 1940. Three days earlier Birman had noted that Italian transit visas were no longer available.
57. YVA, 078/88, Shanghai Municipal Archive. The revised regulations were published in the *Municipal Gazette*, 28 June 1940.
58. CAHJP, 86.4, Braun to DALJEWCIB, 11 November 1940. Japanese ships mostly, or altogether, sailed from Lisbon to East Asia, but these did no longer by November 1940.
59. CAHJP, 86.4, Birman to Reich Association, October 21, 1940. Birman mentions a number of refugees who managed to depart on Japanese ships from the Soviet Union. The most likely port was Odessa where there was a Chinese consulate. CAHJP, DAL 66, Harbin to

Yiddisher Emigranten Hilfskomitet in Bessarabia, 11 March 1938.
60. YVA, JM3755, German Consulate General to the Foreign Office, Berlin, 2 February 1941. The currency question will not be taken up here, involving several foreign currencies, fluctuating exchanges and problems of inflation in China.
61. CAHJP, DAL 95, Birman to Kultusgemeinde Vienna, 20 March 1941.
62. CAHJP, 86.4, JEAS [HIAS] to DALJEWCIB, 22 May, 14 June, 16 June, 17 June 1940.
63. CAHJP, 86.4, JEAS [HIAS] to DALJEWCIB, September 6, 1940. After 4 November 1940 there seemed to be no more letters to and from Warsaw.
64. (Alexander) Kirk, Berlin, to Secretary of State, 18 May 1940, in Mendelsohn, ed., *The Holocaust*, Vol. 6, pp. 234–6; I.A. Eckhardt notification of 23 November 1940, in accordance with the order of 25 October 1940, in T. Berenstein et al., comps., *Eksterminacja ̄ydów na ziemiach Polskich w okresie okupacji hitlerowskiej*, (Extermination of Jews on Polish Soil during the Hitlerite Occupation), Warszawa: ̄ydowski Instytut Historiczny, 1957, pp. 55–6.
65. CAHJP, DAL 99, Birman to HICEM, Marseilles, 20 August 1941.
66. CAHJP, DAL 99, Birman to HIAS, New York, 11 September 1941. There is a slim hope that Judith and Michael survived the war after all. I have checked Serge Klarsfeld, *French Children of the Holocaust, A Memorial*, New York-London: New York University Press, 1996, and neither child appears on the deportation lists.
67. YVA, 078/72, Eber interview with Howard Levin, p. 52.
68. 'Refugees Urged to Remain Neutral', *North China Daily News*, 4 April 1940, p. 2. This had been reiterated in a meeting on 29 March.
69. 'Japanese Bribing Emigres for Votes, Relatives Getting Landing Permits', *Shanghai Evening Post and Mercury*, 3 April 1940, p. 2.
70. *Shanghai Evening Post and Mercury*, 5 April 1940, p. 3.
71. CAHJP, 86.3, Birman to Braun, Reich Association, 15 April 1940; DAL 87, Birman to Kultusgemeinde Vienna, 14 June 1940.
72. PRO, FO/371/24696, no. 364, Kann to Ishiguro, 25 April 1940. (This is a copy of Kann's letter.)
73. *Shanghai Evening Post and Mercury*, 12 April 1940, p. 1; 'Election and War Fevers Compete in Shanghai', *North China Daily News*, 11 April 1940, p. 1.
74. PRO, FO/371/24684, K. Inuzuka to Speelman, 27 August 1940.
75. CAHJP, DAL 94, Birman to Tientsin Hebrew Association, 22 January 1941.
76. CAHJP, 86.2, Birman to Speelman, 14 July 1940; 86.3, Birman to Reich Association, 8 August 1940.
77. CAHJP, 86.3, Birman to Reich Association, 2 September 1940.
78. *The China Press*, August 21, 1940, p. 2; 11 September 1940, p. 3. The five were sentenced to imprisonment in the First District Court of the International Settlement.
79. CAHJP, 86.3, Birman to Reich Association, 2 September 1940.
80. CAHJP, 86.3, Braun to DALJEWCIB, 3 August 1940.
81. JFM, reel 415, frames 2321–22, Kawamura to Foreign Minister Matsuoka, 23 August 1940. I thank Prof. Avraham Altman for making this material available to me.
82. CAHJP, 86.3, Reich Association to HICEM, 18 September 1940.
83. CAHJP, 86.3, Birman to Reich Association, 19 September 1940.
84. Birman here refers to complex aspects of Chinese history resulting from the Sino-Japanese War of July 1937. Following the Japanese attack on Chinese forces, Chiang Kai-shek (Jiang Jieshi) had withdrawn from Nanjing and re-established the Chinese government in Chongqing, Sichuan province. In December 1938 Wang Jingwei defected from the Chongqing government and established his puppet regime in Nanjing in March 1940. Wang's regime was, however, not recognized by the Powers.
85. CAHJP, 86.3, Birman to Reich Association, 12 December 1940.
86. JFM, reel 415, frames 2305–6, Miura to two army and navy addresses in Shanghai, August 12, 1940; reel 415, frame 2312, Miura to two army and navy addresses in Shanghai. I thank Prof. Avraham Altman for making these materials available to me. Deutsch and Haas were either arrested by the Japanese authorities or not caught. They were not brought to trial in the International Settlement as were the other forgers.
87. In the following I include only transit visas issued against permits, and not transit visas issued against visas. The latter applies to different situations with different implications.
88. CAHJP, 86.3, Hilfsverein to DALJEWCIB, 5 January 1940.
89. CAHJP, DAL 87, Birman to Miss Stein, Birmingham, 17 June 1940.
90. CAHJP, 86.3, David Braun to DALJEWCIB, 12 September 1940.

91. CAHJP, 86.3, Birman to Reich Association, 15 August 1940.
92. CAHJP, 86.3, Birman to Reich Association, 19 July 1940.
93. CAHJP, DAL 95, Birman to Reich Association, 10 March 1941.
94. The chronology is based on letters to and from Birman and Berlin and Vienna in the following CAHJP files: 76.1, 72.3, 72.4, 86.2, 86.3, 86.4, DAL 95, DAL 86, DAL 87. The dates of the chronology are those of the letters and are not those of unavailable transit visas.
95. CAHJP, 86.3, Birman to Reich Association, 2 September 1940.
96. CAHJP, DAL 99, Birman to HIAS, New York, 17 August 1941; Birman to Polish Relief Committee, Tokyo, 8 September 1941. The 52 Polish and Lithuanian refugees arrived on the *Arctica*, 2 May 1941.
97. CAHJP, DAL 95, Birman to HICEM, Lisbon and New York, 13 March 1941. The Vladivostok–Tsuruga–Kobe route was taken by the large Polish and Lithuanian contingent which received Japanese transit visas on Curaçao visas. This story is told in great detail by Hillel Levine, *In Search of Sugihara*, New York: Free Press, 1996.
98. CAHJP, 86.3, Braun to DALJEWCIB, 11 July 1940; DAL 87, Birman to HICEM, Paris, 14 June 1940, Birman contacted Canadian Pacific, Dollar Line and the Japanese NYK, but all three refused to lease steamers.
99. CAHJP, 86.3, Birman to Reich Association, 2 September, 12 September 1940.
100. CAHJP, 86.4, Braun to DALJEWCIB, 5 October 1940.
101. CAHJP, 86.4, Birman to Reich Association, 10 October 1940.
102. CAHJP, 86.4, Birman to Reich Association, 25 November 1940.
103. CAHJP, DAL 95, Birman to Reich Association, 17 April 1941. DAL 96, Birman to HIAS, New York, HICEM, Lisbon, 23 May 1941: as late as May, private agents offered freighters under the German flag.
104. CAHJP, DAL 96, Birman to Jewish Community, Kobe, 23 May 1941.
105. YVA, 078/21, Eisfelder, 'Chinese Exile', pp. 13, 170.
106. YVA, 078/56C, for his account of the refugee crisis in 1947–8 in Shanghai Deman collected letters, clippings, and official correspondence. In Shanghai, he organized and headed the Association of Small-Quota Committees. 078/56D, pp. 242, 244.
107. YVA, 078/72, Eber interview with Howard Levin, p. 55.

PART II: OLD TESTAMENT

4

Translating the Ancestors: S.I.J. Schereschewsky's 1875 Chinese Version of Genesis

Partial and complete Bible translations into classical Chinese existed well before Protestant missionaries actually began to work actively among the Chinese. Translation work accelerated once missionaries gained a foothold in the newly opened treaty ports after 1842, and the entire Bible or portions of it were translated into Fuzhou, Amoy, Canton, Hakka, Suzhou, Ningbo, and Shanghai dialects.[1] S.I.J. Schereschewsky's (1831–1906) translation of the Old Testament (OT) into northern vernacular in 1875 opened a new chapter. His translation was accessible to larger numbers of people and, in distinction to the OT in classical Chinese, was readily understood when read to the illiterate. Moreover, unlike previous translations, it was prepared from the Hebrew original.

The purpose of this essay is to examine some of Schereschewsky's views on translating and several of the techniques which he employed in rendering into Chinese the Book of Genesis. My basic assumption is that translation is an interpretative activity. When a text is transposed from one language into another, changes are introduced that are consonant with the receiving language and culture. Translation is affected by interpretations from within the receptor tradition which, in turn, make possible the acceptance of the translation, and the ideas which it contains. Thus the Old (as well as the New) Testament translations represented one of the initial steps in the sinification of Protestant Christianity.[2]

Schereschewsky's OT translation is of considerable interest. It was prepared by a person who was thoroughly familiar with the original Hebrew text and its Jewish commentary tradition. In addition, first the 1875 translation and then the revised 1899 version were widely used until the appearance of the 1919 Union version, which is in use up to the present day. Although the latter represented a new translation effort, even a superficial comparison of Schereschewsky's OT and the

Union text reveals close correspondences both in style and in the use of terms.[3] Earlier printings of the Union text, furthermore, retained portions of the explanatory notes which Schereschewsky had appended to his translation. Precisely when these were deleted in some, though apparently not all, printings must still be ascertained.

But my aim here is not to establish the relationship between Schereschewsky's OT and the Union text's OT. It is rather to examine how the translator transposed the text from one cultural context into another. Toward this end, I shall first take up Schereschewsky's Jewish background and how he viewed the translation enterprise. This will be followed by a brief summary of the 'Term Question' and uses of transliteration and techniques of translating. The essay will conclude with a discussion of the notes he appended to the text to clarify terms and obscure passages.

BIOGRAPHICAL SKETCH

Details about Schereschewsky's early life are scarce since he apparently did not talk much about his childhood and youth.[4] Yet it is obvious that his Jewish education, first in his home town and later in the Zhitomir seminary, uniquely equipped him to undertake the OT translation. His lack of strong family ties combined with the stirrings of the Eastern European Jewish Enlightenment (Haskalah) also played a role in leading him to search at an impressionable age for meaning outside of Judaism. At a later stage in his life he joined, as it were, his Jewish past with his new faith by making the translation enterprise his life's work.

He was born into a Jewish family in Tavrik (Tauroggen, Taurage) in Russian Lithuania. It was a small town, then near the Prussian border, numbering in 1847 410 Jews. He was orphaned early and was brought up in the home of his well-to-do half brother (probably from his father's previous marriage), who was in the lumber business. As an orphan, dependent on the goodwill and care of relatives, his early years seem to have been quite unhappy. Like other Jewish boys, however, he was sent to a *heder* (literally: room), a school where generally underpaid and overworked teachers inculcated in their unruly charges the basics of Jewish learning. He left home, such as it was, in 1846 or 1847, when he was 15 years old.[5]

The next three to four years were crucial in the life of the adolescent boy and must be seen against the background of the Jewish

Enlightenment in Europe. Starting in eighteenth-century Western Europe, the Enlightenment had as its aim Jewish emancipation, participation in Western education and culture, study of the sciences, and a loosening of the hold of orthodox traditions. By the nineteenth century this movement had spread throughout Central and Eastern Europe, leading to widespread educational ferment and open hostility between orthodox Jews and Enlightenment supporters. The first opposed a non-traditional education for Jewish youths and the latter supported the establishment of 'modern' educational institutions. Hardly a Jewish community throughout Eastern Europe remained aloof from the controversy.[6]

During Tsar Nicholas I's reign (1825–55) a number of significant educational innovations took place in Russia and in the lands under Russian rule. Among these were government-sponsored rabbinical seminaries, one located in Vilna, Lithuania, the other, established in 1847, in Zhitomir, in Ukraine. By offering instruction in both traditional and secular subjects, the two seminaries, while abhorred by their elders, were extremely attractive to reform-minded youths.

With no immediate family in Tavrik and no further educational opportunities nearby, it seems no accident that the 15-year- old orphan decided to go to Zhitomir to attend the seminary.[7] There he could choose between a rabbinic or a teaching curriculum, and there he found a window on the world that was not available in Tavrik. In Zhitomir he was for the first time exposed to non-Jewish teachers who taught the secular subjects (there being no qualified Jewish teachers for these), and he probably also encountered the New Testament (NT) in a Yiddish or perhaps Hebrew translation.[8] Schereschewsky's long journey to conversion and high church office in Chinan quite likely began at this time.

His encounter with Christianity in Breslau, where he arrived in 1851 or 1852, was an important milestone. There he came under the influence of a Dr S. (or J.) Neuman, 'a learned Jewish convert', who taught at the Breslau University, and was revising the Hebrew (?) NT translation.[9] Neuman, no doubt, introduced him to German Biblical criticism of the time.[10] Whereas in Zhitomir Schereschewsky was initiated into the Jewish commentary tradition, in Breslau he was introduced to 'modern' methods of OT criticism. From Breslau his road led to the United States in 1854, conversion, and seminary study. He was ordained deacon in 1859 at the age of 28 and immediately sailed for China, having already decided in 1857, according to an interview many years later, that he wanted to translate the Bible into Chinese.[11]

Translation of the Old and New Testaments began in 1864 in Peking together with a group of other missionaries and was completed 11 years later. In the six years that followed, Schereschewsky engaged in raising funds for, and in founding, what eventually became St John's University in Shanghai. He was also elected Missionary Bishop of Shanghai, a post which he actively filled only until 1881. That summer he suffered a sunstroke which left him completely paralysed. He spent the last 21 years of his life revising the complete vernacular Bible and producing a new translation in literary (Easy Wen-li) Chinese.

THE TRANSLATING ENTERPRISE

Missionaries emphasized rendering the Bible into Chinese in order to place the 'word of God' into the hands of the people. The Bible, they argued, was an essential tool for their work. Translating it was sometimes described in extravagant terms and likened to 'what Luther did for Germany' and what the King James version had done for the English-speaking part of the world.[12] But translation as an integral part of the missionary effort was, above all, concerned with the recipient culture. Lamin Sanneh's argument on translating the Bible into African languages also holds true for Chinese. He writes:

> ...that mission was not the instrument for sifting the world into an identity of cultural likeness, with our diversities being pressed into a single mold in preparation for some millennial reckoning. So obedience to the gospel was distinguished from loyalty to a universal cultural paradigm."

Translatability presupposed cultural pluralism by assuming that linguistic variety was needed for the word of God. Far from demanding cultural conformity, missionaries by means of translation encouraged cultural pluralism.[13]

Similar views were expressed by the officiating Bishop of Pennsylvania in 1877, at the time of Schereschewsky's consecration as Episcopal Bishop of Shanghai. The aim of the mission, the Bishop stated, is the creation of a native and thoroughly Chinese Christianity, 'trained on the soil and for the soil'. At a time when ethnicity and identity were hardly subjects of discourse, he argued that nothing must be done to destroy Chinese 'ethnic characteristics'; 'foreign traits' must not be grafted on to the Chinese character. Dislocating Chinese 'from all their social and civil articulations with the body politic in which they were born' must be avoided. 'Instead of weaning him from the dress, the dwellings, the food, the habits and customs, the family circle and the civil obedience due from him... his whole status should be preserved intact....'[14]

Schereschewsky and other missionaries also recognized that in China they encountered a highly literate civilization which attached great importance to the written word. Referring to Chinese schools and the examination system, the Bishop of Pennsylvania had said that '...no nation on earth has such a multiplicity of histories, anthologies, encyclopedias and standard works on archeology, law and letters, as the Chinese'. The Chinese are a 'highly civilized and well-educated people'.[15] Schereschewsky's wife, Susan, wrote in a similar vein that the literature of the Chinese is '...both ancient and immense. Systems of religion, high standards of morality, philosophical treatises composed by the best minds of the nation are theirs.'[16] This respect for China's literary tradition led Schereschewsky, no doubt, to an increased awareness of the importance of the Bible's literary merits in translation. China's literary heritage was intimidating, but so was the diversity of spoken languages and the question of the translators' target audience. Did they want to reach readers as well as listeners? And where, in sheer numbers, was their largest audience?

The importance of vernacular translations to be read to illiterate audiences, in addition to those read by the educated in classical Chinese, was recognized early on. Hence by 1860, when Henry Blodget (1825–1903) arrived in Tianjin, he at once realized that, aside from the several translations into southern Chinese languages, a translation of the Bible into northern vernacular was a major priority. It would be understood by more than half the population of China, he wrote, and in its written form would be understood by everyone.[17] At a later time he again explained that the northern vernacular is:

> ...read everywhere throughout the Empire by all educated men... [and it is] the language of daily life. It is called the Mandarin colloquial because it is the language of all who are in office, spoken in all their official transactions. It is also the language of the common people.... All the provinces north of the Yangtzu river, Yunnan and Kweichow south of it, speak this dialect. It is intelligible to nearly all the people... [and] may be regarded as the general colloquial language of China.[18]

Although a northern vernacular translation could be understood by many millions of Chinese, Schereschewsky was, nonetheless, aware that a vernacular text would not be highly thought of by an educated Chinese. Therefore, he was eventually convinced that separate Bibles were needed for each audience, and that both the vernacular and a literary (closer to classical) translations were equally important.[19] This was especially so after 1879 and the founding of St John's in Shanghai, when he realized that to educate boys by means of a vernacular work, which was, moreover, in idiomatic northern Chinese, was impossible. The differences between spoken northern and Shanghai Chinese were too great.

Professor Fairbank has rightly stressed the importance of close collaboration with Chinese co-workers and teachers as indispensable partners in the translating enterprise. No matter how good a missionary's Chinese – and Schereschewsky's was acknowledged to be superb[20] – the co-workers often rescued translators from embarrassing blunders and outright errors.[21] Henry Blodget's description of the Peking translating committee's working method[22] with their teachers is worth quoting in full:

> Our method is, to apportion to each of the five members certain chapters, or books, that he may prepare a draft. This draft is supposed to be the *best translation he can produce* [underlined in original]. Then his draft is criticized most truly by each of the remaining four, working in his own study, with his teacher. The author... receives these criticisms and... makes out a second draft.... This second draft is sent around to each of the other members who notes every thing, whether in the style, or in the sense, which he wishes to see changed. When this has been done, we meet for discussion... two or three native teachers being present to assist.[23]

Apparently each missionary had his own teacher or teachers. I was not able to ascertain who Schereschewsky's teachers in Beijing were. Mrs Schereschewsky mentions two, unfortunately not by name, one of whom, an older man, 'has served with foreigners for many years'.[24] Blodget mentions a Liang Yunshong, a 45-year-old 'literary man', whom he converted and who became his teacher. Another, Si Xiansong, disappointed him, however, when he smuggled opium into Peking.[25] As a group the Chinese teachers presumably were '...the most competent Chinese scholars such as Peking could afford', in the words of a later commentator.[26]

What was deemed desirable in a translation of the Bible and how did Schereschewsky see his task? In the introduction to the 1875 OT he wrote:

> The original Holy Scripture was written by the Jews (*Youtai*). Afterwards all Western countries (*qinxi*) translated [it] into each language. The present translation into Mandarin (*guanhua*) is profound in meaning and is prepared in accordance with the original. [I]... did not dare add or subtract one word....[27]

At a later time he wrote, 'Idiom and clearness should not be sacrificed to literality. To translate literally Hebrew or Greek into Chinese is often mistranslating.' And, 'It is possible to be faithful to the original without being slavishly literal....' On the other hand, he believed that it was possible to preserve the 'biblical diction' in Chinese, especially the unique characteristics of Hebrew poetry. Hebrew parallelisms could be reproduced in Chinese, and it was essential to retain the differences between the OT prose and poetry portions.[28] Above all, he was already convinced during the initial stages of the translation work that, even if other translations are consulted, he is, '...resolved to adhere to the Hebrew original as much as the nature of the Chinese language... will possibly admit. I believe that the Hebrew text is to be preferred to any version old as it may be.'[29] His principal objections to the two earlier translations was that, whereas the one was idiomatically sound, it deviated from the Biblical text, and the other was too literal and, therefore, not idiomatic.[30]

Finally, although the translators throughout their 11 years of labour felt that they were engaged in one of the most significant tasks of their time, the appearance of the northern vernacular Old and New Testaments was but briefly noted in missionary circles. *The Church News* (*Jiaohui Xinbao*) praised both scriptures for their careful attention to detail calling them a 'meritorious effort'. *The Chinese Recorder* stated the price and assured potential buyers that they now can gratify their desire for a Bible in the 'Mandarin dialect'.[31] The significance of Schereschewsky's accomplishment was fully acknowledged only many years later. Frederick R. Graves, then Bishop of Shanghai, wrote that after its appearance in 1875, Schereschewsky's vernacular OT was immediately adopted. 'Before the publication of the Union Version... Schereschewsky had no rival, and if it has been replaced by the Union Version, his Old Testament in Mandarin in the judgement of the best qualified critics preserves a special value which will be lasting.'[32]

THE 'TERM QUESTION'

In China, the Bible translators' major problem was which term to use for God. The issue was debated at length in numerous publications,[33] and it was raised time and again in the translators' correspondence home. There was (and still is) no easy solution. Not only did British and American missionaries disagree, but Baptists, Methodists, or Presbyterians were also unable to find common ground.

Should an entirely new term be coined, or should an already existing term be chosen? In the first case it was feared that the Chinese Bible reader would have no idea who or what was being referred to, while in the second case he would assume that the Christian message and this God were, after all, no different from the gods he had known all along. Was there in the Chinese vocabulary, others asked, in fact a term which most closely approximated the meaning of God? Although the missionaries' knowledge of the various forms of Chinese religion was far from profound (their teachers were probably also not overly helpful on this subject), they were nevertheless aware that such terms as *Tian* (Heaven), *Shangdi* (Supreme Lord), and *Shen* (god, God, divinity) had significantly different connotations in Chinese religious beliefs. Both those missionaries who knew the language well and their co-workers invested much effort in searching the Chinese classics and dictionaries to establish meanings and usages of the Chinese terms. They cited examples from the *Shujing* (Book of Documents) and the *Lunyu* (Analects), and they defined the terms on the basis of the *Kangxi* dictionary in trying to pinpoint the 'generic' name for God.[34] Others, however, rejected the notion of a 'generic' term, James Legge (1815–97), the translator of the Chinese classics, among them. Bringing his impressive knowledge of the classics to bear on the subject, he supported the use of *Shangdi* for God by citing from the *Shijing* (Book of Songs), the *Yijing* (Book of Changes), as well as the Chinese histories.[35]

Recourse to learned references did not, however, produce a definitive solution because, as George Staunton pointed out, actual worship in temples was of numerous gods (*shen*) and not of one god (*Shangdi*) only.[36] Since the *shen* were many, those who supported this term suggested prefacing it with 'true' (*zhen*). But this was rejected on the grounds that even a *zhen shen* can cease to be *zhen* when it is invaded by a 'wandering spirit' (*cao mu shen*).[37]

Schereschewsky employed a more sophisticated argument in pressing for his term for God, which was *Tianzhu* (Lord of Heaven). *Shangdi* was not satisfactory, he argued, because of *Shangdi*'s identification in some quarters with the Jade Emperor (*Yuwang*) or with Heaven (*Tian*), the latter conveying a pantheistic idea. The search for a generic name for God may in itself not be mistaken, he wrote, but *shen* cannot serve the purpose. The term can be used in the singular or plural, and it can also denote female deities. Therefore, it cannot be used for a monotheistic religion. To preface it with *zhen* contributes nothing. A god is meant to be true, otherwise he is not a god.

His own solution, which he employed in his 1875 OT translation and which had been approved by the Foreign Committee in 1865, was to use *Tianzhu* for Elohim (God), *Zhu* (lord) for YHVH, and *shen* for (other) gods, stating that *Tianzhu* has 'never been used in an idolatrous sense', as none of the Chinese gods are referred to as *Tianzhu*.[38] Schereschewsky's OT translation strictly maintained these distinctions, using in addition *Yehehua* (YHVH) *Tianzhu* whenever YHVH Elohim occurred in the original. Two other terms were also scrupulously differentiated: Almighty God (El Shadai) was translated as *quan nengde Tianzhu*, and YHVH, the Everlasting God (YHVH El Olam) was translated with *Yehehua yongsheng Tianzhu*.

Tianzhu was of course used by the Roman Catholic church, he conceded, and there was the danger that Chinese Bible readers would confuse Protestants with Catholics. He also admitted favouring for a time the use of *Shangzhu* (Supreme Lord), wrote Schereschewsky, but Henry Blodget, one of the NT translators in Peking, persuaded him otherwise. Yet, Schereschewsky by no means dogmatically insisted on his choice of *Tianzhu* as the only possible term. Although in printed matter God will be rendered as *Tianzhu*, in 1878, while serving as Bishop of the Episcopal Mission, he told his clergy to use any term they preferred when preaching.[39]

In 1893, Henry Blodget presented the most cogent argument yet in favour of *Tianzhu*. He believed that the entire Christian church, Protestant, Roman Catholic and Greek, should use uniform terminology. Like Schereschewsky, he felt that it was necessary to distinguish between many gods and the One God. *Shangdi* is not the proper term because of its association with the 'national cult', he wrote. *Tianzhu* is suitable on two counts. The term is mentioned by Sima Qian (c. 145–85 BCE) in connection with the *feng* and *shan* sacrifice, when the First Emperor of the Qin dynasty (221–206 BCE) is said to have worshipped eight gods (*shen*), among them *Tianzhu*.[40] Secondly, 'No word in the Chinese language has more of religious reverence attached to it than the word T'ien, Heaven.' *Zhu* adds the personal element.[41]

Even so, until the appearance of the Union version in 1919, which uses *Shangdi*, the 'Term Question' was not resolved and echoes of the problem continue to linger. In the early years of this century, after Schereschewsky completed both the OT revisions and the translation into literary Chinese, the OT and NT Bibles were printed in three different editions, using *Tianzhu, Shangdi,* and *Shen*.[42]

TECHNIQUES OF TRANSLATING

In his, *The Poetics of Translation*, Willis Barnstone remarked, 'Translation is not a mirror. Nor is it mimetic copy. It is another creation. Of course, every translation owes form and content to its source, yet it has become a new text.'[43] Can this claim be made for Schereschewsky's 1875 Genesis? And if so, which techniques did he use to transform the Hebrew text into a Chinese text? Several examples, though by no means all, will be discussed below.

Schereschewsky had the option of either translating or transliterating names and terms. Whatever method he employed, he and his co-workers had to exercise extraordinary care in choosing acceptable Chinese characters so as not to expose themselves to ridicule for using characters with improper connotations. For transliterating sounds Schereschewsky saw a precedent in Buddhist, Muslim and Roman Catholic translations, and he pointed out that Sanskrit terms especially, though first transliterated, eventually became an integral part of the Chinese language. Hence, aside from the OT translation, he frequently resorted to transliterations, especially of terms connected with church practice and church ritual,[44] assuming perhaps that as China became Christian, these terms would also enter the Chinese language.

In Genesis he transliterated names of plants, place names and personal names. Place and personal names in Genesis generally refer to attributes or characteristics; in transliterated form some semblance of their sound was retained, but not of the meaning. Since he transliterated from the Hebrew, he obviously followed the Hebrew pronunciation. Thus, for example, the Hebrew Hava (Eve) is transliterated as *Xiawa* (Gen. 3:20) and the city Amora (Gemorrah) is *Emala* (Gen. 18:20). Notes are frequently appended to the names explaining their meaning.

I will discuss the notes separately, turning first to a number of terms for which there were no equivalents in Chinese, and terms for which equivalents existed.[45] In both cases, the translator had to carefully balance interpretation and terminology. Several examples will serve to demonstrate how interpretation together with the demands of the Chinese language have left their imprint.

In Genesis, the potential for life commences with the creation of a firmament (*rekiya*) that divides the waters above and below it (Gen. 1:6–7). God called the firmament heaven (Gen. 1:8). Later, after the greater and lesser lights (e.g. sun and moon) as well as the stars were created, they were set on to the firmament (Gen. 1:17).

Schereschewsky had two problems here. One, how to translate firmament, and two, what to do with it once it was said to be the same as heaven. He translated firmament, which in the Hebrew suggests space, expanse, and emptiness,[46] with *kongqi* or air. This was neither an accurate nor a happy choice, leading to confusion for the serious Chinese reader, since air is not heaven. Possibly to avoid compounding the problem and opting for consistency, Schereschewsky then had God place the lights on heaven (*tianshang*, Gen. 1:17), rather than on air. The fact that no equivalent for firmament could be found in Chinese led to necessary changes in the text.

Circumcision, which is included in God's covenant with Abraham (Gen. 17:10–11), presented a similar problem, but was handled differently. The term used for the Hebrew word was *geli*, which may be defined as ritual cutting. In the translation, Abraham is told to circumcise, but the first part of verse 11, specifying what is to be cut, is omitted and the injunction to circumcise is simply repeated. Verse 14 is handled similarly. The omission was of no consequence to either missionaries or converts, and Schereschewsky's decision, based, no doubt, on avoiding embarrassing explanations, is perfectly understandable.

Even where Chinese equivalents could be used, interpretation played an important role. The most obvious examples of the way interpretation influenced translation concern the concepts associated with the three covenants, and how they relate to the process which identified the people of Israel as a separate group. The covenant between Abraham, Isaac, and Jacob includes God's promise to each of the Patriarchs of offspring, nationhood, and land (Gen. 12:1–3; 15:5, 7; 17:5–9; 26:3–4; 28:13–14; 35:11–12). Covenant (*brit*), *yue*, or establishing a covenant, *liyue*, was easily translated, as the Chinese clearly indicates that the person who enters the covenant obligates (binds) himself to do certain things.[47] Similarly, the Hebrew term 'seed' for progeny was translated with various synonyms, signifying sons, and offspring, and also presented no problem.

The promise of land was, however, a different matter because the translator had to interpret whether the world, a country, or a locality was meant. In the majority of cases Schereschewsky translated land or country (*eretz*) with *di*. God tells Abraham that He will give him this land (Gen. 12:7), and to Jacob he says similarly that the land which was given to Abraham and Isaac will be given to Jacob and his posterity (Gen. 35:12). Sometimes also *difang* is used (Gen. 12:1, 17:8), but whether *di* or *difang*, the Chinese terms indicate land as real estate, a place, but not a country. On the other hand, 'all the nations of the earth' (Gen. 26:4) is translated as *tianxia* (all-under-heaven, the world). The translator's avoidance of a more politically slanted vocabulary is especially obvious in Gen. 17:8, where God promised Abraham 'all the land of Canaan' and which is translated as *quandi* (the whole land, or the entire area). The implicit interpretation of the text is thus significant. The reader from another culture is exposed to a different experience and to a new standpoint without, however, being confronted by an altogether incomprehensible situation.[48]

The question of the Israelites' peoplehood versus that of other peoples reveals once more a cautiously used terminology and avoids possible political implications. Genesis has two distinct terms for differentiating people as followers of a ruler or person (*am*), and people in the sense of nation (*goi*). Schereschewsky was clearly intent on retaining the distinction, translating people in the first sense with *min* (Gen. 26:10), or *renmin* (Gen. 14:16, 35:6), and occasionally with *zhongmin* (Gen. 19:4).

When *goi*, or nation, is used in the singular, the Chinese reads *zu*, with its meaning closer to tribe or clan.[49] God's promise to Abraham (Gen. 12:2), Ismael (Gen. 21:18), and Jacob (Gen. 46:3) that they each will become a 'great nation' reads that they each will become a great *zu*. In contrast, the translator used *guo* (Gen. 17:4–5, 35:11) when *goi* occurs in the plural (*goi'im*). The distinction between the singular as tribe or clan, and the plural as states or nations was deliberate and there are few exceptions to the rule. One of these is in Gen. 27:29, where Isaac blesses Jacob: 'Other peoples (*guo*) will serve you, many nations (*wan zu*, 10,000 clans) will kowtow to you....' A more faithful translation should have used *min* for the people in the first phrase, and *guo* for nations in the second. The other example is Gen. 25:23, where God explains to Rebecca, Isaac's wife, that two nations (*guo*) are struggling within her (Jacob and Esau), and 'two sons (*zi*) will be born from your stomach', even though the Hebrew text states that two nations (*goi'im*) and two peoples (*le'umim*) are involved.[50] Hence in Schereschewsky's translation the epic struggle of the brothers does not begin in the womb – Rebecca is merely having a difficult pregnancy.

These translations in what must be considered central portions of Genesis because they contain God's promise of future greatness are not easily explained. The translator deliberately avoided a politically linked vocabulary, which could be the result of the way Schereschewsky interpreted these portions. However, it may also be the result of intentionally eschewing an explicitly political vocabulary, in order not to arouse the suspicion that subversive literature was being produced.[51]

Another technique which Schereschewsky used to good advantage was to be more explicit in the Chinese text where the Hebrew is less so. Following the creation of Adam, for example (Gen. 2:7), the Hebrew reads that 'man was a living soul', whereas the translation states that he was 'a living man having a soul (*linghun*)'. Translating *nefesh* with *linghun* raises the complex question of what is implied by *ling* and *hun*, and *nefesh*. It cannot be discussed here in all its ramifications, but suffice it to say that where *nefesh* denotes life, the *linghun* combination denotes the spirit, or the spiritual *yang* component of the human being. Although obviously a person with a *linghun* is alive, the life of the person is not attributable to the *linghun* alone. For the Chinese reader the text, therefore, had to state clearly that he was a living man having a soul.

On the subject of Eve's creation (Gen. 2:23), the Chinese text states more precisely than the Hebrew that 'she came out from man's body'. According to the Hebrew, 'she was taken from man (*ish*)'. In regard to Adam, Schereschewsky dropped the impersonal *ren*, man (*adam*) already in Gen. 2:19. Thereafter he switched to the named man, Adam (*Yadang*), thus leaving no doubt who is being discussed. In the original, man as *adam* occurs until Gen. 3:17, changing from then on to the named man, Adam.

By making the Chinese text more explicit, the ideas that are conveyed themselves become different. God tells Abraham to leave his country, his birthplace, and his father's home to go to the land that He will show him (Gen. 12:1). The Chinese is considerably more emphatic by adding that God ordered (*fenfu*) Abraham to go. The verse together with the command assumes a harshness in the Chinese that is not present in the original, reading now that Abraham must forsake his 'native place (*bendi*), kinfolk, (*qinzu*), [and his] father's home (*fujia*)'.

A more radical change in meaning occurs in Gen. 17:14. Part of God's covenant with Abraham concerns the circumcision of male children. Abraham is told the consequences of not abiding by the agreement to circumcise: the soul will be cut off from his people because he broke the covenant. As pointed out above, the connotations of soul (*linghun*) being different from the Hebrew *nefesh*, Schereschewsky had to opt for a different translation which, in turn, led to a different interpretation from that implied by the Hebrew text. To make this sentence intelligible in Chinese the translator had to determine what was meant by the soul being cut off. In the Chinese text this became expulsion. Thus the translation reads: 'The male child who is not circumcised, he will be renounced, he will not be permitted (*rong*) among the people, because he abandoned (*fei*) my covenant.' In the 1899 revised version, this passage is interpreted still differently. 'The male child who is not circumcised, abandoned (*fei*) my covenant, he will certainly be destroyed (*miejue*) among his people.'

Both versions omit the word 'soul', punishing the person directly; the 1875 version threatening mercifully only ostracism, whereas the 1899 version foretells death and destruction. Was he overly influenced by interpretations of a wrathful God? Or did Schereschewsky in this place disagree with the Hebrew commentaries? The Onkelos commentary implies that the uncircumcised will be excluded from the community. Rashi, on the other hand, interprets this passage to mean that the person will die childless and before his time.[52] These examples are not evidence of a flawed translation. To the contrary, in the interpreted text Schereschewsky abandoned suggestiveness for the unambiguous statement: Abraham responds to an explicit order; breaking the covenant entails dire consequences.

A brief but closer look at the stories concerning Joseph and his brothers (Gen. 37–50, except for 38) further elucidates Schereschewsky's techniques. These stories, with their alternating themes of fortune and misfortune, the brothers' as well as Joseph's trickery, his skill in managing favourable and unfavourable situations, and the stories' successful conclusion, would surely have had a special appeal to Chinese readers.[53]

Sold to an Egyptian, Joseph had done well in his master's house. But misfortune overtook Joseph when the master's wife tried to seduce him (Gen. 39:7). The Hebrew version that she 'cast her eyes upon Joseph', could not be expressed similarly in Chinese. The Chinese text therefore reads more explicitly: seeing Joseph, she conceived lust (*yuxin*) and said to him, 'let us sleep (*qin*) together'. Joseph resisted and ended up in prison, where he was joined by the Pharaoh's butler and baker whom the two had offended (Gen. 40: 1–3). Translating butler as *jiuzheng* was not a problem, but in nineteenth-century Chinese the word for a baker of bread, implied by the Hebrew *ofeh*,[54] was not in general use, bread not being a staple food. Thus Schereschewsky substituted chief cook (*shanzheng*), clearly understandable to a Chinese reader or listener. The problem was, of course, the same for 'bread', for which the translator had to find a familiar Chinese term. In those portions where *lehem* is referred to (Gen. 41:55; 47:12, 13, 15) and in which Joseph promises to give bread to his brothers and to the famine-stricken Egyptians, Schereschewsky substituted *liangshi*, provisions.

He resorted to still another substitution when the Pharaoh has his dream about the fat and lean cows and the full and thin ears of corn. The dream had to be interpreted, and the Pharaoh sent for 'all the hieroglyphics engravers' (the English text has 'magicians') and wise men (Gen. 41:8). *Hartumei* (engravers) would not have made much sense in Chinese, hence Schereschewsky opted for two nearly synonymous terms: *shushi* (scholars) and *boshi* (doctors).[55] These, as well as many other substitutions, continued to be used by the later translators of the Union version.

Occasionally Schereschewsky must have been as much at a loss as had been Rashi, the commentator of 600 years earlier. Jacob dispatched his sons for a second time to Egypt, reluctantly allowing the brothers to take Benjamin along. Presents are called for (Gen. 43:11), and Jacob advised taking products of the land, including *botnim* and almonds. Rashi did not know what *botnim* were,[56] and neither did Schereschewsky, who translated the word with *feizi*, nuts of the yew tree, that is, types of pine nuts.

The poetic passages and chapters in these stories, like Gen. 49, must have often been a daunting task to the translator, taxing his ingenuity to find similarly poetic expressions in Chinese. I shall cite only one random example, Gen. 47:9, where the aged Jacob is introduced to the Pharaoh, who inquires after Jacob's age. '130 years are the seasons (*nianri*) of my sojourn (*jiju*) in the world… my seasons are not many, [they] do not come up to the seasons of my ancestors' sojourn', answers Jacob. The Chinese not only captures the poetry of this almost regretful statement, sojourn for *megurai* was also well chosen, by conveying a sense of impermanency rather than strangeness.[57] Existence on earth is regrettably brief and longevity is a value, according to the Chinese view.

After 1864, the Peking group of translators had several Bible translations available to them which they could consult for their own work. Even if in classical Chinese, these could serve, at least, as points of reference. The most recent OT versions were the so-called Delegates' Bible, published in 1854, and the variant translation by E.C. Bridgman and M.S. Culbertson, published in 1863.[58] Some of Schereschewsky's transliterations, like *Yehehua*, were quite likely based on Bridgman and Culbertson. Furthermore, not all of Schereschewsky's terminology was new or different from previous translations. *Geli*, for example, for circumcision was probably also borrowed from the Bridgman/Culbertson translation, since earlier versions tended to use only *ge* (to cut).[59]

THE NOTES

Schereschewsky's notes are possibly the most interesting part of this translation enterprise. They do not attempt to present theological interpretations and they are not a vehicle for the Christian message in the OT. The notes provided the reader with technical tools for understanding the text, and the Bible reader and teacher with the means of explaining the text. Above all, the notes demonstrate Schereschewsky's erudition and his profound familiarity with the biblical text and the Jewish commentary tradition.

They generally deal with technical matters of translation, such as the meaning of place and personal names, and they explain or re-word enigmatic and obscure passages.[60] The notes are always placed within the text and directly follow the word or phrase which they explain. The elucidation in many cases is based on Rashi's commentary, although there is also evidence that Schereschewsky resorted to Midrashic materials aside from those included in Rashi.[61]

The following are a number of random examples. Among those notes intended to clarify the text there is Eve's creation from Adam's rib; Eve, according to the translation, 'can be called woman (Gen. 2:23)'. The note reads, 'According to the original Hebrew text, the pronunciation of the two [words] "*ish*" and "*isha*" [man and woman] indicates the meaning of woman being obtained through man.' It is questionable that this explanation was satisfying to an enquiring mind, considering that the crucial issue, the question of that rib, is being evaded.

Another note concerns Lemech, fifth-generation descendant of Cain. In Gen. 4:23 occurs the enigmatic sentence, 'I have slain a man to my wounding, and a young man to my hurt.' The Chinese translation reproduces the Hebrew, but in the appended note Schereschewsky reworded the sentence, 'If I kill a warrior I harm myself, [if] I harm a youth I damage my [own] body.' The note reflects Rashi's explanation (obtained from a Midrash) that Lemech inadvertently killed Cain, his forebear, and, utterly distraught, then killed his own son, Tubal-Cain.[62]

Almost as faithfully as Rashi had done earlier, Schereschewsky glossed over minute points of the text. In Gen. 31:46–47, Laban and Jacob, after the latter's sucessful flight, erect a cairn to seal their agreement. Laban calls the cairn Yegar Sahaduta, Jacob calls it Galed. For both names there are notes; the first, Schereschewsky explained as an Aramaic (*Yalan*) word, meaning a stone heap as testimony; the second, he wrote, is a Hebrew word with the same meaning.[63]

Plants, fruit, types of wood, animals, or fabrics for clothes – all these

Schereschewsky tried to explain in notes. A few examples will suffice. Pharaoh dresses Joseph in 'shesh' clothes' (*bigdei shesh*, Gen. 41:42). Schereschewsky, not differentiating between the name of the cloth, *shesh*, and the Hebrew construct for clothes, *bigdei*, transliterated both words as *bishu*. In the appended note he explained that the fabric was of the whitest and finest kind; in antiquity it was most expensive, and was worn only by the high-born. Schereschewsky knew that descriptions of this fabric (a fine wool?) occur elsewhere in the OT and his note was based on these.

At harvest time, Reuben brings home mandrakes (*duda'im*), a plant or fruit (Gen. 30:14), widely thought to have been an aphrodisiac. The name of the plant is transliterated in the text as *dudai*, and the appended note explains it as the name of a plant. Some of the extensive literature on mandrakes must have come to Schereschewsky's attention in the next two decades, for in the revised 1899 edition there is the added information that this is a kind of tomato. Indeed, mandrakes, which were said to have erotic qualities and enhanced the charms of women, were identified with tomatoes after the latter became known in Europe.

A somewhat different kind of explanation concerns Gen. 47:21, which reports rather laconically that during the famine, Joseph moved his people from Egypt's borders to the cities. Rashi's lengthy explanation that Joseph wanted to remove from the people the stigma of emigrants by settling them in the cities[64] is only partly reproduced. According to the note, Joseph caused his people (*min*) to be removed to, and to settle, in cities from one border to the other.

Finally, the meaning of transliterated names of people is frequently given. Thus Hava's name (Gen. 3:20) is explained as mankind's mother. The name Cain (Gen. 4:1) refers to his occupation. Noah (Gen. 5:29) means 'peaceful'. Abraham (Gen. 17:5) means that he is the ancestor (*zu*) of many nations (*guo*). Jacob's name (Gen. 27:36) can be translated as 'cheating' (*chipian*). The appended notes attest to Schereschewsky's intimate acquaintance with the OT and its Jewish commentary tradition. But, the notes also add a new dimension to the text. Names, which in transliteration can be considered devoid of all meaning, become concrete when explained; passages which are otherwise obscure often make more sense in the receptor language. By means of the notes the translation became a teaching tool that could be used by the newly converted to instruct others.

This examination of Schereschewsky's Chinese Genesis translation has shown that, aside from other considerations, the background of the translator is important. In the attempt to determine what kind of a translation he produced, Schereschewsky's Jewish antecedents and early training are evidently also significant factors. Moreover, that Jewish scholarship had a role in the incipient beginnings of Chinese Protestant Christianity has larger implications. These cannot be explored here, but they surely are an element in the reception of the OT in nineteenth and twentieth century China.

By the same token, the assumptions that inform the translating enterprise must be considered. Schereschewsky profoundly respected Chinese civilization, and it is a pity that his extant correspondence reveals so little on this subject. Still, it is this respect, I would suggest, that led to his firm belief that becoming Christian did not mean becoming westernized, that a genuinely Chinese Christianity was both possible and desirable. His belief was, no doubt, reinforced by his own experience of becoming a Christian. Conversion had not changed him into an Anglo-Saxon. The respect for Chinese civilization and learning was, however, not some vague notion of what China was about. It is hard to say how widely read he was in the Chinese classics and histories. Yet his deep appreciation for the Chinese language and his highly unusual grasp of its complexities could only be gained on the basis of a wide-ranging acquaintance with China's literary heritage. Clearly, he never doubted the translatability of scripture, or the suitability of the Chinese language as its vehicle.

Perhaps for this reason the 'Term Question', which so exercised most missionaries, did not seem to trouble him once he decided that the use of neologisms was unavoidable. Yet, I find that, aside from God and a few other key terms, these are kept at a minimum in Genesis and that he preferred to use standard, idiomatic Chinese together with the device of explanatory notes. Schereschewsky was above all interested in creating a standard, unified, and consistent terminology, eliminating the arbitrary usages of earlier translations. The 'Term Question' may not have bothered him, as it did others, for still another reason. In his translation work he was concerned with understanding a text and with conveying this understanding, and not with questions of theology. The absence of theological overtones in Genesis in either the choice of vocabulary, or in the notes, was noted earlier.

Schereschewsky's techniques for translating have been described in some detail. As concerns the transliterating of place and personal names, the obvious drawbacks, as noted by Arthur Wright, are that transliterations are awkward, uncouth, and destructive of rhythm.[65] There is no quarrelling with this judgement; the Biblical names look and sound supremely clumsy and must have given difficult moments to readers and listeners alike. Yet, short of translating names according to their meaning, which would have led to the loss of their sound, Schereschewsky had no alternative.

It is to Schereschewsky's credit that he confined transliterations to place and personal names, translating everything else, whether Chinese equivalents existed or not. As a result, he did not make good on his promise in the introduction of neither adding nor subtracting a word. Quite the opposite is true. The examples cited from Genesis show that the translation is not literal; there are omissions, and the choice of language and idiomatic expressions often changes the text's connotations. There is, in addition, the tendency towards transforming opaque into explicit statements which in part, at least, is due to the linguistic peculiarities of northern vernacular. However, precisely because literalness was not attempted, and omissions, changes, and vocabulary choices were made, the transposed text was not merely a translation into another language. More than any other early scripture translator, Schereschewsky recognized and tackled the problem of Chinese cultural and linguistic factors in expressing foreign ideas.

NOTES

1. For a fairly comprehensive listing of translations, see Hubert W. Spillett, comp., *A Catalogue of Scriptures in the Languages of China and the Republic of China*. British and Foreign Bible Society, 1975. See also Alexander Wylie, *Catalogue of the Chinese Imperial Maritime Customs Collection at the United States International Exhibition, Philadelphia 1876*. Shanghai: Statistical Department of the Inspectorate General of Customs, 1876. Appendix, 'Catalogue of Publications by Protestant Missionaries in China'. And H.R. Hykes, *Translations of the Scriptures into the Languages of China and Her Dependencies, Tabulated to December 31, 1915*. New York: American Bible Society, 1916, pp. iv, 1–11. By courtesy of the Burke Library of the Union Theological Seminary in the City of New York.
2. John Fairbank notes the importance of the Chinese collaborators in the sinification process, in addition to the Chinese vocabulary that came to be used for religious terms. John K. Fairbank, 'Introduction', in Suzanne W. Barnett and J.K. Fairbank, eds., *Christianity in China, Early Protestant Missionary Writings*. Cambridge: Harvard University Press, 1985, pp. 7–9.
3. The Union version continues to be used widely in Protestant churches. See Thor Strandenaes, *Principles of Chinese Bible Translation*. Stockholm: Almqvist and Wiksell, 1987, p. 15, n. A recent effort by the Bible Societies of Taiwan and Hong Kong, *Shen jing: xiandai Zhongwen yiben* (The Holy Bible: Today's Chinese Version). Hong Kong Bible Society, 1975, although widely used, has not replaced the Union Version. For a valuable contribution on the topic of the Union version see Jost Zetzsche, *The Bible in China, The History of the Union Version or the Culmination of Protestant Bible Translation in China*. Sankt Augustin: Monumenta Serica Institute, 1999.
4. James A. Muller, *Apostle of China, Samuel Isaac Joseph Schereschewsky 1831–1906*. New York: Morehouse Publishing Co., 1937, is a biographical account which emphasizes his missionary career. Most of the documentary sources used by Muller, including Muller's correspondence with a number of valuable informants, are now housed at the Archives of the Episcopal Church in Austin, Texas. I have resorted to the archival collection rather than to Muller's account. A different biographical approach was taken in I. Eber, *The Jewish Bishop and the Chinese Bible, S.I.J. Schereschewsky, 1831–1906*. Leiden: E.J. Brill, 1999.

5. Domestic and Foreign Missionary Society (hereafter DFMS). China Records, 1835–1951,RG64-185, Caroline Schereschewsky's biographical statement which had been in the possession of Sister Emily Faith and was forwarded to J. A. Muller, ms. 5 pp. In the above I have enlarged somewhat on Caroline's bare facts.
6. Among the Russian, Hebrew, and Yiddish literature on the subject of the Jewish Enlightenment, see Azriel Shochat, *Mosad Harabanit Me'ta'am, Parasha Bama'avak-ha Tarbut bein Haredim l'bein Maskilim* (The 'Crown Rabbinate' in Russia, a Chapter in the Cultural Struggle between Orthodox Jews and 'Maskilim'). Haifa: University of Haifa, 1975, which details the arguments on both the orthodox and enlighteners' sides, Michael Stanislawski, *Tsar Nicholas I and the Jews, The Transformation of Jewish Society in Russia, 1825–1855*. Philadelphia: The Jewish Publication Society of America, 1983, explores government policies and their effects on Jewish life.
7. Neither Caroline Schereschewsky's written statement, DFMS, RG-64-185, nor Muller's notes on his talk with her, DFMS, RG-64-185, 5 January 1929, mention the Zhitomir seminary. The sole evidence is found in DFMS, RG-64-185, letter from James A. Kelso, President, the Western Theological Seminary, Pittsburgh, Pennsylvania, to Muller, 16 December 1933. Kelso wrote that, according to Schereschewsky's registration, he studied at the Zhitomir Rabbinical Seminary.
8. NT translations were prepared by the London Society for Promoting Christianity Amongst the Jews. Their intensive proselytizing activities began after 1818 in the lands under Russian control. The translation of the Hebrew NT was completed in 1817, and the Yiddish in 1821. William T. Gidney, *The History of the London Society for Promoting Christianity Amongst the Jews from 1809 to 1908* London: London Society for Promoting Christianity, 1908, pp. 55–6. Although I have found no evidence in the yearly reports of the London Society about active missionaries in Zhitomir, from their stations in Warsaw, Lublin, and Kalish the missionaries covered considerable distances to other towns. However, the NT need not have been brought to Zhitomir by missionaries. New and Old Testaments were liberally distributed throughout the areas of the missionaries' activities and pupils could have easily brought copies to the seminary from elsewhere.
9. London Society for Promoting Christianity, 19th Report, 1827, p. 36.
10. DFMS, RG64-28, Schereschewsky letter to the Reverend S.D. Denison, 21 July 1865. For his translation of the OT, Schereschewsky mentions consulting works by De Wette, Rosenmüller, Eichhorn, and Genesius. See John W. Rogerson, *Old Testament Criticism in the Early 19th Century: England and Germany*. London: Anchor Press, 1984, for a discussion of these authors and the German scholars' controversies.
11. [Bishop McKim and Bishop Partridge], 'How the Bible has been Translated for the Millions of China', *Spirit of Missions* (henceforth *SM*), 68, no. 4 (April 1903), p. 233.
12. DFMS, RG64-29, John R. Hykes, (?), 1903 (?).
13. Lamin Sanneh, *Translating the Message: The Missionary Impact on Culture*.' Maryknoll: Orbis Books, 1990, pp. 170, 205.
14. 'Consecration of the Missionary Bishop of Shanghai', *SM*, 42 (December 1877), p. 672.
15. Ibid., pp. 670, 673.
16. DFMS, RG64-30, Mrs Schereschewsky letter to the Reverend S.D. Denison, 21 January 1876.
17. American Board of Commissioners for Foreign Missions (henceforth ABCFM), Vol. 302. *North China Mission*, 1860–71, 'Letters and Papers Addressed to the Board', Vol. I, Houghton Library, Harvard University, Henry Blodget letter to the Reverend R. Anderson, 4 November 1861, Tianjin, ms. 127. By permission of the Houghton Library, Harvard University, and the United Church Board for World Ministries.
18. ABCFM, ibid., Henry Blodget letter to the Reverend N.L. Clark, 12 October 1867, Peking, ms. 186.
19. DFMS, RG64-29, Schereschewsky letter to Dr Langford, 18 May 1895.
20. DFMS, RG64-185. Sister Emily Faith, Deaconess, Sisters of the Transfiguration, St. Lioba's Convent, Wuhu, letter to Muller, 19 December 1933. She wrote that Max Müller ranked Schereschewsky as one of the six most learned Orientalists in the world.
21. Fairbank, 'Introduction', in *Christianity in China*, p. 7.
22. The committee was formed in 1864 and consisted of three Americans, Henry Blodget, W.A.P. Martin, and Schereschewsky, and two Englishmen, Joseph Edkins and John Burdon.
23. ABCFM, *North China Mission*, Vol. I, Henry Blodget, 'Occasional Notes', 20 March 1867, ms. 181.

24. DFMS, RG64-30, Mrs Schereschewsky letter to ?, 27 December 1871.
25. ABCFM, *North China Mission*, Vol. I, Henry Blodget letter to ?, 28 December 1861, Tianjin, ms. 129, and letter to the Reverend R. Anderson, 29 January 1863, Peking, ms. 147.
26. Marshall Broomhall, *The Bible in China*. London: The China Inland Mission, 1934, pp. 83–4.
27. *Jiuyue quanshu*. Peking, 1875. The full English title is: *The Old Testament in the Mandarin Colloquial*. Translated from the Hebrew by the Reverend J.I.S. Schereschewsky, D.D. of the American Episcopal Mission, and Printed for the American Bible Society at the Press of the A.B.C.F.M., Peking, China, 1875.
28. DFMS, RG64-29. 'Translation of the Scriptures into Chinese'. Also, in *Bible Society Record*, April 1890.
29. DFMS, RG64-28, Schereschewsky letter to S.D. Denison, 21 July 1865.
30. DFMS, RG64-29. 'The Bible, Prayer Book, and Terms in Our Mission', Addressed to the House of Bishops, pp. 4-5. Pamphlet. Schereschewsky was referring to the Morrison translation and the Bridgman and Culbertson OT. Robert Morrison (1782–1834) published his translation in 1823; Elijah C. Bridgman (1801–61) and Michael S. Culbertson (1819–62) published their OT translation in 1863.
31. 'Shengjing yi guanhuaben gaocheng (Translation of the Bible into *Guanhua* is Completed)', *Jiaohui Xinbao*, 14 (13 July 1872), p. 225. 'Missionary News', *The Chinese Recorder*, 5, no. 4 (August 1874), pp. 223–4. Mandarin and *guanhua* were synonymous before 1911. When the latter term was abolished, Mandarin continued to be used for *guoyu*, as the Beijing dialect was referred to before 1949. In both cases the spoken northern Chinese language is meant. See Strandanaes, *Principles of Chinese Bible Translation*, p. 15, n.
32. DFMS, RG64-29, Frederick R. Graves letter to John H. Wood, 30 June 1937. Although Bible sales generally had sharply increased in the second decade of the twentieth century, Mandarin Bibles (that is, northern vernacular Bibles) outstripped all others. Most of the OTs sold must have been in Schereschewsky's translation. See Milton T. Stauffer, ed., *The Christian Occupation of China*. Shanghai: China Continuation Committee, 1922, p. 453.
33. How to translate the Holy Spirit was equally vexing. But since this is a NT problem, it will not be discussed here. For a summary of the early stage of the 'Term Question', see Douglas G. Spelman, 'Christianity in Chinese: The Protestant Term Question', *Papers on China*, Vol. 22A (May 1969), pp. 25–52. For a more detailed discussion, see I. Eber, 'The Interminable Term Question', in I. Eber, S.K. Wan, K. Walf, with R. Malek, eds., *Bible in Modern China: The Literary and Intellectual Impact*. Sankt Augustin: Monumenta Serica Institute, 1999, pp. 135–61.
34. For example, B. Helm, 'Shen and Shang-ti', *The Chinese Recorder*, Vol. 7, no. 6 (December 1876), pp. 436–42, and Sir George Thomas Staunton, *An Inquiry into the Proper Mode of Rendering the Word 'God' in Translating the Sacred Scriptures into the Chinese Language*.... London: Lionel Booth, 1849, pp. 5–6, 34.
35. James Legge, *The Notion of the Chinese Concerning God and Spirits: With An Examination of the Defense of an Essay, on the Proper Rendering of the Words Elohim and Theos, into the Chinese Language, by William J. Boone, D.D.* Hongkong: Printed at the 'Hongkong Register' Office, 1832, pp. 7–64. Ch'eng Wen Reprint, 1971.
36. Staunton, *An Inquiry*, p. 18.
37. *The Chinese Recorder*, Vol. 7, no. 4 (August 1876), pp. 294–7.
38. DFMS, RG64-28, Schereschewsky letter to S.D. Denison, 21 July 1865.
39. Schereschewsky, 'The Bible, Prayer Book and Terms', pp. 9–11, and 'Terminology in the China Mission', *The Churchman*, Vol. 57, no. 6 (14 January 1888), pp. 34–5.
40. *Shiji*, 28, in *Ershiwu shi* (Twenty-five Histories). Kaiming Edition, 1934, Vol. I, p. 115.
41. Henry Blodget, *The Use of T'ien Chu for God in Chinese*. Shanghai: American Presbyterian Mission Press, 1893, pp. 1, 4, 10, 20. Pamphlet. By courtesy of the Burke Library of the Union Theological Seminary in the City of New York.
42. DFMS, RG64-29, John R. Hykes letter to John Fox, 29 August 1903.
43. Willis Barnstone, *The Poetics of Translation, History, Theory, Practice*. New Haven-London: Yale University Press, 1993, pp. 261–2.
44. Schereschewsky, 'Terminology in the China Mission', pp. 60–2.
45. I am using the *Jiuyue Quanshu*, 1875 edition, although I will sometimes refer to the *Jiu Xinyue Shangjing* (The Old and New Testament Holy Scriptures), 1899 revised edition as well. For the Hebrew I am using the standard Masoretic text.
46. See M. Rosenbaum and A.M. Silbermann, trans., *Pentateuch with Targum Onkelos, Haphtaroth*

and *Rashi's Commentary*. New York: Hebrew Publishing Co., n.d., Vol. I, pp. 3-4 (hereafter *Rashi*). Rashi ingeniously explained that the firmament was needed to solidify or stabilize heaven. He does not, however, have a satisfactory reason for the firmament then being called heaven. Rashi (Solomon Yitzhaki ben Isaac, 1040-1105) was a French rabbinical scholar whose authoritative commentary on the Pentateuch has been universally studied for centuries past.

47. Compare, for example, the *Lunyu*, 6:25, '*Yue zhi i li*', bind oneself with *li*.
48. Eugene Chen Eoyang, *The Transparent Eye, Reflections on Translation, Chinese Literature, and Comparative Poetics*. Honolulu: University of Hawaii Press, 1993, pp. 157-8.
49. *Rashi*, p. 115, explains *goi* as *le'um*, or nation.
50. The 1899 revision corrects sons (*zi*) to read clan (*zu*), which is, however, also not in keeping with the Hebrew text. The 1899 rendering is retained in the later Union Version.
51. DFMS, RG64-30, Mrs Schereschewsky letter to the Rev S.D. Denison, 22 August 1870, and 25 October 1870. The tragic incident involving the Catholic mission at Tianjin and the subsequent massacre in June 1870, had apparently led to considerable tension in the capital, and relations between Chinese and foreigners were severed. By 1870, Schereschewsky was well along in the translation. In a letter to the Rev. S.D. Denison, 14 October 1864, DFMS, RG64-28, he mentioned being nearly done with Genesis. However, there is no way of knowing whether he decided to make editorial changes afterwards and when these were made.
52. *Rashi*, p. 67.
53. See *The Cambridge Bible Commentary, Genesis 12-50*. Commentary by Robert Davidson. Cambridge: Cambridge University Press, 1979, p. 211. Devidson describes the stories as 'masterpieces of storytelling'.
54. See Joseph Elchanan Greenberg, *Foreign Words in the Bible, Commentary of Rashi* Jerusalem, n.d., p. 194. Rashi explained *ofeh* as pistor or petrisseur (a French loanword), defined by Greenberg as 'kneader', that is, one who kneads dough.
55. Although *shushi* can in some instances also mean conjurer or magician, this is not the case here, since *hoshi* is invariably a learned person and a contradiction is not intended here.
56. *Rashi*, p. 214, thought that *botnim* were pistachios and thought that they are like peaches. In modern Hebrew *botnim* are peanuts.
57. *Rashi*, p. 233, glosses *megurai* as 'the days of my being a stranger'. The English version translates, however, 'my pilgrimage'.
58. See Spillett, *A Catalogue of Scriptures*, p. 21. Part 2 of the Bridgman and Culbertson version was published in 1861, the other parts in 1863. I have consulted the 1865 edition, *Jiuyue quan shu* (The Old Testament). Shanghai: Meihua, 3 Vols., in the ABCFM collection at the Harvard-Yenching Library.
59. For example, Robert Morrison, trans., *Chuangshi lidai chuan* (Genesis), 1832, in the ABCFM collection at the Harvard-Yenching Library.
60. In the 1875 edition there are altogether 41 notes for Genesis; the 1899 edition has 53 notes, omitting some of the earlier ones and adding new ones to other verses. In some instances briefer notes were expanded. The Union version omitted most of Schereschewsky's notes.
61. Midrashic literature refers to a large collection of writings dealing with interpretation, and it includes a rich body of imaginative works.
62. The English wording is according to the Masoretic text, which is not faithful to the Hebrew. However, due to the terse and obscure nature of this sentence, a faithful translation is practically impossible. For the story, see *Rashi*, pp. 20-1. I thank Dr Uri Melammed for pointing out that Lemech's statement is probably a line from a long poem, perhaps a dirge, which he addressed to his two wives.
63. The note is based on *Rashi*, p. 153.
64. *Rashi*, p. 236.
65. Arthur F. Wright, 'The Chinese Language and Foreign Ideas', in Arthur F. Wright, ed., *Studies in Chinese Thought*. Chicago: University of Chicago Press, 1953, p. 296.

5

Several Psalms in Chinese Translation

Perhaps because the 'Bible has always been a translated book', as Stephen Prickett remarked,[1] an abundance of studies deal with questions of the Bible's translatability and its translation into European languages. In comparison, even though the history of Christianity in China has been studied in considerable detail, research on the Bible, especially its translation into Chinese, is still scarce.[2] Impressive beginnings are made, to be sure, by scholars like Marián Gálik, Liang Gong, Jost Zetzsche and others in recent years.[3] Nonetheless, a host of unresolved questions about the Chinese Bible remain. We need to be better informed about the beginnings of Bible translating by the Jesuits and the later Protestants in the nineteenth century; the source languages used by the missionary translators; and who the Chinese scholars and co-workers were who participated in the translating enterprise. What were the translating strategies and how are the earlier translations related to later efforts? What about the context of the translators' times as it may have affected the nature of the translation?[4] What differences might we find in, say, style or language among various books of the translated biblical text and to what can such differences be attributed?

The present chapter will address some of these larger questions briefly. But my major concern here is more specifically with a number of Psalms in the 1875 *guanhua* translation by S.I.J. Schereschewsky (1831–1906).[5] Three reasons in particular were important for choosing this translation. Schereschewsky used the Hebrew Masoretic text as his source language.[6] His was, furthermore, the first attempt at casting the biblical text into the northern spoken language. His Old Testament (OT) translation, together with the Peking Translating Committee's New Testament (NT) version, was in circulation for over 40 years until superseded by the 1919 Union version. Clearly the subsequent Union version translators were, therefore, able to use and improve upon the earlier rendition.

Aside from other examples, several Psalms that I want to take a closer look at are those which deal in part (usually) with Jerusalem or Zion, also known by names such as the holy city, city of God, city of righteousness (*ir hakodesh, ir Elohim, ir hatsedek*). The main reason for choosing these

Psalms is the unique place Jerusalem holds in Jewish history and memory throughout the centuries and the range of emotions connected with both the place and its name. Emotions, like the longing for Jerusalem, mourning the city's loss, joy at having regained it, rejoicing at its rebuilding, anxiety over threats to it, prompt echoes in those who recite, listen, or read the Psalms. Has this emotional content been conveyed in the Chinese translation? How meaningful can Jerusalem be to those whose collective memories are not associated with the city by this name? What means and devices, which strategies, did Schereschewsky and his co-workers use to evoke and convey the emotional content attached to Jerusalem?

Aside from prose, although too in need of a closer examination,[7] the poetry of the Psalms must have represented a daunting challenge to the translator.[8] How well did Schereschewsky and his co-workers understand the poetic principles of the Psalms? Could they make the Psalms 'sing' in Chinese? Are we reading 'Chinese' poetry when we read the Psalms? Keeping in mind that those I have chosen to discuss can by no means be considered a representative sample of all 150 Psalms, I hope, nonetheless, to be able to suggest answers to several of the questions raised. But first, some brief remarks about how the work of translating the Psalms started.

Schereschewsky was ordained deacon in 1859 in New York and sailed almost immediately for Shanghai with Bishop William J. Boone (1811–64). During the two years that he was in Shanghai and while learning Chinese, Schereschewsky began translating the Psalms. He apparently did not make much progress and, after an adventurous journey up the Yangzi gorges, he left for the capital with Boone's blessing. He remained in Beijing from 1862 to 1874.

The Peking Translating Committee, consisting of British and American missionaries, which he joined, had constituted itself in 1864 for the purpose of translating the Bible into northern colloquial Chinese. It was soon decided that Schereschewsky should work by himself on the OT using the Hebrew Masoretic text as his source. By 1866 he had completed the Psalms,[9] and by the end of 1873 or early 1874 he had translated the entire OT, leaving that year for a well-deserved furlough in the United States. When he returned to Shanghai in 1878, it was as bishop and as founder of St John's College.

We have no way of knowing whether Schereschewsky resumed translating the Psalms soon after his arrival in Beijing, or only after the translating committee began work. Nor do we know who his Chinese co-workers in Beijing were. Their names are not mentioned in the correspondence to the home office, or in published letters in the missionary journal, *The Foreign Missionary*. The names of his co-workers in Japan, when he was confined to a wheelchair and with whom he collaborated on the revision of the entire biblical text are, however, known. Lian Yinghuang worked with Schereschewsky for almost five years, Yu Baosheng for about two years, and Zhang Jiezhi for about one year. Nothing much is known about these men or their subsequent careers. Apparently, Schereschewsky got along best with Lian Yinghuang, who was a Christian and very much devoted to the work.

Schereschewsky's effort at translating the Psalms was not the first such undertaking. Indeed, Gálik argues that the Psalms were more frequently translated than any other biblical text.[10] Aside from their inclusion in complete Bibles, others had tried their hand at Chinese renditions, the earliest being by a Protestant missionary, William C. Burns (1815–68). Burns, of the English Presbyterian Mission, was in Beijing from 1863 to 1867, when the translating committee's work got under way. According to Joseph Edkins (1823–1905), Burns translated from the Hebrew original but in metrical form.[11] No doubt, the missionaries knew of Burns's effort, though in any event Schereschewsky would not have benefited from it.

ZION AND JERUSALEM

Some general observations might be useful. Compared to other books of the OT, Schereschewsky wrote very few explanatory or interpretive notes for the Psalms; four in all in the 1875 edition (Psalms 84, 115, 139 and 147) and 20 in the 1899 revised edition, of which most are merely glosses. He did not, of course, revise all biblical books to the same extent, but the Psalms are nearly identical in both versions, except for occasional changes of vocabulary. Both Schereschewsky and Liang Yinghuang, who worked with him in Japan, were apparently satisfied with the initial rendition.

As had earlier (as well as later) translators, Schereschewsky carefully differentiated terms for Elohim and YHVH throughout the OT as well as in the Psalms. He used *Zhu* for the latter and *Tienzhu* for the former.[12] When both terms are used together, as in the 'Lord our God' (e.g. Ps. 122), he opted for transliterating YHVH, obviously for stylistic reasons. Other terms occur occasionally in the Psalms, such as *Elyon* (Most High) in Ps. 87:5 or 46:5 [4][13] for which Schereschewsky preserved the difference by translating it as *Shangzhu*. Finally, aside from the headings of the Psalms, which are often problematic allowing for a variety of interpretations, two recurring terms, *sela* and *halleluiah*, deserve our attention. The meaning of the former is uncertain,[14] and the latter means *hallel*, to praise YHVH. He transliterated *sela* as *xila* (e.g. Ps. 52:5, 54:5 [3]), and he also transliterated *halleluiah* (e.g. Ps. 106:1), though one might have assumed that he would have preferred to translate the term.

As mentioned earlier, Zion is often used in place of Jerusalem. Yet there are also Psalms where the mountain rather than the city is indicated. To differentiate city from mountain, when this seems important, Schereschewsky added *cheng* or *shan* to Zion *xun*. He may have had two reasons in particular for wanting to clearly specify whether city or mountain is meant.[15] Mountain imagery is an important element in the Psalms and mountain or mountains are not mere geographic designations, as Ps. 121:1–2 states so beautifully:

> I will lift up mine eyes unto the mountains:
> From whence shall my help come? My help
> cometh from the Lord,
> Who made heaven and earth.[16]

The mountain is thus associated not only with God Himself but with creation and with God's care for His creatures. Therefore, the frequent reference to Zion as the holy mountain (e.g. Ps. 2:6), that is, the mountain holy to God as well as the seat of the ruler.[17] There is here an interesting similarity to the Chinese concept of the mountain as a cosmic centre, not of holiness but of life-dispensing forces.[18]

That Zion as city, or Jerusalem, is referred to should, however, be specified in those Psalms which speak about the 'gates of Zion' (Ps. 87:2), the 'children of Zion' (Ps. 149:2), or the 'daughters of Zion' (Ps. 9:15 [14]), lest the reader or listener is led to erroneous assumptions. In such cases Schereschewsky did not translate literally, adding simply 'city' to Zion in all three cases, *xuncheng de men*, *xuncheng de jumin*, and *xuncheng*, making it perfectly clear that Jerusalem is meant. Still, complications can occur when both the city and the mountain are mentioned together as in Ps. 48:2. 'In the city of our God, His holy mountain' becomes in the Chinese version: *Wo Tienzhu Yehehua zai ziji chengnei shengshanshang*, which is the not quite felicitous: 'Our God, YHVH is in his city on the holy mountain.'

Let me take a closer look at the well-known Ps. 137. The psalmist states that he is now back in Jerusalem, back from exile in Babylon where:

By the rivers of Babylon,
There we sat down, yea we wept,
When we remembered Zion.[19]

The translator indicates that Zion is Jerusalem by having added 'city' here as well as in verse 3 where the exiles are asked to sing a song of Zion. The word order is reversed in the first line of verse 5, lending emphasis to, 'If I forget thee, O Jerusalem', by stating, *'Yelusaleng, wo ru wangji ni'*.

The terse Hebrew of the second line of verse 5, *tishkakh yemini*, forget right ('Let my right hand forget her cunning') was translated with nine Chinese characters as in the first line, thus making both lines of equal length. As in Western language translations, 'hand' was added as well as 'cunning'. For the latter, Schereschewsky chose *zhineng* with its implication of skill rather than cunning. The second line in this way matches the first in emphasis: *'qingyuan wo youshou wangji jineng'*, 'Let my right hand forget its skill'. The reader or listener would have had no doubt that Jerusalem refers to a place to which the exile has strong attachments and that he must not forget.

The centrality of Zion and Jerusalem to the life of the state and the family, to the well-being and prosperity of both as well as to future generations is related in Ps. 128. It is a brief Psalm and yet tells a potent story: a total vision, as it were, of peace and personal happiness, veneration of the Lord, and family life connected to the centre. In this Psalm the order of lines two and three in the first verse is reversed and the word order is changed, which leads to a slight shift in meaning. It is not so much to fear the Lord as to venerate Him and to faithfully follow His ways, that is, follow His Dao. A comparison of the English with the Chinese translation reveals the shift in meaning. The Chinese reader would be well aware of the transcendental and all-encompassing implications of following the 'Lord's Dao':

Happy is everyone that feareth the Lord,
That walketh in his Ways.

Jingwei Zhu zunxing Zhudao,
Zhaideng ren bianwei you fu.

Revere the Lord and obediently follow the Lord's Dao,
Those people will then be happy.

In verse 5 of Ps. 128 Schereschewsky indicates the difference between Zion and Jerusalem. The Lord will bless the people from Zion mountain, that is from His dwelling, and the people all their lives will see with their own eyes Jerusalem's blessing in the city where they dwell. It is not clear why the translator departed here from the Hebrew text, which states that it is the goodness (good qualities, or beauty) of Jerusalem that its inhabitant will see. The short closing line 'Peace on Israel' is more explicit in the Chinese version: let the people of Israel enjoy peace. The psalmist's vision includes the welfare and prosperity that necessarily exists in the state when peace prevails.[20]

The few examples cited thus far reveal several translating strategies. Obviously Schereschewsky did not aim for a literal translation, interpreting wherever necessary in order to produce as understandable a text as possible. He neither hesitated changing the word order nor reversing lines to achieve the desired poetic effect. As will be discussed below, this strategy was, however, borrowed from the earlier Bridgman/Culbertson translation. Finally, he employed the couplet form to good advantage wherever possible.

TEMPLE AND KING

The centrality of Jerusalem in the life of the people began with King David and his conquest of the Jebusite citadel, as related in Sam. II, 5:7. He then brought the Ark that had accompanied the people throughout their wanderings by stages to Zion. David did not build the Temple; the Ark was placed in a tabernacle and there it remained until King Solomon, David's son, built the Temple as the sacred centre of the mountain-city. The destruction of the Solomonic Temple by the Babylonian King Nebuchadnezzar occurred in 586 BCE and was considered a national catastrophe, ending only with the return of the exiles from Babylonian captivity and the rebuilding of both the Temple and the city under Ezra and Nehemiah. Sanctity of the structure together with the presence of the transcendental and the mundane king are, therefore, closely associated with Jerusalem and Zion in the Psalms. A number of Psalms celebrate the rebuilding of the Temple.

The psalmists used two terms to designate the Temple: *heikhal*, which can also mean palace depending on context, and *bayit*, meaning house, which, however, can also be used in place of family, that is, someone 'from the family of...' or 'house of...' In both cases the translator had to rely on the context, though he was often aided by the addition of the adjective 'holy' in making the proper choice.

1. Ohel Rachel Synagogue in Seymour Road, Shanghai established in 1921 by Sir Jacob Sassoon. (Courtesy Beth Hatefutsoth)

2. Main synagogue in Harbin at the corner of Artilliriskaya and Connaya Streets. The synagogue was built in 1907 on a plot of land allotted to it by the Chinese Eastern Railway Company. (Courtesy Beth Hatefutsoth)

3. Gathering near the synagogue upon hearing the news of the establishment of the State of Israel, Tianjin, 1948. (Courtesy Beth Hatefutsoth)

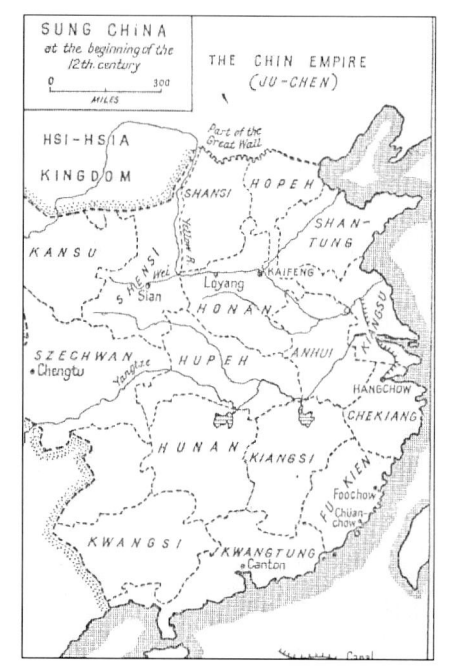

4. Map of Sung China. (Jacques Gernet, *Daily Life in China on the Eve of the Mongol Invasion, 1250–1276*, Stanford: Stanford University Press, 1962, p. 20)

5. Rubbings of the stelae erected in the courtyard of the Kaifeng synagogue, which relate the history of the Kaifeng Jews. The one on the left dates from 1489, and on the right from 1512. (From the exhibit catalogue, *The Jews of Kaifeng, Chinese Jews on the Banks of the Yellow River*, Tel Aviv: Beth Hatefutsoth, The Nahum Goldmann Museum of the Jewish Diaspora, 1984)

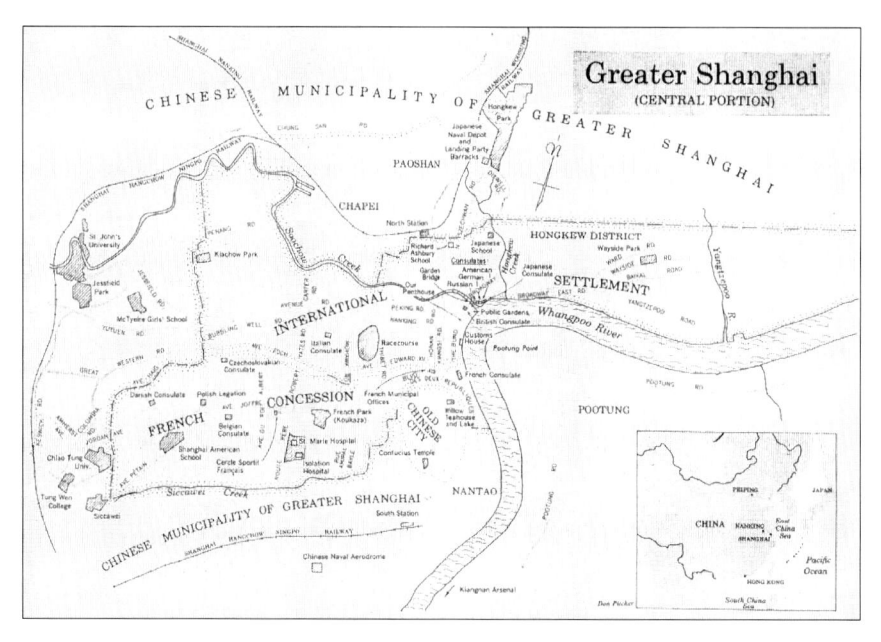

6. Map of Greater Shanghai, 1930s. (Georges Spunt, *A Place in Time*, London: Michael Joseph, 1969)

7. The Heim, or shelter, on Ward Road, Hongkou, Shanghai, 1939. This was the first of several such shelters established to ease the housing shortage of the refugees. (Courtesy Beth Hatefutsoth).

8. Marble Hall, the home of the Kadoorie family in Shanghai. (Courtesy Beth Hatefutsoth)

9. First page of the Yiddish newspaper *Dos Vort* (The Word), no. 6, December 5, 1941, printed in Shanghai

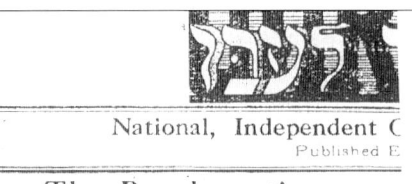

10. The infamous February 1943 'Proclamation' ordering stateless refugees into a portion of Hongkou, called the 'designated area'. Published in *Undzer Lebn* (Our Life), no. 36, February 26, 1943

11. Samuel Isaac Joseph Schereschewsky, 1877. (Courtesy of the Archive of the Episcopal Church, USA)

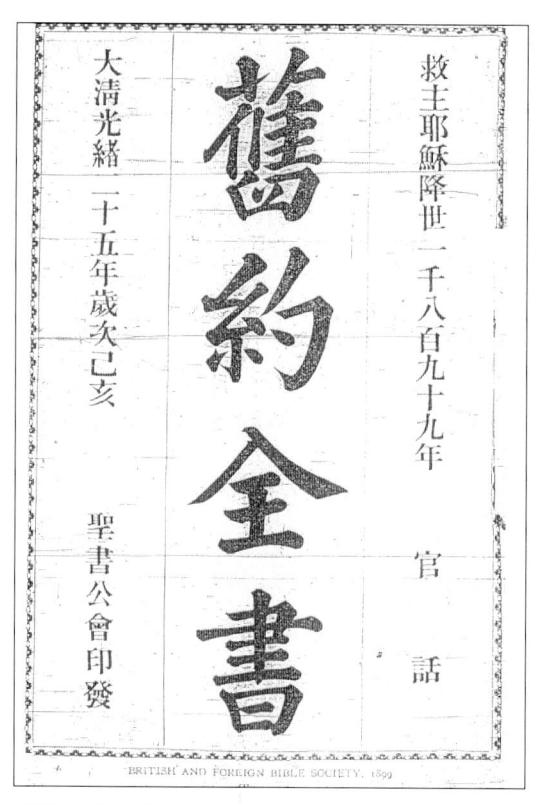

12. Title page of the 1899 revised Chinese translation of the Bible into *guanhua* (Mandarin)

異邦人亦當如此萬物皆當如此主於鄰至聖至義仍宜稱至聖雖可畏至聖公有人其恩慈心敬拜蒙以勉古樂叩拜主為仍勉主獨一無二主當知主乃謝人欣然讚主當至善恩惠永存詩人頌美主之仁義自言

第九十九篇

我上帝所施的拯救普天下人都當向主歡呼發聲欣然歌頌彈琴歌頌主用琴聲並用歌聲用此民也當如此在主面前江湖聲如拍手山嶺音像歡呼因為主必來審判天下按公義審判世界照正直判斷萬民。

主執掌王權萬民須悚懼主坐在基路伯上大地動搖主在郇城極大無比在萬民上惟主至高人當頌揚你大而可畏的名你的名至聖也當頌揚喜愛公義的大君的權力你堅定正理向雅各家施行公平義理你當讚美我上帝耶和華為至上叩拜在主足凳前主為至聖在主的祭司中有摩西亞倫在禱告主名的人中有撒母耳他們禱告主主常應允他們在雲柱裏諭他們他們遵守主的法度和所賜與他們的典章我上帝耶和華常應允他們為他赦罪的上帝若有過犯主也懲罰他們你們都當讚美我上帝耶和華為至聖。

第一百篇 這是稱謝的詩〇普天下人、都當向主歡呼欣然事奉主、到主面前歡樂歌唱、應當知道惟耶和華是上帝、創造我們的乃是主、並非自造、我們是主的民是主牧場的羊當進主的門稱謝入主的院讚美主稱頌主的名主為至善主的恩典永遠長存主的

舊約全書 詩篇 第九十九篇 第百零一篇 八百零七

第百有一篇 這是大衛所作的詩〇我要歌頌仁慈公義、主阿、我要向你奏樂歌詩我存智慧心

13. Psalm 100 in Chinese translation by S.I.J. Schereschewsky in the 1899 revised edition of the Bible. This Psalm contains an annotation (double column) and a header (theological explanation)

一個餓人的故事

猶太　賓斯奇（David Pinski）著

陳　振羣　譯

　　伊惡一連兩天沒有東西到嘴了，換句話說，他換了兩天餓了。到得第三天，他拿了三個賣銅紐子，買了在他住的大院裏賣賣的希伯來小學學生一頓點心。——兩塊小牛油餅。——他餓餓餓的吞下肚去，於是他助了氣力，兩塊餅子，在他真是一口東西，但他至少提起一點氣力來曉得生氣並且引起他做嗟嘆的衝動。這個題心一起，手指頭兒擅自爬爬的起來第音第一下，對準這個懶兒一個踢去。這小狗乃是他的女居停銅匠萎的。她愛這狗比愛着自己子女還要加甚。「薩西克」帶着一路叫喊着逃走了。伊惡還要加甚。他在地下撿起一塊石頭，用盡他平生之力，追着狗後邊打去；他結論如何，這塊石頭乱沒打着那狗，却打到酒門銀律師豪門上去了。很響的一聲回音，伊惡捉捉待痛快。綠他初不願應這石頭究打在酉門銀律師或律師夫人的

　　但是這些作為並沒有藉平他的飢火，也沒有使他澆熄的心胸平靜一點點的，他還是怒加怒因為他覺得這些都不過是些小孩並沒有到於他們做出什麼事來他們的仇敵。尤其是那些坐在草的人們的仇敵。他用驕奇到的話咒詛他們；在自己手裏加一個很厲利，那是滿痕快的。

　　另又一個小學生走近這門邊家來穿了一雙大人的鞋子，胖着手誠在圍巾裏大概因為太冷他也不用手抹抹鼻子，他的紫黑蒼色包皮，伊惡見了，雖活不過但是這房孩子的顔色不許他的他任怒憑尋來自排的方法却不由的要勁怒反對這孩子正和他反對基世界是一樣那末他

　　一個餓人的故事

1

Schereschewsky generally translated Temple with *dian* (e.g. Ps. 11:4), 'The Lord is in His holy Temple', and palace with *gong* (e.g. Ps. 45:16). But sometimes there were slips. The girls who are as graceful as 'Corner pillars carved after the fashion of a palace' (Ps. 144:12) is translated as in the fashion of the Temple (*dian*), when obviously 'palace' would have been more appropriate.

Although the 'house of the Lord' generally referred to the Temple, there are exceptions and the translator should have been aware of this. The last line in Ps. 23:6: 'And I shall dwell in the house of the Lord forever', can be understood as an example of figurative language alluding to 'spiritual sustenance and protection', rather than to actually dwelling in the Lord's Temple (*Zhu de dian*).[21] More problematic is the first line of Ps. 36:9 [8] where figurative language is also used to indicate God's abundance with the phrase 'fatness of your house'. This is translated rather inadequately and too literally with '*ni fengfnei de feigan*'. In Ps. 76:3 [2] still another term, 'tabernacle', is used:

> In Salem also is set His tabernacle,
> And his dwelling-place in Zion.

> *Ta de gongdian zai Saleng*,
> *Ta de jusuo zai Xunshan*.

> His palace is in Salem,
> His dwelling is in Zion.

Apparently Schereschewsky did not want to translate *sukka*, tabernacle (a covered place), with a humbler term like tent and decided to use palace instead. The translation also retains the parallelism, to be discussed below, of the Hebrew, but not as an intensification, which the Hebrew text suggests by using 'tabernacle'.

Until the destruction of the Solomonic Temple, Jerusalem was the royal capital from where the king ruled his domain whatever its size. A number of Psalms refer to the king as ruler and sometimes they also refer to God as king. How successfully did Schereschewsky sort out the heavenly from the earthly king? He had no problem when king was prefaced by 'my Lord', as in Ps. 145:1. There, instead of using king (*wang*), he used a much more suitable term, *huanghuang*, perhaps August Ruler, followed by *wo Tienzhu*, my Lord. By reversing the word order of the sentence, 'I will extol Thee, my God, O King', *Tienzhu cong gu wei wode wang*, the Chinese version becomes more emphatic. Although *wang* as king occurs more frequently, especially when referring unequivocally to the Lord (e.g. Ps. 44:5[4], 47:7, 74:12) Schereschewsky also resorted to *jun* occasionally (Ps. 29:10, 105:20). This term with its meaning of ruler or sovereign has, however, mundane rather than transcendental connotations and one cannot be certain exactly how the translator used it. Aside from translating king as *wang* (e.g. Ps. 21:2, 45:2, 6, 10, 12), Schereschewsky also used *junwang* (Ps. 33:16). In Ps. 48:3[2], where a question can arise about which king is referred to, he used *da jun* for the Hebrew *melekh rav*.[22] But the two lines together are ambiguous, as has been noted by a number of scholars.[23] Schereschewsky, trying to make sense, may have resorted here to the Midrash on the Psalm.[24] The English translation of the Masoretic text reads:

> Even Mount Zion, the uttermost parts of the north,
> The city of the Great King.

The Chinese translation differs:

> *Junshan beicheng*
> *dajun jingtu.*

> The northern city of Zion,
> The capital of the great ruler.

Thus the Chinese text indicates rather that the northern city of Zion is the capital where the great king resides.

QUESTIONS OF POETRY, STYLE, AND IMAGERY

The importance of the Psalms as poetry has been widely noted. According to Jerome Walsh, poetry:

> ...is words: the music of their sounds, the rhythm of their cadences, the interwoven patterning of their placement. What the words are is what the poem is. Poetry is image: sounds and sights and shapes to appeal to all the senses. [And] Ultimately, poetry is experience: a poet's experience made articulate in language hewn to engender experience in its hearer.[25]

Regarding the three types of biblical poetry (Psalms, Songs of

Solomon, Lamentations), Gao Bolin has argued similarly that this 'Poetry is the product of the imagination and the manifestation of mature feelings. [When it] has artistic life, it has a natural soul.'[26] And Robert Alter has cautioned readers not to divorce form from content: '...the spiritual, intellectual, and emotional values of the Bible... are inseparable from the form they are given in the poems.'[27]

Form is, however, exceedingly complex in the Psalms and the specific feature of parallelism has a special role, involving a combination of semantic, prosodic, syntactic, morphological, and sound elements as well as rhythm determined not by fixed but by changing principles. Biblical Hebrew, being both laconic and condensed, endows each word in a line with special prominence.[28] The importance of parallelism for the appreciation of the poetry of the Psalms is noted by most scholars.[29] And, significantly, Andrew Plaks has directed attention to the construction of parallelisms in both the poetry portions of the Bible and Chinese literature, describing it as 'repetition as the basic grid of literary patterning'.[30] Schereschewsky was certainly aware of having to consider parallel construction when translating the Psalms. He argued that this was not at all difficult as Chinese literature too employs parallelisms.[31] That the earlier renditions by Bridgman and Culbertson (more about this translation below) also did not neglect parallel construction was, no doubt, helpful to Schereschewsky's efforts.

In the following I will be less concerned with technical explanations of Schereschewsky's parallel construction, but will confine my remarks to the techniques he employed. Let me begin with the brief Ps. 133:1:

Behold, how good and how pleasant it is
For brethren to dwell together in unity!

The parallelism of the first line is preserved differently by the translator, who reversed the lines and created a rhythmic couplet of 6,3,3 characters:

Sixiong hemu tongju,
he ji shan,
he ji mei.

[When] brothers peacefully dwell together
How good this [is]
How beautiful this [is].

The second verse is also rearranged, although somewhat differently from the first in order to retain the rhythmic parallelism:

> It is like the precious oil upon the head,
> Coming down upon the beard;
> Even Aaron's beard,
> That cometh down upon the collar of his garments.

Jiu xiang Yalun toushang zhi meide gaoyou,
Liu dao xuxu,
Liu dao yijin.

> Like good oil on Aaron's head,
> Flows down [his] beard,
> Flows down [his] garments.

The rearrangement of both verses has not changed the meaning of the psalmist's message with its rich imagery of people together who are likened to naturally flowing oil, spreading, permeating Aaron's beard (it presumably was very long), and flowing along the length of his garment. We might also note that the Chinese translation is closer to the terse Hebrew than the English translation, which adds words that are not in the Hebrew, and there is, in fact, an additional line, 'Even Aaron's beard'.

Schereschewsky employed a similar technique of reversing and/or changing the order to create a parallelism in other Psalms. Here is 48:2[1] where, however, a subtle change has occurred in the meaning, the emphasis having shifted to the Lord who is in Jerusalem that is on Mount Zion:

> Great is the Lord, and highly to be praised,
> In the city of our God, His holy mountain.

Wo Tienzhu Yehehua zai ziji chengnei shengshanshang,
Zhita wubi,
Jidang songyang.

> My Lord YHVH is in His city on the holy mountain,
> Incomparably the greatest,
> [To be] extremely praised.

The two examples cited represent a parallelism, which is not invariably based on repetition, as can be seen. In Ps. 48 it is rather an intensification, as pointed out by Alter, or concretization of the first part.³² The major feature is the couplet where each line consists of the same number of characters, no matter how many words were in the Hebrew Psalm. Schereschewsky used the same method for a different kind of parallelism where a contrast is established, as in Ps. 56:4[3]:

In the day that I am afraid,
I will put my trust in Thee.

Wo kongju shi,
wei yilai ni.

When I am afraid,
I will trust Thee.

These few examples are not meant to suggest that the poetic features were worked out in all and every Psalm. Some are certainly not as successful as these. Yet it cannot be denied that the attempt to endow the translated Psalm with poetic features in the target language was a significant achievement. As poetry with familiar forms it, no doubt, contributed to the impact these poems must have had on nineteenth-century literati readers. One other feature seems to me significant, and that is the feeling of immediacy conveyed in many Psalms when God is addressed directly at the very beginning of the poem, even when his name occurs in the middle of a line in the Hebrew text. *Zhu'a*, asks the psalmist in Ps. 10:1, or *Tienzhu'a* in Ps. 42:1, depending whether it is YHVH or Elohim. This immediacy, or foreshortening of the distance between the speaker and God, introduces an element of intimacy; the Psalm is the means for conversing with the divine presence.

Whereas the wonders and abundance of God's creation of the cosmos and nature are evocatively portrayed in a number of Psalms (e.g. Ps. 104) as well as the miracles He had wrought in the people's history, the psalmist seems reticent when it came to descriptions of Jerusalem and Zion. That about Jerusalem wonderful things are said (Ps. 87:3) or that it is beautifully situated (Ps. 48:3) seems insufficient. Robert Alter thinks otherwise. The poetic medium, he suggests, is precisely suited to imagining what this city was like. Combining disparate, interlocking, elements it allows for the 'intricate progression of images and ideas'.³³ This is indeed the case when the psalmist sings the praises of rebuilt Jerusalem (Ps. 122:3):

> Jerusalem, that art builded
> As a city that is compact together;

> *Yelusaleng cheng,*
> *jianli jiangu,*
> *lianle zhengqi.*

> Jerusalem city,
> Established [and] firm,
> Joined in good order.

The translator here somewhat embellished the terse Hebrew description. But in doing so did he sufficiently convey the implications of unity and coherence indicated in the Hebrew text? This unity is not so much the city's physical appearance, rather it is the coherence, the 'togetherness' of its inhabitants; the coming together of all of Israel, implying the end of divisiveness. This is echoed in Ps. 147:2:

> The Lord doth build up Jerusalem,
> He gathereth together the dispersal of Israel;

The Chinese version actually accords better with the Hebrew:

> *Zhu zhongqian Yelusaleng,*
> *Juhui Yisalie zhongbei qusan de ren.*

> The Lord rebuilt Jerusalem,
> Gathers and returns [to it] Israel's dispersed peoples.

Jerusalem's strength as a fortified city, Ps. 48:13–14 [12–13], is given a somewhat different interpretation in the Chinese translation:

> Walk about Zion, and go round about her;
> Count the towers thereof.
> Mark ye well her ramparts,
> Traverse her palaces;
> That ye may tell it to the generation following.

> *Nimen dang raobian Xucheng,*
> *Siwei Xunle,*
> *Shushu chenglou.*

Jiren chengyuan,
Chakan gongdian,
Shi nimen chuanshuo dao houshi.

Walk round about Zion city,
Circle all around and inspect,
Count the city towers.
Take note of the city walls,
Examine the palaces,
So that you can transmit it to posterity.

This Psalm, which reflects the joy over the aborted Assyrian invasion,[34] alludes to the effectiveness of Jerusalem's fortifications – its towers and ramparts – as a deterrent. The aspect of the city's hopefully awe-inspiring defensibility is, however, not emphasized in the translation. Rather, Jerusalem is a walled city (as the Chinese would be familiar with) with palaces or mansions of the wealthy. The towers might be watch-towers, but they might also be other kinds of towers within the walled city. Possibly here as elsewhere, Schereschewsky projected the prophetic image of Jerusalem on to the Psalm, an image of a tranquil city of peace and well-being as described in Ps. 128.[35]

SCHERESCHEWSKY'S REFERENCES

Both Schereschewsky and the Peking Committee translators referred to earlier translations in preparing their own renditions. They would have had at their disposal several complete and partial Bibles rendered earlier into Chinese. The Morrison/Milne translation was published in 1823,[36] and the later Bridgman/Culbertson version appeared in 1863.[37] Aside from several New Testaments, there was also an Old Testament translated by Karl F. A. Gützlaff (1803–51), published in 1838. Schereschewsky had arrived in China, moreover, with a number of works of German biblical criticism acquired, no doubt, during his Breslau student days.[38] Among works by Wilhelm Gesenius and E.F. K. Rosenmüller, he also had Wilhelm M.L. de Wette, *Commentar über die Psalmen*, the work he most likely consulted when translating the Psalms. Although he makes no mention of it, he probably brought along a multi-volume edition of the Masoretic text with commentaries, *Mikra'ot Hagedolot*, also called the Rabbinical Bible. The commentary that he apparently consulted for the OT was the one by Rashi

(1040–1105).[39] Whether this was also the source for some of his interpretations of the Psalms must still be explored.

Although Schereschewsky had the Morrison/Milne translation of the Psalms at hand, it is doubtful that it would have been of much use to his own efforts, being based in its entirety or in very large part on the King James version. It is a very literal translation and, like the Bridgman/Culbertson version, was rendered into classical Chinese. Still, Schereschewsky may have borrowed some of Morrison's terminology and transliterations, like *dian* for temple and *Yelusaleng* for Jerusalem. He did not, however, use Morrison's transliterations of names for biblical personages or for Israel. Still, some features of the earlier punctuated text may have appealed to Schereschewsky and been modified by him, such as differentiating between personal and place names. Morrison enclosed place names between lines while Schereschewsky used a double line. For personal names both translators used a single line.

The Bridgman/Culbertson version may have been of greater use to Schereschewsky. From it he probably adopted a number of transliterations, and he would have paid special attention to the parallel construction which this version employed in many Psalms. However, the translation is more often than not too literal to the neglect of meaning. One obvious example is the Lord's house (e.g. Ps. 26:8), which is translated literally with *shi*, dwelling; another is Ps. 134:1–3, where the house of the Lord clearly refers to the Temple, but where the translator did not use *dian*. This overly literal rendition sacrificed clarity, even when no more than terminology is considered.[40]

De Wette's commentary was, no doubt, of considerable help. For example, differentiating Zion-mountain from Zion-city may have been suggested by de Wette's extensive comments to Ps. 2:6 and 87:2, where he pointed out the relationship of one to the other.[41] His comments may have been similarly useful when translating Ps. 5:8[9], where both house and temple occur. Despite not offering an explanation, de Wette had pointed out that a difference is intended, thus alerting the translator to the importance of carefully choosing his terminology.[42] Although clearly synonymous, Schereschewsky used *tang* for the former and *dian* for the latter. But he did not consistently follow de Wette, whose commentary suggests a figurative meaning for 'dwelling in the house of the Lord' in the last line of Ps. 23:6,[43] but which Schereschewsky translated literally: *Wo yao yongjiu zhuzai Zhude dianzhong*, 'And I shall dwell in the house of the Lord forever'.

Would Schereschewsky also have had the benefit of his fellow translators' criticism? Even if the question cannot be answered with any degree of certainty, we have fortunately an excellent description by Henry Blodget (1825–1903) of the Peking Committee's working method. According to Blodget, each translator's first draft of a biblical portion was criticized by the others and their Chinese co-workers. On the basis of this criticism, the translators prepared a second draft, which was again criticized by the others. Thereafter, a meeting was called when the second draft and comments were discussed by all the translators, including their Chinese co-workers.[44] No doubt, Schereschewsky's translation was subjected to the same routine scrutiny when suggestions for changes and improvements were made. We do not know to what extent suggestions were accepted or rejected, or how binding on the translators the committee's decisions were. However, there is no evidence of either acrimony or antagonism among the committee members throughout the long years of their association, and I am led to believe that they had harmonious working relationships. In the final analysis, Schereschewsky's missionary colleagues respected and acknowledged his superior acquaintance with the Hebrew text and most likely deferred to his judgement on most matters. It is nonetheless important to realize that the translated text, including his, had to pass careful scrutiny.

SOME COMPARISONS WITH THE UNION VERSION

Translating the Union version had not been a simple matter, as pointed out in Jost Zetzsche's excellent study, and the work of the Mandarin translation committee progressed far from smoothly. Work on the Psalms had begun under Calvin W. Mateer (1836–1908) of the American Presbyterian Mission, who headed the committee until his death. It was finished under Frederick W. Baller (1852–1922) of the China Inland Mission. Absalom Sydenstricker (1852–1931), Mateer's successor on the committee for a short time, was highly critical of the way the Psalms were translated under Baller's direction. Among others, Sydenstricker charged Baller with deficient knowledge of Hebrew and for wanting to impose the use of his own translation on the committee. This may have been so, for even though only 34 Psalms had been completed by 1908, the other 116 Psalms were finished by 1909 and the book of Psalms appeared in print in 1910.[45]

Like Schereschewsky's rendition, the Union version distinguishes between YHVH and Elohim, consistently transliterating, however, the former and using *Shangdi* for the latter, depending on the version. The transliteration of Zion is an improvement over the earlier transliteration by being more phonetic as *Xi'an*, even if perhaps somewhat mysterious as a geographic location. By omitting the designation of either city or mountain, the Union version does not indicate clearly what is being referred to. Ps. 48:2, for example, was as unsatisfactorily translated in the Union version as it had been by Schereschewsky; the difficulty being that city and mountain are one and the same place, even if with differing functions. The first line of the couplet contains an additional problem by seemingly stating that YHVH is in the Lord's city, and on His holy mountain:

...zai women Shangdi de chengzhong,
zai tade sheng shanshang.

Our God is in His city,
He is on His holy mountain.

An interesting innovation to Schereschewsky's 1874 version is the handling of *sela*. Transliterated as earlier, it is, however, printed in smaller type as if it were an appended note. On the other hand, *halleluiah* (e.g. Ps. 106:111–113) is omitted and was neither translated nor transliterated. As did Schereschewsky, the Union version translators used *dian* for Temple and did so similarly when the 'house of the Lord' was referred to. Palace was usually rendered as *gong*.

Aside from introducing grammatical changes, stylistic, and other improvements (more than 40 years of language change had after all taken place) many sentences and portions of sentences appear from the earlier rendition in the Union version.[46] Some random examples will demonstrate the intertextual relationship of both texts. In the later version of Ps. 133:1, discussed above, the first two lines are also reversed, but the Hebrew *hineh*, behold (*kan'na*), which Schereschewsky had omitted, is restored. While retaining the parallelism of the earlier version, the later translators abandoned the couplet in favour of a more colloquial form:

Kan'na, dixiong hemu tongju,
Shi he deng de shan,
He deng de mei.

Behold brothers dwelling together harmoniously,
How good,
How beautiful.

A similar intertextuality can be also seen in Ps. 137:5. The Union version introduced only minor changes with the addition of the subordinate particle *de* and the substitution of *jiqiao* (perhaps cleverness?) for *jineng*:

> *Yelusaleng'a,*
> *Wo ruwangji ni,*
> *Qingyuan wode youshou wangji jiqiao.*

> Jerusalem,
> If I forget you,
> Let my right hand forget [its] cleverness.

The Union version, on the other hand, tends to be more literal than its predecessor, and generally lacks the interpretive qualities of the earlier version. Ps. 48:13–14[12–13] is a good example where the translation indicates, as does the Hebrew text, that Jerusalem is a fortified city:

> *Nimen dang zhou you Xu'an,*
> *Siwei xuan rao,*
> *Shudian chenglou.*
> *Xikan tade waiguo,*
> *Chakan tade gongdian,*
> *Weiyao chuanshuo dao houtai.*

The translation of the Chinese text differs from the earlier version on page 20:

> Circle about Zion,
> Circle all around,
> Count the city towers.
> Carefully note its fortifications,
> Examine its palaces,
> Tell it to future generations.

Compared to the prose portions of the Bible and their more colloquial style, Schereschewsky's Psalms utilized expressions and forms of classical poetry, thus reproducing the terseness and economy of the Hebrew as much as possible. Pronouns are added in many places as is the subordinate particle *de*, but the translator did so sparingly, mindful of the poetic form he was striving to achieve. Lines where parallelisms occur in the original are transformed into couplets and, far from attempting a literal translation, Schereschewsky reversed the word order in lines and reversed lines for greater effectiveness. This is a reader-oriented translation and is aimed at engaging the listener as well. Some of his techniques are innovative, but the construction of couplets to highlight parallelisms is borrowed from the Bridgman/ Culbertson translation. The Union Bible translators similarly borrowed from Schereschewsky's version. It may, therefore, be that Bible translating from Morrison to the Union version can be regarded as an interlocking, intertextual process, each new translation benefiting from its predecessor.

Views may be divided on the extent to which Schereschewsky conveyed the emotional content commonly associated with Jerusalem. Yet I would suggest that the topographical differentiation, indicated by 'mountain' and 'city', the holiness of the one, the orderliness of the other, and God's presence in both, are all factors in underlining the uniqueness of the place for the reader from a different culture. When we add to these the terseness of poetic language, its suggestiveness rather than description, one can well imagine a reader (or listener) grasping Jerusalem's sacred and mundane majestic power. Form and content are firmly joined in the Chinese translation of the Psalms, for only a genuine Chinese poem could have given expression to the Jerusalem of the psalmist. But in the final analysis, how skillful a poet Schereschewsky was and whether his Psalms are 'good' poetry must be addressed by the literary critic.

There is still the question of how much credit for poetic diction and form can be assigned to Schereschewsky and how much to his co-workers. According to accounts by his contemporaries, Schereschwsky's knowledge of Chinese was outstanding at the time. But knowing Chinese does not necessarily make for a good poet. Although any answer can only be conjectural, I shall nonetheless suggest the following. Due to his background, Schereschewsky's early exposure would have been to Hebrew poetry, both as reader and listener. His other encounters with poetry were in acquired languages – Russian, German, English – but only much later. In Chinese poetry would he have heard an echo of the powerful suggestiveness of the Hebrew? Moreover, like a Chinese of his day, he was accustomed to reciting and hearing poetry recited, to hearing a poem's rhythms and cadences. It is, therefore, entirely possible that much of the credit for translating can go to Schereschewsky. Even the highly educated Lian Yinghuang, as was pointed out, saw no need for introducing major changes in the revised edition.

NOTES

1. Stephen Prickett, 'The Changing of the Host: Translation and Linguistic History' in David Jasper, ed., *Translating Religious Texts, Translation, Transgression and Interpretation*, New York: St. Martin's Press, 1993, p. 4.

2. Chen Mai-wang, review of *Bible in China*, in *China Review International*, Vol. 7, no. 2 (Autumn 2000), pp. 441–5. The reviewer further remarks on the neglect of such topics as the Bible's role in the Chinese church and its manner of circulation.
3. Aside from the several articles on the Bible which have appeared in print, there is Marián Gálik, *Influence, Translation, and Parallels, Selected Studies on the Bible in China*, Sankt Augustin: Monumenta Serica Institute, 2004; Jost O. Zetzsche, *The Bible in China*, Sankt Augustin: Monumenta Serica Institute, 1999; Liang Gong, *Shengjing zhinan* (A guide to the Bible), Shenyang: Liaoning renmin chubanshe, 1993. 'The Bible has burst upon the China studies field' writes Daniel H. Bays in his review of Zetzsche's volume, *The China Quarterly*, no. 164 (December 2000), p. 1094.
4. See, for example, Gerbern S. Oegama, 'On the Contextuality of Translation and the 'Inspiration' of Scriptures', in *Translation of Scriptures*, Philadelphia: Annenberg Research Institute, 1990, pp. 103–16.
5. *Jiuyue quanshu* (The Old Testament in the Mandarin colloquial). Translated from the Hebrew by the Rev. S.I.J. Schereschewsky, D.D. of the American Episcopal Mission and Printed for the American Bible Society at the Press of the A.B.C.F.M., Peking, China, 1875.
6. For an excellent summary of works discussing problems of translating the Hebrew text into European languages, see Edward L. Greenstein, *Essays on Biblical Method and Translation*, Atlanta: Scholars Press, 1989, pp. 125–9.
7. Some translating techniques were briefly examined in I. Eber, *The Jewish Bishop and the Chinese Bible, S.I.J. Schereschewsky (1831–1906)*, Leiden: E.J. Brill, 1999, pp. 164–98.
8. Unfortunately, Zhu Weizhi, 'Shipian wenxue jianshang (A literary appreciation of the Psalms)', in *Zhongjiao wenyi lunji* (Collected works on religion, literature and art), 1951, was not available. It would have been useful to have Zhu's insights on this topic.
9. They were published in 1866, but a copy of this publication apparently no longer exists.
10. See his *Influence, Translation, and Parallels*, pp. 85–92.
11. Zetzsche, *The Bible in China*, p. 145. In 1890 a partial and experimental translation was prepared by John Chalmers (1825–99). He too used the metrical form, but modelled his translation on the *sao* style of the *Chuzi* where an emphatic interjection *xi* divides line, pp. 212–13.
12. The categorization of the Psalms with each category having special characteristics cannot be a concern in this paper. Suffice it to say that Ps. 42–83 are assumed to be 'elohistic', and may have been an independent collection. For an excellent discussion of the problem of categorization and terminology, see Nahum M. Sarna, 'Psalms', *Encyclopedia Judaica*, Jerusalem: Keter, 1971, Vol. 13, pp. 1303–34,
13. Schereschewsky's numbering of verses differs from those Psalms which have ascriptions. Where pertinent, I have added his number in brackets.
14. Sarna, 'Psalms' p. 1321. The author suggests that *sela* may be understood as a synonym for eternity (*netsakh*).
15. Differentiating Zion as city or mountain is especially relevant in the later portions of the Psalms. Possibly Schereschewsky felt, after he began translating again in Beijing, that greater clarity was called for. Or it may have been the other committee members' suggestion.
16. All English translations are according to A. Cohen, trans., *The Psalms*, London: The Soncino Press, 1965.
17. Richard J. Clifford, *The Cosmic Mountain in Canaan and the Old Testament*, Cambridge: Harvard University Press, 1972, pp. 7–8 suggests that Zion's imagery is that of a cosmic mountain from where the world is stabilized, 'the point where the earth touches the divine sphere'.
18. See Richard Wilhelm, I. Eber, trans., *Lectures on the I Ching, Constancy and Change*, Princeton: Princeton University Press, 1979, pp. 123–4.
19. See Michael D. Goulder, *The Psalms of the Return (Book V, Psalms 107–50)*, Sheffield: Sheffield Academic Press, 1998, pp. 224–9, for an excellent discussion about the several problems connected with this Psalm. He suggests dating it to between 537 BCE, when Cyrus authorized the return, and 516 BCE, when the walls of Babylon were partly destroyed.
20. See Goulder, ibid., pp. 68–73 and his useful comment on this Psalm. This vision, though differently expressed, is also that of the *Great Learning* (*Daxue*).
21. Cohen, *The Psalms*, p. 78, gloss for Ps. 27:4.
22. Ibid., p. 149. The gloss states here that *rav* was used in Assyrian titles. In this place the reference is probably to God.
23. The occurrence of '*tsafon*', is especially problematic. See, for example, A. Robinson, 'Zion and Saphon in Psalm XLVIII 3', *Vetus Testamentum* 24 (1974), pp. 118–23.

24. William G. Braude, trans., *The Midrash on Psalms*, New Haven: Yale University Press, 1959, Vol. I, pp. 460–3. Midrash literature is a large body of writings from various periods on books of the Bible, which attempts to find meanings other than literal ones.
25. Jerome T. Walsh, 'Melitzeha Pash'u bi, Theology and the Translation of Poetry', in *Translation of Scriptures*, pp. 239, 240.
26. Gao Bolin, *Shengjing yu wenxue yanjiu* (Bible and literature studies), Commercial Press, 1940, p. 23.
27. Robert Alter, *The Art of Biblical Poetry*, New York: Basic Books, Inc., 1985, p. 205.
28. Benjamin Hrushovski, 'Prosody', *Encyclopedia Judaica*, Vol. 13, pp. 1200–02.
29. See, for example, Zhu Weizhi, *Xibailai wenhua* (Hebrew culture), Zhejiang: People's Publishing, 1988, pp. 177–89; Pius Drijvers, *The Psalms, Their Structure and Meaning*, Freiburg: Herder, London: Burns and Oates, 1965, p. 32; W.M.L. de Wette, *Commentar über die Psalmen*, Heidelberg: J.C.B. Mohr, 1836, pp. 32–57, discusses at length rhythm and parallelism.
30. Andrew H. Plaks, 'Where the Lines Meet: Parallelism in Chinese and Western Literatures', *Chinese Literature Essays, Articles, Reviews*, Vol. 10, nos. 1,2 (July 1988), pp. 43–60. I thank Amira Katz for bringing this article to my attention.
31. S.I.J. Schereschewsky, 'Translation of the Scriptures into Chinese', in *Records of the General Conference of Protestant Missionaries in China 1890*, Shanghai: American Presbyterian Mission Press, 1890, pp. 41–42. Schereschewsky unfortunately did not provide examples nor a more detailed explanation.
32. Alter, *The Art of Biblical Poetry*, p. 19.
33. Ibid., p. 121.
34. Cohen, *The Psalms*, introductory statement, p. 149.
35. See, e.g. Isa. 32:18, 33:20-21. Moshe Weinfeld, 'Zion and Jerusalem as Religious and Political Capital: Ideology and Utopia', in Richard E. Friedman, ed., *The Poet and the Historian, Essays in Literary and Historical Biblical Criticism*, Chico, Ca: Scholars Press, 1983, p. 103. Weinfeld considers the Jerusalem at peace view the prophetic-utopian transformation of the idea of Jerusalem.
36. Robert Morrison (1782–1834) was apparently the major translator. It is not clear which portions William Milne (1785–1822) translated. The Psalms were printed already in 1815. The entire Bible, printed in 1823 by the British and Foreign Bible Society in 21 volumes, was entitled *Shentian shengshu*. See Zetzsche, *The Bible in China*, pp. 41–3.
37. For the complex history of the OT version by Elijah C. Bridgman (1801–61) and Michael C. Culbertson (1819–62), see Zetzsche, *The Bible in China*, pp. 97–107. Their Psalms and several other OT portions appeared in 1861.
38. Domestic and Foreign Missionary Society, China Records, 1835–1951. The Archives of the Episcopal Church USA, Austin, Texas, RG64-28, Schereschewsky's letter to S.D. Denison, 21 July 1865. Unfortunately, we do not know which books were in the Beijing missionary library, otherwise a better idea could be had about various sources missionaries were able to consult.
39. Solomon Yitzhaki ben Isaac. Rashi was a French rabbinical scholar whose authoritative commentaries are studied to the present day.
40. John Werry criticised the translation as too literal and therefore frequently more ambiguous. See his comments, 'Historical Summary of the Different Versions of the Scriptures', in *Records of the General Conference of the Protestant Missionaries*, 1890, pp. 45–58.
41. Wilhelm M.L. de Wette, *Commentar über die Psalmen*, Heidelberg, 1811.
42. Ibid., p. 101.
43. Ibid., p. 228.
44. American Board of Commissioners for Foreign Missions, 'Letters and Papers Addressed to the Board', Houghton Library, Harvard University (ABCFM), Vol. 302:I, Blodget, Occasional Notes, 20 March 1867, ms. 181. See also I. Eber, 'The Peking Translating Committee and S.I.J. Schereschewsky's Old Testament', *Anglican and Episcopal History*, Vol. LXVII, no. 2 (June 1998), pp. 212–26.
45. Zetzsche, *The Bible in China*, pp. 307–10, 315, 406. Sydenstricker also objected to 'italicized words', that is, words not in the original text, their addition being marked with a dotted line in the translation, p. 309, n. 47. Baller's translation of the Psalms was published privately in 1908.
46. In her study of the first chapter of the Book of Ruth, Lihy Yariv-Laor also noted this fact. See her 'Linguistic Aspects of Translating the Bible into Chinese', in I. Eber, S.K. Wan. K. Walf, R. Malek, *Bible in China, The Literary and Intellectual Impact*, Sankt Augustin: Monumenta Serica Institute, 1999, pp. 101–21.

6

Notes on the Early Reception of the Old Testament

The reception of the Bible was preceded by its translation into Chinese, and its translation, in turn, is part of China's encounter with the West, with Christians and with Christianity. The merchants who came to trade in the thriving markets of the Tang dynasty (618–906) capital, Chang'an, may have been Persians and Central Asians of various religious persuasions, but in their wake in the seventh century came Nestorian Christians, who founded churches and received permission to preach. Nestorian Christianity disappeared in the anti-Buddhist sweep between 841 and 845 – reappearing but briefly at the Mongol court centuries later – yet they were only the first among other Christians who followed in subsequent centuries. In the Yuan dynasty (1279–1368), when the Mongols controlled the vast area from China to the gates of Western Europe, we know of a number of Christian visitors who made the long journey from Europe to China. There were the Venetian merchants, the Polo brothers Maffeo and Niccolo, and Niccolo's son, Marco. Marco Polo's popular account of his sojourn in China often eclipses the vivid stories of other intrepid travellers, the Franciscan friars who, braving the dangers of deserts and seas, arrived in China about the same time as the Polos.[1]

The first translator of portions of the Bible in China was, it seems, John of Montecorvino (1247–1328). His translations, apparently into Mongolian rather than Chinese, have long since disappeared, as did other vestiges of the Catholic Church introduced by the Franciscan friars. Not until centuries later, following the arrival of Portuguese and Spanish traders in Asian waters in the sixteenth century, did Chinese once more have contact with Christians, the Jesuits, whose encounter with the thought and culture of the Chinese literati was to have profound repercussions in Europe.[2] The Jesuits were the first to translate into Chinese, but they too translated only those portions of the Bible which they used in liturgy and preaching. Less well known and indeed not often mentioned was the encounter with Russian orthodox Christianity which brought to China monks, priests, and traders across the Inner Asian frontier. Both trade and the Russian Orthodox Church were institutionalized by the Kiakhta Treaty of 1728, after the Russians attempted in the 1720s to increase trade with China and to gain a firmer foothold in the empire. But despite their uninterrupted presence in the capital since the time of the Jesuits, the Russians did not write an edifying chapter in the annals of mission, and they made few converts.[3]

Matters were different when Protestant Christians arrived in the mid-nineteenth century, either preceded by or together with gunboats and merchants determined to open China to Western trade. Taking advantage of Chinese political and military weaknesses, and its simmering social unrest, Protestant and Roman Catholic missionaries were active in most parts of China. They were encouraged by the pervasive evangelism of their home churches, especially British and American, and they often expressed the Christian message in stridently militant terms.

The history of Chinese–Western contacts has been discussed in numerous works, but one dimension in need of greater attention, aside from the translation of the biblical text, is its reception in China in the nineteenth and twentieth centuries. In China, Christian missionaries came into contact with a highly literate civilization, where the Christian message could not remain a verbal message only, conveyed in preaching. Thus Protestant missionaries applied themselves vigorously to Bible translation, and by the 1870s a number of Chinese translations of the Old Testament (OT) were available in various parts of the Chinese empire, especially in areas where mission stations had been established. There was the 1823 classical, though even then rarely used, text translated by Robert Morrison (1782–1834); there was the more popular, so-called, Delegates' version of 1852–54, also in classical Chinese; and there was the 1865 classical Bridgman/Culbertson translation, as well as various OT portions in one or another southern vernacular. Samuel I.J. Schereschewsky's OT translation of 1875 into pre-eminently readable northern colloquial (*guanhua*, later *guoyu*) was becoming increasingly popular; unlike previous versions, it was prepared from the Hebrew.

If translation is considered the first step in the Bible's 'sinification',[4] the second step concerns its reception. By reception, I mean the comments by Chinese readers on the OT that represented initial attempts to understand and interpret a text in which new and different ideas about human life, the transcendent, and the relationship of the human being to the divine were expressed. In this essay I want to explore several themes found in these interpretations. For it is reception that led in time to the third step of appropriation, when writers and intellectuals integrated the biblical text in their creative works and polemical writings.[5]

Where the Bible is concerned one must, of course, consider the importance of the religious motivation, but a major prerequisite for both reception and appropriation of a text is its readability. The two prime examples for readability were the Delegates' Bible in classical Chinese and Schereschewsky's *guanhua* translation which, until the appearance of the 1919 Union Bible, was the most widely read OT.[6] Readability is not only clarity of language for understanding the ideas expressed in the text. By readability I mean the power to evoke a response, be it a creative act, like writing poetry, or a philosophical inquiry.[7]

THE TEN COMMANDMENTS

Let me begin with a small portion of a rather long poem on the Ten Commandments, published in 1869:

> Moses went forth from Egypt
> To carry out God's will.
> Crossing the Red Sea, God's miracle
> parted the waters like rocks,
> sent manna and bestowed a fiery pillar
> which Israel respectfully received.
> [Amid] Mt. Sinai's blazing flames
> The ten commandments were established.
> The first commandment proclaims:
> The True God is only One
> Outside of God there is no second lord
> All peoples, take note.[8]

Not great poetry, to be sure, but worth noting for combining all the essential facts of the Exodus in one compact verse, and for stating the quintessential meaning of monotheism in four brief lines.

A prose poem by another writer interpreted the fifth commandment in terms of Chinese moral maxims:

> To nourish both parents when resting and active, is to be since antiquity a worthy filial and respectful person. In their conduct the former sages displayed fear of Heaven.

The poet's reference to filiality and former sages supplied the commandment with a Chinese context, as was also the case with the ninth commandment:

> One word lightly spoken is hard to return [even] by force. Those who profit from deception and cheating, cheat the spirits (*shen*), cheat God (*Shangdi*).

Contrasting these verses to missionary interpretations in Chinese, one cannot help but be struck by the difference. No poetic frills for a man like J. Lewis Shuck, who wrote a slim pamphlet in 1841 on the Ten Commandments, where the fifth proclaims sternly and in no uncertain terms:

> [Treat] both parents with filiality (*xiao*) and respect (*jing*). This commandment forbids people to be unfilial toward father and mother [and exhorts] supporting fathers and mothers.

Here is Shuck's ninth commandment:

> Do not tell lies and cheat. This commandment forbids people to create disorder (*luan*) by bearing false witness and inciting others to do evil.[9]

Chinese writers were apparently inspired to use poetic forms for the Ten Commandments rather than prose, and there are quite a number of expository poems from the 1870s on this theme. In one final example the poet left no doubt that the fifth commandment was part and parcel of China's culture, by stating that since the beginning of time everyone has been filial to those who lived formerly, praising them, and fearing to offend them.[10] For these men – literati, educated by means of the Confucian Classics – it was important to prove that the new ideas in no way contradicted the cultural assumptions they had acquired as part of their earliest and most recent education. Referring to the *Four Books* (Si shu) and five Classics, Liu Changxing wrote that when the commandments which God gave to Moses on Mt Sinai are examined, it will be found that they accord with the principles transmitted in the Classics.[11] Thus, instead of stern prohibitions, these initial interpreters chose not only a gentler form, poetry, for conveying the Bible's messages, but attempted also to show that these messages were no different from what the Chinese themselves had practiced since the hoary past.

RECEPTION OF GENESIS

Whereas poetry may have been especially suitable to the kind of reception at issue here, reception was by no means confined to verses, and the prose essays written by the Chinese often tended to raise intriguing questions. This was especially true for the Book of Genesis, which invited more comments than other OT books. Among essays that take up the creation of the world, the biblical account was usually accepted without questioning. God existed before heaven and earth. Creation began when God separated the original chaos (*huntun*). There was light, then plants and trees; there was the earth, then sun and moon. Among animals, first were fish, then birds, then large and small insects, and so on. Man was created last. Creation was gradual, step by step, and occurred because of God.[12] The question was apparently asked, however, how this monumental task could be accomplished in six days. The answer given was that one day was not the day we know. One day was a very long time, as if 10,000 years, 'untold springs and autumns'.[13]

Others asked more penetrating questions, perhaps as a result of the new knowledge inquiring minds gained from science. The Bible contradicts astronomy, wrote Chen Dayong. The earth rotates about the sun, and to assure rotation, earth, sun, and moon must attract one another. Yet, according to the Bible, the sun was created on the first day, whereas the moon was created only on the fourth day. But even if we assume that the earth did not begin to rotate until the fourth day, how could vegetation survive which was created on the third day?[14]

The Garden of Eden and Adam and Eve's misconduct came in for scrutiny. In view of Eve's transgressions (the writer does not mention her name), how can she be considered the ancestral mother (*shizumu*) of humankind? The author considered her to have committed not one, but four sins. First, she did not believe God's (*Shangzhu*) prohibition and listened to Satan (*mogui*). Second, she was determined to do as she wished, and did not obey God's command. Third, she was neither satisfied with, nor grateful for all the trees in the Garden of Eden; she did not distinguish the existence of other trees in relationship to the one tree, the fruit of which she wanted to taste. Fourth, having received her human body from God, she nonetheless wanted to be divine (*chengshen*). But ultimately, it was not she, it was Satan-as-snake which caused the expulsion from the Garden of Eden by God. In spite of her sins, therefore, Eve can be absolved, according to the writer, from the guilt of having lost paradise.

Adam, in this account, is somehow less sinful; he was ashamed, stated the author, and did not manage to find the words to reprimand Eve, or talk about her actions. This human couple then was as human as we are, he concluded, and they, like we, were prone to transgressions. We, however, can repent, be redeemed from our sins, and prepare for Paradise.[15] How to interpret Adam and Eve's disobedience and the subsequent Fall presented, nonetheless, a problem, and not every commentator was as charitable. Even if, claimed another author, the first ancestors were endowed with wisdom, thus preparing the way for loving, knowing, and venerating God (*Shen*), they also gave in to the temptation of opposing God's decree. With this act they brought calamity on their children and their descendants.[16]

In Genesis it was, however, most frequently the human story which engaged the interpreters' attention, the values the ancient Hebrews held, what might be gained in reading about them, and how these can be related to Chinese history and the values of the Chinese people. 'During China's Xia dynasty [traditionally dated to around 2000 BC]', begins one essay, 'Israel's ancestor, Abraham, dwelled together with his nephew Lot, their children, their herds, and their possessions.' But, as related in Genesis 13–14, the amiable relationship went sour when the two men's herdsmen quarrelled; therefore, not wishing the strife to get out of hand, Abraham proposed they go their separate ways. Lot moved on to the Jordan plains with its cities, including Sodom and Gomorrah, and Abraham remained in Canaan. When, later, Lot was captured in battles between kings of the plain cities, Abraham came to his rescue. Why was this significant? Because, explained the writer, 'Abraham first [reached] a compromise with his nephew and then he rescued him. This can be called the utmost of humanity (*airen*).'[17] The writer's intent in this brief essay is to show that Abraham's conduct was comparable to that of China's ancient paradigmatic figures. Yet, we should note that there seemed to be little interest in Judges or Joshua or Samuel, although these books certainly contain powerful examples of positive images reminiscent of those found in Chinese history.

Bu Wangbian set himself the task of commenting in detail on a number of selected Genesis verses that could be taken to contradict the evidence of science. His explanation of Genesis 1:6 is especially interesting because he used scientific reasoning to prove the accuracy of the creation story. When examining the results of the Lord's creation, wrote Bu, we find that He first created light and then air (*qi*, also ether). And what is air? 'It is the vapours (*tianqi*) within emptiness (*kong*).' Air holds things together, and air is vast and limitless, as everyone knows. Air is the source of the vitality of grass, wood, or grain. Air divides the waters into those above and those below, according to Bu. Water rises as clouds due to the sun's evaporation and it descends as rain due to the air's power in emptiness. Western countries investigate (*kewu*) water, fire, wind, and earth because the usefulness of air is so great that its principle must be completely understood.[18]

OTHER ISSUES CONCERNING THE OT

That some writers chose to discuss only certain chapters or verses was not due to lack of knowledge of the OT. Rather, it would seem that some focused on smaller questions, while others did indeed take up larger ones. Such is the question, why read the Bible? What kinds of benefits can possibly be gained from reading the entire OT? Listing each book of the OT (which I shall not do here), the writer answered:

> Reading Genesis [one will] know the benefit of following ancestral [ways] (*juiyuan*)... reading Leviticus [one will] know the benefit of offering sacrifices; reading Numbers [one will] know the benefit of family registers (*puxi*)... reading Judges [one will] know the benefit of repentance... reading Samuel I and II [one will] know the benefit of establishing rules....[19]

Some of the benefits listed strike one as far-fetched. Most, however, reflect values that are meaningful within the Chinese cultural context. Who could negate the importance of family registers or ancestral ways?

The question of authenticity was also raised. Where Williamson had stated unequivocally that Moses had written the Pentateuch, others asked whether Moses was indeed the author of the Five Books (*wu jing*). Some claim that the Pentateuch was completed in the time of Moses. Others say the Five Books were completed later; some say they were written in the time of King Josiah (fifth century BC), and some assign their composition to the time of the prophets. Some deny altogether that they could have been written in the time of Moses. Yet, went the argument, according to Kings I, 2:1–4, Moses was the author of the Five Books, and according to Kings II, 23:25, King Josiah embraced God and the law with all his heart and soul. Therefore, the Five Books must have existed in his time.[20] Finding proof for knowledge of the law within the Bible marks the writer as a critical reader of the text and as one who was familiar with its several books.

Missionaries writing in Chinese also contributed, however, to the reception of the OT. Although their essays are often dry, more intent on conveying information rather than interpretation, they should not be ignored. Thus an article serialized in several issues of the *Globe Magazine* (*Wanguo gongbao*) by Alexander Williamson was meant to introduce readers to the Pentateuch and the book of Genesis. He began with Moses, identifying him as a man from the tribe of Levy. Moses was born, according to Chinese reckoning, in the 66th year of the Shang dynasty King Taiwu, or in 1578 BCE. Williamson summarized events from the life of Moses: he saved the Israelites, led the Exodus, went up to Mt Sinai, but in the end was prevented from entering the land of Canaan. Each brief summary is followed by the biblical chapter and verse. In another instalment, Williamson took up three different themes. First he described a number of early books from several traditions, like the Indian Vedas, comparing them to the three Chinese Classics, the *Shu* (History), *Shi* (Songs), and *Yi* (Changes). He next supplied brief one- or two-sentence descriptions of the 50 chapters of Genesis, ending the essay with an excursus into the treacherous byways of the 'Term Question'. Babylonians, Persians, Romans, wrote Williamson, all had different names for God, though each had a different meaning. In the Jewish country (*Youtaiguo*) two names were used: *Hela* and *Yehehua*. The first means 'utmost omnipotence' (*dingda zhi liqi*), the second: 'is as is' (*ziran er randi*). Westerners, he concluded, have used equally *Tianzhu, Zhen Shen, Shangdi,* and *Yehehua*.[21]

I have not found an account by a Chinese writer of this early date which attempts a similarly abbreviated overview of the Five Books. However, one essay written four decades later was precisely what the missionary seemed to have ever so clumsily attempted earlier. Instead of launching into an account about Moses' connection with the Pentateuch as Williamson had done, Li Yongfang wrote, 'The Bible has been from the very beginning spiritually influenced and has, in turn, had spiritual influence.' Men felt this influence in antiquity, and others listened to their ideas thereafter,[22] thus explaining to the reader why the Bible should be of interest. Li's essay is of special interest, as he apparently knew Hebrew and was well acquainted with the arrangement and content of the OT.

To turn to another issue, the 'Term Question' controversy, that is, the problem of which Chinese term to use for God, had raged among missionaries since the late 1840s.[23] Numerous polemical articles and pamphlets had appeared in China, Europe, and America, involving also a number of Western theologians in the debate. Chinese writers too took up this issue, but apparently neither they nor the missionaries noted one another's arguments. Like their commentaries on the OT, which employed an essentially different approach from the missionaries to the text, the Chinese writers on the 'Term Question' also tackled the issues in a distinctive manner. Like the missionaries, they often invoked the Chinese Classics to prove a point, but most of their essays were explanatory rather than polemical. This much debated question reveals once more the uniqueness of the Chinese exegesis.

By 1878, perhaps a dozen or more articles on terms had appeared in *Globe Magazine*, which led one author to write a review article with a summary of the various issues that were raised. Some of these are as follows: Heaven and *Shangdi* are synonymous, and the Tetragrammaton should be translated with *Shangdi*; it is erroneous to argue that the True God (*Zhen Shen*) is in the country of China, for then it need also be argued that the teaching of Jesus is in the country of Jesus; the teaching of the Bible is not much different from that of the Six Classics,[24] since both teach the Way of Heaven (*Tiandao*).[25]

We might take a closer look at some of the arguments advanced on behalf of the term *Shen*. In the sense of deity, stated the writer, *Shen* was the same as the Tetragrammaton, Creator of heaven and earth and all things. From heaven, *Yehehua* oversees His creation, He is transcendent as well as immanent, is Deity as well as Lord (*Zhucai*).[26] Westerners, another believed, do not sufficiently understand the wider implications of the term *Shen*. As Deity, the term refers to YHWH, who was introduced from the West. And as Deity, *Shen* is omnipotent, omniscient, totally benevolent (*ren*), bestows grace and blessings, was in the past, is in the present, beginningless and endless, self-so (*ziran er ran*): this is *Yehehua Shen*. Lord the Creator (*Zhuangzaozhu*) of the OT is the same as the Tetragrammaton. But *Shen* can also be used in another sense: divine, even spiritual, or divinity. The *Zhouli*, for example, speaks of heavenly divinities (*tianshen*) who go by different names, and Zhu Xi[27] wrote that a person's heart/mind (*xin*) is his *shenming*. Therefore, it is important to distinguish between the name and the appellation (*hao*). This had also been the missionaries' argument – the need to distinguish between the generic name and the appellation – except that their search for both led them into countless thickets. For the Chinese writer the matter was simpler. Just as each person has an honorific, his *hao*, so each *shen* has an appellation which cannot be applied to another. *Yehehua* is the name given to the *Shen* who was brought from the West;

Yehehua Shen is One, not two. When people pray, they pray to *Yehehua Shen*, the true Ruler (*Zai*) who created heaven and earth. He is the True Ruler (*Zhen Zai*) of the OT, and the self-existent Name revealed to men. As to the term *Shangdi*, it is an appellation; it is not synonymous with *Shen*, and is certainly not the same as the Tetragrammaton.[28] Although left unstated, the implication is that the Tetragrammaton is an appellation, and is, therefore, neither synonymous nor interchangeable with another appellation.

These and other interpretive poems and essays on the meaning of the Protestant Bible and God are the initial building blocks which subsequently made possible the entrance of biblical concepts and imagery into a wider discourse. Even if later theologians, writers, or intellectuals were not actually aware of, or had not read these early works, ideas once expressed tend to assume a life and dynamic of their own, spoken of or mentioned perhaps in random conversations. They are transformed into new, or different and more developed forms by others in another place and at another time. Perhaps not a mighty stream, but also not a mere trickle, Chinese biblical scholarship has developed apace since the end of the nineteenth century, as Professors Liang Gong, Márian Gálik, and others have shown. The Bible's connection with literature was explored more than 60 years ago,[29] and biblical images and imagery were creatively transformed in literary works even earlier.[30] If these can be taken as signs of the biblical text becoming part of the larger cultural context, then we should again remind ourselves that it began with the Bible's readability, progressing from there to interpretability.

NOTES

1. Less well known but equally as interesting as the Polos' journey is, for example, the journey of William of Rubruck, W.W. Rockhill, *The Journeys of William of Rubruck to the Eastern Part of the World, 1235–55, As Narrated by Himself, With Two Accounts of the Earlier Journey of Pian de Carpine*. Lichtenstein: Kraus Reprint, 1967. First published 1900.
2. Among the many works about the Catholic Mission, see J.D. Young, *Confucianism and Christianity – The First Encounter*. Hong Kong: Hong Kong University Press, 1990.
3. I am grateful to Yuri Pines for reminding me of the Russian Ecclesiastical Mission in Beijing and the recent numerous Russian sources on this topic. The major source in English is still Eric Widmer, *The Russian Ecclesiastical Mission in Peking During the Eighteenth Century*. Cambridge: Harvard University Press, 1976.
4. John K. Fairbank, 'Introduction', in Suzanne W. Barnett and J.K. Fairbank, *Christianity in China: Early Protestant Missionary Writings*. Cambridge: Harvard University Press, 1985, p. 9.
5. A number of essays by Lewis Robinson, Márian Gálik, Raoul Findeisen, and Sze-kar Wan

deal with appropriation in fiction and intellectual history. See I. Eber, S.K. Wan, K. Walf, with R. Malek, eds., *Bible in Modern China, The Literary and Intellectual Impact*. Sankt Augustin: Monumenta Serica Institute, 1999.

6. The problem with the Delegates' Bible was that it sacrificed fidelity to readability, while the Union version, although widely hailed by Chinese readers, often sacrificed readability to literalness.
7. Regarding poetry, the Polish poet, Czesaw Milosz, calls this the adapting of a work to 'a modern sensibility'. See *The New York Review of Books*, 15 February 1996, p. 26.
8. Wu Chunqiao, 'Zhen Shen Shijie Ge', *Jiaohui Xinbao* (henceforth *JHXB*), Vol. 1 (26 June 1869), p. 192.
9. Chen Shenxiu, 'Shangdi shijie shi (Verses on God's Ten Commandments)', *JHXB*, Vol. 2 (18 December 1869), pp. 79b–80a. J. Lewis Shuck, *Shangdi zhi Ming* (God's Commandments), Shuyuan Cangban, 1841. The English title is *The Ten Commandments, Stated and Explained, with Additional Running Comments*. Pamphlet in the ABCFM collection of the Harvard-Yenching Library.
10. Yang Yongzhi, 'Hankou jilai fuyin shijia shi (A Poem on the Gospel's Ten Commandments Received from Hankou)', *Wanguo Gongbao* (henceforth *WGGB*), Vol. 8 (8 July 1876), pp. 629a–29b.
11. Liu Changxing, 'Moxi Shijia yu Rudao Xianghe Shuo (Moses' Ten Commandments Agree with Confucianism)', *WGGB*, Vol. 8 (18 March 1876), p. 405. The *Four Books* consist of the *Lunyu* (Analects), *Mengzi* (Mencius), *Da Xue* (Great Learning), and *Zhong Yong* (the Mean). The five Classics are: *Shujing* (History), *Shijing* (Songs), *Yijing* (Changes), *Chunqiu* (Spring and Autumn Annals) and *Liji* (rites).
12. 'Chuang shiji zhuan, erpian zhiwu (Story of the creation of the world, chapters two to five)', *WGGB*, Vol. 15 (16 September 1882), pp. 50a–50b.
13. 'Shengshu jiuyue yizhen (Some questions about the Old Testament)', *WGGB*, Vol. 12 (24 January 1880), pp. 210a–11b.
14. Chen Dayong, 'Dasheng jing yiwen (Answers to Difficult Questions of the Bible)', *JHXB*, Vol. 3 (26 August 1871), p. 205b.
15. Bu Gangbian, 'Shengshu tiwen (A Scripture Subject)', *WGGB*, Vol. 10 (10 November 1877), pp. 177a–8a.
16. Wu Chunqiao, 'Shenlun (About God)', *JHXB*, Vol. 2 (13 November 1869), p. 581.
17. 'Xianzhi rang shu (A Nephew's Compromise with Uncle)', *WGGB*, Vol. 12 (23 August 1879), p. 13.
18. Bu Wangbian, 'Shangzhu shuo yao kongqi jiao shangxiade fenkai (The Lord Said, Let there be the Firmament. Causing the Waters Above and Below to Divide)', *WGGB*, Vol. 10 (22 December 1877), pp. 256b–7b.
19. Yang Yongzhi, 'Shengshu lun (The Bible)', *WGGB*, Vol. 11 (17 May 1879), p. 506.
20. 'Some Questions about the Old Testament'.
21. Weilianchen Laigao, 'Chuang shiji xiaoyin (A Brief Introduction to Genesis)', *WGGB*, Vol. 14 (13 May 1882), pp. 347–8, and (20 May 1882), pp. 375a–5b. Williamson's reference to *Hela* may be Eloah, which missionaries used as the singular for Elohim.
22. Li Yongfang, 'Jiuyue dao yan (Introduction to the Old Testament)', *Shangming*, Vol. 1, no. 6 (January 1921), pp. 1–13.
23. For a summary of the issues raised, see I. Eber, 'The Interminable Term Question', in Eber et. al., *Bible in Modern China*, pp. 135–61.
24. The Six Classics are mentioned at an early time and include the *Shi* (Songs), *Shu* (Documents), *Yi* (Changes), *Li* (Rites), *Yue* (Music), and *Chunqiu* (Spring and Autumn). Their canonical status derives from the assumption that they were edited by Confucius.
25. Zhou Shungui, ' Yuege shenghao lunjin chenbi jian (Review essay of articles on holy appellations)', *WGGB*, Vol. 10, no. 491 (1 June 1878), 562a–3b (5025–5027).
26. Wu Chunqiao, 'Shenlun (About God)', *JHXB*, Vol. 2 (13 November 1869), pp. 581–2.
27. Zhu Xi (1130–1200) was the most important philosopher of the Confucian revival in the Song dynasty. His commentaries on the Classics have remained authoritative.
28. Kao Zhenzi, 'Cheng Shen liyi (Meaning of the term *Shen*)', *WGGB*, Vol. 10, no. 463 (November 1877), 169a–75b (4287–4300).

29. Gao Bolin, *Shengjing yu wenxue yanjiu* (Bible and literature studies). 1940.
30. I especially like the poem by Zhou Zuoren (published under the name Zhongmi), 'Qilu (Crossroads)', *Xiaoshuo yuebao*, Vol. 13, no. 4 (April 1922), pp. 3–4. Bewildered by the many roads one can take, Zhou wrote:

> I love Jesus
> But I also love Moses.
> Jesus said, "When people strike your right cheek, turn the left...
> Moses said, 'An eye for an eye, a tooth for a tooth.
> Had I the strength, I [would] certainly walk on Jesus's road, carrying the cross on my back.
> Had I more than a little strength, I [would] also walk on the road of judge Moses.

An innocent perplexity lands the poet in a delightfully incongruous juxtaposition.

PART III: LITERATURE

7

Translation Literature in Modern China: The Yiddish Author and His Tale

Translation literature – the product of different cultures and different perspectives – has played a significant role in modern China's intellectual life. This body of translation work, which began in the latter part of the nineteenth century, is broadly concerned with scientific, humanistic, behavioural, philosophical, and literary subjects. The group of translations from literary works is a particularly fascinating subject.

Translating from another people's literature poses several highly interesting problems. First there is the question of the selection of works for translation. For what a translator will choose is often related to specific values, concerns, and even goals of his own period. Secondly, the translator's ideological, philosophical, or political point of view is bound to influence the choices he makes. And thirdly, when a translator translates from a literature with whose language he is not familiar – thus using an intermediate translation – his selection is in fact already preselected.[1] Notions gained and views developed, on the basis of translations, regarding other peoples are, therefore, sometimes distorted. Another people may be idealized or condemned. Similarities may be seen where none exist, and differences may be glossed over because they are not understood.

Translations from Yiddish literature have a place in Chinese translation literature generally. Although numerically not large – 40-odd stories and plays in all [2] – the importance of these translations is due to the fact that they supported a variety of ideas current among Chinese intellectuals, particularly in the 1920s. Among these was the idea that Chinese intellectuals ought to be concerned with the plight of the so-called 'weak and small peoples' (*ruo xiao minzu*). And, of course, Jews, in addition to Poles, Hungarians, or Czechs, were such a people. Perhaps more important, however, was the idea concerning the use of Yiddish. For it was thought that Yiddish was the true vernacular of the Jewish peoples. Chinese writers, wanting to use their own vernacular, were urged to take note of what the use of Yiddish had done for the Jewish people.

Chinese writers did not translate from original Yiddish, a language which for obvious reasons they did not know. Rather, the translations, with some possible exceptions, show that English or Esperanto sources were used in the 1920s and 1930s. Most of the stories which have appeared after 1949 in the People's Republic of China, however, were translated from Russian. English translations of Yiddish literature were readily available in China before 1949 and English, moreover, was apparently favoured by many as a language of translations.[3] More interesting is the considerable use of Esperanto works, for these were used not only for preparations of translations from Yiddish, but also from Polish and other minor European languages.[4]

The bulk of the translations from Yiddish literature appeared in the 1920s.[5] A few translations were, however, published in the first half of the 1930s, and 13 stories appeared in the late 1950s. Alongside the translations were also a number of articles discussing either the nature, history, and content of Yiddish literature, or individual authors and their works. The last such article dates from 1959. When the stories and plays are grouped into patterns of themes, the basis of the selection process as well as current concerns emerge; the critical and descriptive articles in turn indicate how interest in Yiddish literature was related to Chinese intellectual problems and change.

The purpose of this paper is to attempt to answer several questions. What did Chinese writers know about Yiddish literary history and about Yiddish authors, and how did they evaluate them? What kind of stories were chosen for translation, who were the translators, and why were they interested in Yiddish literature? And finally, what sort of problems did the translators encounter with specifically Jewish idioms and expressions?

BACKGROUND

The initial interest in translating Yiddish literature must be understood within the general context of China's literary revolution, which can be roughly dated to 1917, but blossomed fully only after 1919. As part of the general intellectual ferment, the literary revolution was a complex phenomenon. Its two central issues were, firstly, the abolition of the written literary language (*wenyan*) and the use of the vernacular (*baihua*), and secondly, the creation of a new literature in the vernacular which would be original in form as well as in content.

In 1918, Hu Shi (1891–1962), the 'father' of the literary revolution, described these twin goals as the development of tools and the development of methods. The first involved a thorough acquaintance with vernacular usage and also practice in writing in the vernacular. The second consisted in new methods of collecting materials, new methods of composition, and new methods of description. In order to use new methods for collecting materials, wrote Hu Shi, old themes must be discarded. Materials for writing literature should be drawn from the lives of the common people – farmers, workers, storekeepers, and the impoverished strata of society. In order to use new methods of description, writers must describe people, their environment, their affairs and feelings.[6]

The proponents of the literary revolution looked to Western literature as a model and guide. Reading Western literature had led Chinese intellectuals to two conclusions. One, both China and some European nations faced similar political and social problems. Moreover, even China's intellectual ferment was also found elsewhere, though in a different form. And two, knowledge of foreign literature was vital in the creation of China's new and 'human' literature (*ren de wenxue*). Human literature must be concerned with the universal experiences of men and women; Chinese writers, in order to write this literature, must be able to 'perceive humanity as a whole'.[7]

But this was not all. The most important reason for the creation of a new literature was that literature can be used as a tool for the transformation of society. Zhou Zuoren (1885–1956), essayist and literary critic, writing in 1917, explained that he had planned to transform society through literature and art while still a student in Japan prior to 1912. Toward this end he had been translating and publishing the new literature of foreign countries.[8]

Notions such as these concerning literary creativity were first publicized in *Xin qingnian* (New youth, founded in 1915), the highly influential journal of the intellectual revolutionists. By 1920 these tenets were further elaborated by the Literary Research Society (*wenxue yanjiu hui*), a loosely organized group of writers and scholars. From 1921, men like Mao Dun (pen-name of Shen Yanbing, 1896–1981), Zheng Zhenduo (1898–1958), and Zhou Zuoren publicized their views in *Xiaoshuo yuebao* (Short story magazine), the organ of the Literary Research Society. Throughout the 1920s, the journal set the tone for the literary revolution and the new literature, and it became the major vehicle for the publication of Chinese translations of Western literature.

In the early 1920s, contributors to *Short Story Magazine* expressed increasing interest in the literatures of the 'weak and small peoples'. Chinese writers were struck by the fact that the small European peoples had not only waged a desperate struggle for independence and identity, but that they had also produced great literary figures who articulated this struggle. Such, for example, had been the poet-patriot Adam Mickiewicz (1798–1855) in Poland[9] and A. Petoefi (1823–49) in Hungary.[10] Apparently, Chinese writers not only felt a kinship with such nations, identifying with their struggle, but they also found the literary figures very attractive personalities.[11] When, in October 1921, an entire issue of *Short Story Magazine* was devoted to the literatures of the small peoples, the 'Introduction' specifically stressed this feeling of kinship.[12]

However, it was one thing to assume ties of kinship with people deprived of political independence and national identity, and another to identify with a people without a land and without national cohesion, like the Jews. As will be shown below, Yiddish literature had a somewhat different and specific attraction, found only peripherally or not at all in the literatures of other weak and small peoples. This attraction, as Chinese writers saw it, was the portrayal of an oppressed society, oppressed by its own tradition and a hostile environment. Secondly, it was the portrayal of a society faced with the necessity for change and modernization in order to survive. And thirdly, Chinese writers saw the development of Yiddish literature as a result of a literary revolution similar to their own. And this literary revolution, according to Chinese writers, was related to a Jewish cultural renaissance.

INFORMATION ABOUT YIDDISH WRITERS AND THEIR WORKS

In order to understand more clearly how Chinese writers arrived at these conclusions, it may be useful to take a closer look at the extent to which Chinese writers were informed on the subject of Jewish literature. The following is a summary of the contents of descriptive and critical articles on Yiddish literature which appeared between 1923 and 1959.

The available materials show that pre-nineteenth century literature in the Hebrew language was of little concern.[13] The literary developments that interested Chinese writers began with the use of Yiddish. They ascribed to Mendel Levin (1741–1819, also called Lefin, Satanower, or Mendel Mikolayover) and Israel Axenfeld (1787–1866) the beginnings of the revolution of the written language (*wenzi keming*). Mendel Levin was of special importance because, by translating the Psalms into Yiddish in 1817, he created a new written language (*xin wenzi*). Both men discarded Hebrew, the dead language, wrote Mao Dun, or the 'old literary language' (*wenyan*) and substituted for it the living spoken language. By using this new medium, Jewish writers once more made available the Jewish national heritage.[14]

The social content works of Mendele Mocher Sforim (Shalom Jacob Abramovich, 1836–1917) are superb examples of the literature in the new language, and with the works of the prose writers I.L. Peretz (1852–1915) and Sholem Aleichem (Sholem Rabinovich, 1859–1916) Yiddish literature reached its height. Peretz, declared Mao Dun, is the best short story writer among the new Jewish writers and his use of the method of realism is unequalled. Neither he nor Sholem Aleichem, who is the Jewish Mark Twain, indulges in obtuse or idealized descriptions. Indeed, Sholem Aleichem's influence extends beyond Jewish literature, having influenced world thought and world arts.[15] Adding a small embellishment, Li Nianpei remarked in 1957 that both Peretz and Sholem Aleichem first wrote in Hebrew, but later switched to Yiddish, abandoning the 'learned' language of the Jews.[16] Sholem Aleichem, moreover, comes from among the people; he writes of the small places and the small people, of oppression, and the oppressed.[17]

David Pinski (1872–1962) is another writer who is primarily concerned with the oppressed. His works, wrote the Japanese author Chiba Kameo, reflect an exceptional bias and sympathy for the impoverished classes. His superlatively realistic descriptions portray all aspects of life of the labouring and destitute; their wickedness and their temptations. But Pinski does not presume to judge. He weeps over man's weakness and his inability to relieve the distress of the soul. Chiba Kameo saw in Yiddish writing a strong humanistic (*rendao zhuyi*) trend, as well as oneness of humankind. No matter whether one speaks of men and women in Poland, or men and women in East Asia, all act basically alike.[18] Other Jewish prose writers, whose works were known although not translated, were Leo Kobrin (1873–1946), and David Frischman (1886–1922).[19] Regarding Kobrin, Mao Dun approved of the fact that Kobrin's socialist leanings did not lead him to condemn Jewish culture, and that he developed naturalistic and realistic descriptive techniques to a high point.[20]

When discussing Yiddish poets and poetry Chinese writers, although acquainted with some Yiddish poetry, confined themselves simply to mentioning the existence of Yiddish poets and added little or no critical analysis. Thus, there are discussions of Morris Jacob Rosenfeld's (1862–1923) *Songs of the Ghetto*, and the work of Joel Linetzki (1839–1916), Jacob Dienesohn (1856–1919), and of Simeon Frug (1860–1916). The latter's poetry was enthusiastically praised. Although for the most part unacknowledged among modern Jewish writers, Frug is perhaps the greatest Jewish poet of the past 80 years, wrote Mao Dun. He spent his whole life among peasants, loved nature, and is a naturalist poet with a modern egalitarian outlook. Frug's poetry, therefore, consists of a deep appreciation of nature, and of profound sympathy for his fellow man.[21]

Closeness to the people, or a feeling for the masses and their language, was also stressed as a significant attribute of Moishe Nadir (Isaac Reiss, 1885–1943). Nadir, stated one Chinese writer, is unlike others in his use of language. He avoids elaborations, uses direct speech, and prefers common expressions.[22] The group of young Jewish poets (*die yunge*), the so-called *Insikhists* (Introspectives), was not neglected and the influence of French symbolism on writers such as A. Leyeless (Aaron Glantz, 1899– ?) was mentioned.[23]

Dramatists and dramatic literature were more closely scrutinized. In addition to noting the general historical development of Yiddish drama,[24] Pinski and Sholem Asch (1880–1957) were especially noted as dramatists. Pinski, wrote Mao Dun, points out the illness of modern man. His ideas are particularly useful when expressing his doubts regarding civilization and man's capacities, and when he reflects on human existence. What is more, Pinski has been influenced by socialist thought, which can be seen in his utopian (*datong shijie*) leanings. Asch, in contrast, is completely Jewish. His thinking is Jewish and some vestiges of the old Jewish literature – its obtuseness and symbolism – continue in Asch's writings. Both Asch and Pinski represent the two poles of world Jewry today.[25]

Aside from these discussions about Yiddish literature, it seems fairly obvious that the social and political realities of Jewish existence were not completely unfamiliar to Chinese intellectuals and writers. Hence these writers could supply a certain, if limited, context for their discussions on Yiddish literature. Periodic notices of persecutions of Jews had been appearing in Chinese missionary publications towards the end of the nineteenth and in the early years of the twentieth century,²⁶ while Zionism and its role were discussed in the 1920s and 1930s.²⁷ Improvement in American Jewish life was also reported, and one optimistic writer observed in 1921 that former contempt for Jews is disappearing; there is a great change in attitudes at present. He unhesitatingly suggested that this may be due to the export of Jewish literature to the literary world at large.²⁸ In a more cautious vein, Mao Dun felt that Jews are the only people in the world today without a country of their own, whose religion being different from that of other people, often subjects them to cruel treatment. Still, no matter where they are, they keep to their faith, their customs, and their Eastern thought.²⁹

Interest in the Bible, specifically the Old Testament (OT), among these intellectuals and writers provided some background in early Jewish history. Aside from the Bible's literary qualities, which were much appreciated by men like Zhou Zuoren and Mao Dun, stories about heroic figures of the past also aroused interest. So inspired by these was the latter, for example, that he re-worked the biblical Samson materials into a poignant tale of resistance and revenge.³⁰

Finally, Chinese writers were not only concerned with bringing the works of Yiddish writers to their readers. They also frequently supplied information about the authors of the short stories and plays they had translated. Mao Dun was especially conscientious about injecting this human element into his translation work. Aside from brief biographies, included in *Short Story Magazine* and other journals, he also wrote longer ones on Pinski, Peretz, and Sholem Aleichem in anthologies such as *Xueren* (Snowmen) and *Xin Youtai xiaoshuo ji* (Collection of Yiddish fiction). In the latter he also discussed Z. Wendroff and Sholem Asch.³¹

Several highly interesting points related to the questions of language and literary creativity, and to the significance of new literary methods are stated in these discussions. Before proceeding, however, it should be pointed out that Chinese writers held an entirely mistaken notion of the place of Yiddish in Jewish literature. Although the use of Yiddish certainly opened a new chapter in Jewish letters, Hebrew by no means fell into disuse, nor indeed can Hebrew be described in terms of classical Chinese. In fact, together with Yiddish, Hebrew was itself assuming a new literary significance during this period. The impression which was created in the early 1920s in Chinese writings, namely that Yiddish had displaced Hebrew, was never corrected, despite Mao Dun's essay on Hebrew poetry published in 1924, which clearly speaks of a Hebrew literary restoration (*fuhuo*).³² Thus the impression that Yiddish was the Jewish *baihua* has continued to persist. The mistaken idea that the literary revolution of Yiddish led to the disuse of Hebrew offered, if nothing else, the comforting certainty that literary revolutions can succeed. But, more significantly, it confirmed the relationship between language and literary creativity.

In addition, Yiddish literature was seen as socially relevant literature because the miserable lives of the common people were depicted by means of naturalistic and realistic methods. These methods made it possible for readers to understand this literature, and to identify with its contents. Hence Chinese writers were also comforted by the fact that their own efforts were not taking place in isolation, but in conjunction with efforts elsewhere. Implied here is a kind of universalism, a universalism of the human condition, as it were, which writers everywhere describe, and which writers everywhere can understand.

But what is naturalism and what is realism? And why was Yiddish literature so consistently described in terms of method? Obviously, it was not without reason that Peretz and Pinski were said to use the method of realism, that Kobrin was considered a naturalist and realist, and that Frug was described as a naturalist poet. The labels naturalism and realism are often used interchangeably (or together), especially by Mao Dun.³³ Their use in relationship to Yiddish writers reflects both the intense discussions on literary criticism at that time, and the attempt to understand Yiddish literature from the point of view of modern literary criticism. Literary naturalism was considered an ephemeral but necessary development. The creation of new literature necessitates that writers pass through the 'naturalist baptism', as Mao Dun put it. But a precise definition is lacking. Apparently, naturalism in 1921 and 1922 China was considered as being simply truthful description based on thorough and minute observation. The discussions of Chinese writers show that realism was not much different from naturalism. It, too, was thought to be a method of truthful description based on observation. But in addition there was the demand to find the typical; and most frequently, realism in literature was didactic.³⁴ When Chinese writers referred to Yiddish authors as naturalists or realists, they apparently wanted to indicate their modernity. By means of criteria such as naturalism or realism, they expressed their conviction that Yiddish writers were indeed within the mainstream of modern European literature.

Accordingly, Chinese writers saw a definite relationship between literary creativity and the use of new literary methods. Changes in language make possible increased literary creativity. Both language and literature can reflect the condition and concerns of a period of change. The resort to new literary methods is due to the use of the new language. And, therefore, the new literature rests, on the one hand, on new uses of language and, on the other, on the adoption of new methods of expression. Chinese writers pointed to the universality of literature when there was a confluence of these phenomena.

The question of universality is particularly significant. Chinese writers implied that relevance is equivalent to universality. New methods are relevant. Literary creation which utilizes new methods to create relevant literature is tantamount to the creation of universal literature. The universality of this literature consists in the fact that, although a particular condition is depicted, it is universally accessible. Yiddish literature confirmed for those who became acquainted with it, the belief in a universality joined with cultural identity and a commonality of human values.

Within the context of pre-1949 Chinese intellectual history these assumptions are both valid and acceptable. But how are we to understand the fact that writers after the establishment of the People's Republic have continued to translate and comment on Yiddish literature, at least until shortly before the onset of China's catastrophic Cultural Revolution (1966–76)? What does it mean that Sholem Aleichem is lauded as a 'people's' writer in 1959? The answer to these questions has once more much to do with the notion of universality. Relevant literature was still seen as universal literature in the People's Republic. But relevant literature was more narrowly defined then as 'people's' literature. The writer who wrote 'people's' literature created universal literature. Joseph Levenson's distinction here of the 'people' in terms of an international class (*renmin*) and the 'people' as national entities (*minzu*) is particularly significant.[35] For Sholem Aleichem, who comes from the people (*renmin*) and writes of the people, need not be relegated to ideological impurity. With a slight twist in the definition of universality, Sholem Aleichem was able to maintain his honoured position.

CATEGORIES OF STORIES AND DRAMA TRANSLATED

The translations from Yiddish literature in the 1920s and 1930s include both short stories and drama, but no full-length works. These were apparently translated only at a later time. The stories and dramatic pieces which I was able to identify can be grouped into the following categories of themes:[36]

Author	Title	Year	Translator	Language

A. Social Criticism and Social Injustice

Author	Title	Year	Translator	Language
Pinski	Forgotten Souls	1920	Zhou Zuoren	English
Peretz	The Fast*†	1921	Mao Dun	?
Wendroff	Zerach and Bulani†	1921	Shen Chemin	?
Pinski	In the Storm	1924	Chen Gu	English
Pinski	Tale of a Hungry Man	1925	Chen Gu	English
Pinski	Down with the Burden	1926	Wang Luyan	?
Sholem Aleichem	Gymnazya	1926	Wang Luyan	?
Sholem Aleichem	Treasure	1926	Wang Luyan	?
Sholem Aleichem	A Pity for the Living	1929	Nanming	English
Libin	Picnic	1934	Zhao Zhongqian	English
Asch	God of Vengeance	1936	Tang Xuzhi	English
Peretz	The Devout Cat	1957	Xi Zi	Esperanto
Peretz	A Weaver's Love	1957	Li Nianpei	English
Peretz	The Messenger	1957	Xi Zi	?
Sholem Aleichem	Eternal Life	1957	Tang Zhen	English
Sholem Aleichem	Three Little Heads	1957	Tang Zhen	English

B. Philosophy of Life

Author	Title	Year	Translator	Language
Asch	Winter†	1921	Mao Dun	English
Pinski	Rabbi Akiba's Temptation*	1922	Xi Zhen [Mao Dun]	English
Pinski	The Cripples	1922	Hu Yuzhi	?
Peretz	What is the Soul?	1924	Wang Luyan	?
Peretz	Seven Years of Plenty	1926	Wang Luyan	?
Peretz	Pidjon Shwuim	1926	Wang Luyan	?
Peretz	Ormuzd and Ahriman	1926	Wang Luyan	Esperanto
?	The Jew's Dance	1931	?	?
Nomberg	In the Mountains	1935	Yin Yan	?
Peretz	Bontshe the Silent	1941	Ji Jianbo	?

Author	Title	Year	Translator	Language
C. Entertainment				
Sholem Aleichem	The Person from Buenos Aires*†	1921	Mao Dun	?
Sholem Aleichem	Rabchik	1924	Wang Luyan	Esperanto
Sholem Aleichem	Miracle of Hoshana Raba	1925	Wang Luyan	Esperanto
Sholem Aleichem	Bad Luck	1926	Wang Luyan	?
Sholem Aleichem	The Passover Guest	1934	Huang Yi	English
Sholem Aleichem	Song of Songs	1959	Chen Zhenguang	?
Sholem Aleichem	Joseph	1959	Huang Zuohan	?
Sholem Aleichem	Menachem Mendel, Agent	1959	Zhou Zuolun	
Sholem Aleichem	If I Were Rothschild	1959	Chen Zhenguang	?
Sholem Aleichem	Methusela	1959	? Wenwei	?
Sholem Aleichem	Poor and Happy	1959	Chen Zhenguang	?
Sholem Aleichem	Bad Luck	1959	Zhang Luobei	?
D. War				
Pinski	The Beautiful Nun	1921	Dong Fen [Mao Dun]	English
Pinski	Poland 1919	1922	Xi Zhen [Mao Dun]	English
Pinski	Diplomacy	1924	Hu Yuzhi	English
E. Jewish Existence				
Sholem Aleichem	Passover in a Village	1929	Nanming	English

As can be seen from the above table, translations from Yiddish were published between 1920 and 1959. Most appeared in the 1920s; fewer in the 1930s; two (amazingly) in the Liberated Areas, under Communist control in the 1940s; five stories were published in 1957, and eight more in 1959. The categories dealing with social criticism and social injustice (A), with philosophy of life (B), and simply entertainment (C), although the latter often contained a moral message, are larger than war (D) or Jewish existence (E). The reason for category A's size is clear. The theme of social injustice found a strong echo in China in the 1920s as well as in the 1950s. On the other hand, stories dealing with philosophy of life seem to have little relationship to the concerns which made themes of social injustice so popular. One explanation that suggests itself is that interest in this theme was somehow related to the concern with evolving a *Weltanschauung*. The protracted controversy among intellectuals, known as 'The controversy on science and a view of life' (*kexue yu rensheng guan*), was one expression of this concern.[37] The translation of literature on this theme may very well have been the expression of a similar concern in another area.

It is important that only two stories can be described as dealing unequivocally with the problem of Jewish existence (E). The absence of such purely 'Jewish' stories or plays no doubt strengthens the conclusion that the Jewish content of the translated works was largely incidental to other messages conveyed.

Three other facts should be mentioned. Only a small number of Yiddish writers were translated into Chinese, nine or ten in all.[38] The stories and plays translated deal, furthermore, with a restricted number of themes, indicating a high degree of selectivity, and a relatively large number of translators and writers had an interest in Yiddish literature.

The last point requires further explanation. There were 20-odd translators. However, since many writers translated pseudonymously, the exact number cannot be established with certainty. Most important among them was Wang Heng (Wang Luyan, 1901–40), who usually signed his stories Luyan. He published two anthologies of translations from Yiddish,[39] of which some also appeared in various journals. Wang, a writer in his own right, translated principally from Esperanto. Zhou Zuoren was an essayist and a well-known literary figure. Like his brother, Lu Xun (Zhou Shuren), he was interested in Eastern European literature. He translated only one, or possibly three stories.[40] Mao Dun, who was especially interested in the literature of the 'weak and small peoples', translated altogether six stories, three of these under the pen-names Xi Zhen and Dong Fen.[41] Hu Yuzhi (1900–?), who translated one drama, was a literary critic and translator. The remaining translators cannot be identified with certainty.

Chinese translators, as pointed out above, did not translate at random. They seem rather to have carefully selected whatever they wanted from a variety of available works, omitting such themes as did not serve their purpose. Thus there are no plays or stories that deal specifically with romantic love (Sholem Aleichem's 'Song of Songs' comes closest perhaps), industrialization, and problems of the working class (except for one 1957 translation – a story of social injustice – which has a working-class setting). Furthermore, works whose content was totally unfamiliar, and works which did not even have a 'familiar ring'[42] were not translated. Although it was not possible to trace all the translations to their sources (especially the 1959 collection of eight stories), it might nonetheless be useful to list the few works which are known to have been used. The number of stories or plays which they contain, and those actually translated, will show more clearly that only certain examples were chosen for translation.

Author	Title	Place Publisher	Year	Details
Berman, Hannah, tr.	*Jewish Children From the Yiddish of Sholem Aleichem*	New York, A.A. Knopf	1922	19 stories altogether; 3 stories translated.
Frank, Helena, tr.	*Yiddish Tales*	Philadelphia, Jewish Publication Society of America	1912	48 stories altogether; 2 stories translated.
Frank, Helena, tr.	*Stories and Pictures* by Isaac Loeb Peretz	Philadelphia, Jewish Publication Society of America	1906	35 stories altogether; 3 stories translated.
Goldberg, Isaac, tr.	*Six Plays of the Yiddish Theater*	Boston, J.W. Luce & Co.	1916	2 plays translated.
Goldberg, Isaac, tr.	*Ten Plays* by David Pinski	New York, B.W. Huebsch & Co.	1920	4 plays translated.
Goldberg, Isaac, tr.	*Temptations. A Book of Short Stories* by David Pinski	London, G. Allen & Unwin	1919	8 stories altogether; 3 stories translated.
	'Jewish Life' Anthology, 1946–1956, A Selection of Short Stories, Poems and Other Essays, Drawn from the Magazine	New York, Jewish Life	1956	43 stories, essays and poems; 1 story translated.
Salem-Alehem, Mucnik, Is., tr.	Perec, *Hebraj Rakontoj*	Leipzig, F. Hirth	1923	(Esperanto). 11 stories altogether; 4 stories translated.

Turning now to the stories themselves, I want to briefly discuss their contents in order to show the variety of treatment of the different themes. As it is impossible to describe all the translations, some representative examples only will be chosen.

The theme of social criticism and injustice is discussed in the translations in many different ways, either as corruption, religious and secular bigotry, exploitation, or social oppression. Sholem Aleichem's 'Eternal Life'[43] is an attack on the social system as a whole, the corruption and indifference of both the Jewish and Russian establishments. A young man journeys to another town. At an isolated inn, overcome by compassion and lured by the promise of eternal life, he is persuaded by the innkeeper to take the body of his dead wife for burial to the next town. However, when the young man suggests that the town's burial society bury the dead woman, they suspect that the dead woman is in fact his own wife, his mother-in-law, or worse. No one believes the truth. At last he is forced to fabricate a tale for the Russian authorities. The young man is swindled out of his money for burial expenses and jailed. In the end, his mother-in-law is summoned and the affair is straightened out. Eternal life may be his in the next world, but in this world there is only misfortune.

Criticism of the hypocrisy of religious piety forms a basic substratum of a number of translated works by Peretz and Asch. Peretz's 'The Devout Cat' and Asch's 'God of Vengeance'[44] are superb examples of attacks on a superstitious and religiously bankrupt society. In the first story – a biting fantasy – a religious cat kills three singing birds in the name of piety. Filled by holy zeal, the first bird was killed in order to save it from committing further sins. The second bird was killed for the same reason, but now gently and kindly. The third bird, however, died because of the cat's pious breath, which was to instil in the bird remorse and repentance. In the stifling atmosphere of religious piety, the bird suffocated. For obvious reasons Peretz's indictment of religious hypocrisy was a welcome message to convey to Chinese readers in 1957. Asch denounced religion and religious Jews more forthrightly, showing mercilessly the clash of religious and human values. In 'God of Vengeance', the Jewish keeper of a house of prostitution has an only daughter whom he protects and educates in order to erase the sinfulness of his occupation. He commissions the writing of a Torah (Pentateuch) which to him signifies a holy talisman that will protect his home from misfortune. To the leaders of the Jewish community, however, this commission means money in the form of various contributions. The drama ends on a distressing note when, despite the Torah's presence in the household, his daughter turns to the path of prostitution. Although a simple and ignorant Jew, the father is overwhelmed by the tragedy of his family's existence. On the other hand, the community leaders' single thought is to preserve the outward form of Judaism and not let it be known that the daughter has strayed. Asch masterfully shows that this sort of Judaism is only an empty shell. Its outward forms do not coincide with human values.

Peretz's 'A Weaver's Love'[45] has a strong proletarian flavour and depicts the problems of the working class. Written in the form of a series of letters, Peretz tells of the abysmal conditions of workers who, underpaid and overworked, try to organize in order to improve their lot. But the weavers are no match for the powerful manufacturers who simply fire the workers when they become troublesome. In an ever-growing market of the unemployed, ten other workers are waiting to find one place. And even if a weaver gives no thought to collective welfare, slaves at his trade and does not lose his job, he will still not earn enough money to marry and support a family.

Without doubt, one of the most forceful and moving stories in this category is Pinski's 'Tale of a Hungry Man'.[46] Itsye, the subject of the story, is a total outcast. Hungry, filthy, hopelessly impoverished, he goes to his inevitable doom. However, despite misery and degradation, Itsye is neither compliant nor meek. Angry and quarrelsome, he strikes out at society. At last he quarrels with a policeman and lands in jail. Although he has reached the end of the road, Itsye does not give in to the oppressive society which has brought him to this state. Defiantly and mockingly, he will not let them kill him; instead he hangs himself.

Preoccupation with social injustice apparently led Chinese writers to search for stories that would describe social oppression in its many different forms. Their concern, therefore, is always with the little man who suffers when a religious law loses its human value, when factory owners exploit labour, when a heavy-handed bureaucracy plays with the human being as with a pawn, or when ruthless landowners exhaust a peasant's last ounce of strength. The different situations depicted in this group of translations were all well known to Chinese writers. They ring as true in the Chinese as in the original. And they certainly reflect the concerns of the various periods when they appeared, including the more political and ideologically Marxist purposes which obviously prompted the 1957 translations.

Nonetheless, a strongly pessimistic story, like 'A Weaver's Love', raises the problem of how this story accorded with the literature of socialist realism which writers were required to use in Mao's China.

Although it deals with the exploitation of the proletariat, it did not, as was expected of socialist realism, end on an up-beat note. Woven into the proletarian theme is the author's question whether this new world which is in the making is better. In a poignant passage, the weaver explains that in the factory new cloth as well as new customs and standards are being woven. More than that – shrouds for the old world in which it will be buried. But will this new world be a better place? No, says Peretz. In place of the old, 'will arise another world, rotten through and through'. Socialist realism demanded a different answer. What was required, if not in actuality, at least potentially, was the suggestion of a new world with new men. The weaver may be a 'new man' in one respect, since against many odds he does attempt to organize the workers. But he does not succeed. And in the last letter he announces his return home.

The stories in the next category are very diverse, all raising the question of human existence or the meaning of life. In 'Ormuzd and Ahriman',[47] Peretz deals with the dangers of excesses, be it nationalism which turns into jingoism, or simple living transformed into some sort of ideal. Sholem Aleichem in 'A Pity for the Living',[48] expresses concern for all life, be it a cock to be butchered, a bird killed by two boys, or a dog inadvertently scalded by the maid. This is a beautifully sensitive story which, told through the eyes of a child, points to the insensitivity of adults. 'Winter'[49] raises two crucial problems, one concerning self-sacrifice for family, the other perpetuation of customs. A matchmaker has persuaded a mother to marry off her younger daughter while the older one remains unmarried. The mother's feelings are in turmoil, since this is contrary to traditional custom. The older sister, in touching self-denial, bows to necessity and helps prepare the younger sister for the suitor.

Compared to the category of social injustice, these stories, concerned with some aspect of the philosophy of life, were all published between 1921 and 1935. The group of stories often verge on the sentimental; they are gentle and leisurely. In trying to understand the appeal of these contemplative stories, it may be that part of their attraction consisted in the utilization of interesting and imginative literary devices: two of the stories are told through children's eyes, and four have a fairy tale-like setting. Their appeal might have been, therefore, the result of combining a serious theme with a playful literary device. It is perhaps also significant that seven out of ten pieces were translated in the 1920s when many intellectuals were precisely preoccupied with the question of the meaning of life.

Stories in the third category are entertaining, light in spirit, and are told by the master storyteller Sholem Aleichem. Whether about a runaway locomotive, as in ' Miracle of Hoshana Raba', about a dog, as in 'Rabchik', or about a misfired business venture, as in 'Bad Luck', they fully display the art of the master in all its variety.[50] The eight stories from the 1959 collection *Poor and Happy*[51] fit best into this category, despite the great differences of treatment of such stories as the lyrical 'Song of Songs' or the tragic outcome in 'Methusela'.

The translations concerned with war are a series of plays by David Pinski. 'Poland 1919'[52] tells of suffering and death, when a group of people is trapped in no-man's land between two opposing armies. 'The Beautiful Nun'[53] portrays the ultimate dehumanization of men in war. But 'Diplomacy'[54] is somewhat different. In this drama Pinski shows how unscrupulous politicians manipulate events. He describes growing war hysteria as the masses are incited to hate and kill. With superb irony, Pinski mocks the symbols of God, fatherland, honour, or religion, in the name of which wars are fought and people die.

The last category deals with Jewish existence. Here, there is only one story, Sholem Aleichem's 'Passover in a Village',[55] which describes the friendship of two children, one a Jew, the other a gentile. The story is told against the implied background threat of blood libel.[56] Feitel and Fedoka have gone to the hills to share a piece of *matzah* (unleavened bread). Delighted with their treat, the friendship, and spring itself, they stay out longer than intended. Meanwhile, the villagers surround Feitel's house and the blood libel accusation is in the air. Luckily all ends well when the children at last return. This story, then, contains the sinister overtones of instant violence as well as the precariousness of Jewish existence, despite the subtle joys of a spring holiday and of friendship.

The fact that there seem to be no other translations which deal with the vicariousness of Jewish existence is not surprising. Stories of religious persecution would not have the same kind of meaning within the Chinese context as in Europe, except perhaps where they communicate the universality of suffering and oppression. However, the issues most likely to have made Jewish existence intolerable would have remained largely incomprehensible to a Chinese reader. Moreover, the problems such issues raised for translators might have been impossible to overcome. In the final analysis, the objectives of this translation literature were less to inform Chinese readers of Jewish life and its problems. Rather they were to show the communality and concerns of human values in China and elsewhere.

TECHNIQUES OF TRANSLATING

What kinds of problems did Chinese translators encounter in translating terms that were specific to Jewish culture? Evidently, most of the translators tried to choose equivalent terms. Much effort was spent on attempts to convey all such terms in a clear and precise way, or to append explanations, either in footnotes or in the text itself. A random sampling, based mostly on Chinese translations of English translations, will show the different techniques of handling problems.

The term, rabbi, was usually transliterated as *labi*. In 'Poland 1919', Mao Dun added the parenthetical explanation that a rabbi was a pastor superintending education (*zhangjiao chi mushi*), and in 'The Temptation of Rabbi Akiba'[57] that he was a Jewish pastor (*Youtai mushi*). Apparently, Mao Dun understood the educational function of the rabbi, despite choosing the term *mushi*, which is derived from Christian usage. Wang Luyan, in his appended glossary to 'What is the Soul?'[58] reveals a more sophisticated insight, by describing a rabbi as a Jewish doctor who explains the law (*Youtai jiangfa boshi*), thus avoiding the Christian implication. On the other hand, the 1957 translator of 'A Weaver's Love' discarded the transliteration, and translated rabbi as *Youtai fashi*, or Jewish priest.

In 'Rabbi Akiba', Mao Dun transliterated Torah as *tula*, explaining it as the Jewish teaching of righteousness (*Youtai jiaoyi*). Wang Luyan, in 'What is the Soul?' also transliterated Torah, but described it more specifically as the traditional five-part Mosaic code of Hebrew law. The 1957 translator was more precise. In 'A Weaver's Love', Torah is translated in the text itself as the Five Books of Moses (*Moxi wushu*), and a footnote explains that this is the holy scripture of the Jews. In 'Eternal Life', however, Torah is translated in the text as the teaching of righteousness (*jiaoyi*), and the footnote describes it as the Five Books of Moses.

Still another way of handling transliterations meaningfully was to add the English term, parenthetically, after the first mention. Hu Yuzhi did this in 'Diplomacy' when dealing with names which were difficult to explain. On the other hand, when neither an explanation nor the original term were added, meanings could be easily obscured. This, for example, was the case when Zhou Zuoren transliterated *Yahrzeit* as *ye'erzaide* in 'Passover in a Village' without explaining that it was the annual commemorative prayer for a departed family member. The Chinese reader had no way of knowing what father and son were doing in the synagogue.

Another method in addition to transliteration was either to coin a new phrase or choose a familiar term. Pogrom, for example, was translated literally as searching out and destroying (*soujiao*) as well as killing (*tusha*) in 'A Pity for the Living'. A similarly literal translation was used for People of the Book, rendered as *shuzhong de ren*, and chosen people is clearly recognizable in *tianxuan zhi min*. Synagogue was translated either as church (*libai tang*) as in 'Winter' and in 'A Weaver's Love', or as Jewish church (*Youtai jiaohui*), as in "Picnic".[59] Church (*jiaotang*) was similarly used by the 1959 translator of 'Song of Songs'.[60] Rather an exception was meeting hall (*huitang*) for synagogue in 'The Passover Guest'.[61]

Huang Yi, the translator of the latter story, has, however, several careless mistranslations. Reb, a form of address commonly used in Eastern Europe, was transliterated by him as *leibai*, as if it were part of a name. He translated *kiddush* as prayer before eating (*shiqian daogao*), and the Haggadah as a scriptural Bible comment (*shengjing xunhua*). The translator of 'Eternal Life' also misunderstood the nature of the Haggadah. Transliterating the word as *hajiada* in the text, he explained in a footnote that this is the legendary part of the law. Both translators were apparently ignorant of the fact that the Haggadah is the book of the Passover story traditionally read before the festival meal.

The word God occurs frequently in Yiddish stories. Generally, the word was translated with *Shangdi* (High Lord),[62] as in the 1957 translations, even when other words, such as Almighty, Lord of the Universe, or His Name, had been used in the versions from which the translations were prepared. But there are exceptions. In 'In the Storm'[63] the term is omitted from the translation whenever possible. It occurs only once and then as *Laotianye*. Zhou Zuoren, it seems, was also reluctant to translate the term. In 'Forgotten Souls',[64] there is only one mention of God in the translation and the Chinese chosen for it is *foshen*, which has Buddhist connotations.

A few other terms are of interest. In 'Three Little Heads',[65] the spring festival of Shavuot (Weeks) is transliterated as *jianwuxun* and explained in a footnote as one of the important Jewish holidays, which comes 50 days after Passover. In the same story, Sukkot (Tabernacles) is, however, not transliterated but translated as festival of greens (*maojie*) and explained as the Jewish autumn festival. In 'Eternal Life', *tefillin* (phylacteries) is translated as scripture box (*jingxia*) and their use is described in a footnote. But in the same story *kaddish*, the prayer for the dead, is simply translated as hymns (*zanmeishi*), without further explanation. The ingenuity of the last story's translator is altogether admirable. For the pious utterance, 'Blessed be He who gives, and He who takes', he found perhaps a more prosaic, but nonetheless suitable Chinese proverb, 'Life and death are caused by fate' (*sisheng you minger*). He was undaunted even by *shlemazel* (this is quite untranslatable, perhaps 'dolt' is best), which became unlucky one (*daomei jiahuo*).

On the whole, the translations are faithful and read smoothly. If, occasionally, a translator found it useful to omit a phrase, the general meaning was not impaired. The immediacy of Sholem Aleichem's Yiddish, for example, is frequently recaptured with a Chinese idiomatic expression. The 1957 translators tended to take their task more seriously by annotating their translations carefully, and even supplying references for biblical citations, something none of the earlier translators had done, apart from Wang Luyan. Still, a random comparison of Chinese translations with their Yiddish originals shows that in some instances the Chinese departs more drastically than it should from the original. This is especially true in translations that were prepared from Esperanto. Therefore, in so far as all translations were secondary, they could only be as good as the translations from which they were translated.

The major objective of this study has been to show the uses to which literature can be put, or the ends it can serve. But literature also has the power to move people to new thoughts and new perceptions. Literature, in the sense that it allows a person of a given time and place to participate in the lives of others of another time and place, is a door to the world and a bridge. It is pleasing to think that for moments in time Yiddish literature bridged the gulf that separates culture from culture and man from man. It is pleasing to know that at such moments Chinese readers could participate in the joys and sorrows of a people so different – and yet in some ways so like themselves.

POSTSCRIPT

We saw earlier that Chinese writers and translators in the 1920s and 1930s held erroneous views about the nature of Hebrew literature and were, in fact, not much interested in the innovations then taking place in Hebrew letters. Certainly, a major reason for the Chinese neglect was the non-availability of Hebrew literary works in English translation. But our story would not be complete if I were not to mention, however briefly, recent Hebrew fiction in Chinese translation: when it began and the course it has taken so far.

Until recently, translating from world literature in the People's Republic of China was not divorced from political considerations. The politics of culture had much to do with what was and was not translated and when it was translated. China's chilly relations with Soviet Russia and the Iron Curtain countries after 1960 also affected translating activities, and interest in Yiddish writers was greatly diminished. Thus, even before the start of the Cultural Revolution in 1966, when translating nearly ceased altogether, the tendency was to translate Third World fiction, preferably by Marxist writers, and not the fiction of bourgeois Eastern European authors.[66]

The cultural wasteland that China had become between 1966 and 1976 was but gradually transformed and, together with the recall and rehabilitation of purged writers, new translation journals as well as discontinued older ones also slowly appeared. Some of Sholem Aleichem's works were reprinted, others, like *Guguo* (The old country), were newly translated and published in 1981. But nineteenth-century literature was apparently not what translators wanted to translate or readers to read in the new cultural climate. Current American literature was of far greater interest, and was at long last accessible. Putting their thin diet of Mark Twain, John Steinbeck, and Ring Lardner behind them, translators turned to the up-to-date fare of the twentieth century, which included Jewish American fiction. Labelled invariably 'American' (which avoided possible embarrassing implications as long as China and Israel had no diplomatic relations), the works of Isaac Bashevis Singer – 1978 Literature Nobel prize winner – Philip Roth, Saul Bellow, and Bernard Malamud were the first Jewish writers to be translated. As soon as the *Waiguo wenxue* (Foreign literature) journal resumed publication in 1980, short stories by Singer were featured in its fourth and fifth issues. *The Manor* was published in 1981 and *Enemies, A Love Story* in 1982. Malamud's *The Assistant* appeared in 1980, and *The Fixer* in 1984.

Politics also determined the translating of Hebrew fiction by Israeli authors. Following the 1991 establishment of diplomatic relations between China and Israel, translations of works by Israeli authors finally began to be published. Although an (no doubt, officially sponsored) interest in Israel, Zionism, Jewish antiquity, and the Central European refugee community in Shanghai was already in evidence three years earlier,[67] it did not include the translating of fiction. A pioneering effort was Xu Xin's translation in 1990 of S.Y. Agnon's novella, *In the Heart of the Sea*.[68] He has since published an anthology of Israeli short stories, introducing the works of 21 major writers.[69] In

1994, the journal *World Literature* devoted an entire issue to Israeli literature, featuring A.B. Yehoshua, Amos Oz, Yehuda Amichai, and others.

Unlike 60-odd years ago, however, when translators also attempted to bring their readers literary criticism of 'new Jewish literature', the current translating effort has little of interpretive value to offer. This may change as more Hebrew fiction is made available to Chinese critics and readers. Yet, like their predecessors in the 1920s and 1930s, Chinese translators still continue to be dependent on secondary languages for their sources.

NOTES

1. Wolfgang Bauer, *Western Literature and Translation Work in Communist China*. Frankfurt/Main-Berlin, 1964, p. 1.
2. It is entirely possible that a number of translations had escaped my attention at the time of writing. Chinese bibliographies are notoriously incomplete, and some major journals in which translations appeared, especially in the 1920s, were unavailable. Two collections probably contain additional short stories. They are: Dai Cong, trans., *Meinahan Mante'er* (Menahem Mendel). Jiangxi chubanshe 1980, and Yang Zhen, trans., *Guguo* (The Old Country). Shanghai: Shanghai yiwen chubanshe, 1981.
3. Shen Yenbing [Mao Dun], *Yinxiang ganxiang huiyi* (Impressions, reflections, and reminiscences), Shanghai, 1948. 2nd ed., p. 52.
4. Several Esperanto collections of Polish literature were widely used by Chinese translators. These are described in my 'Poland and the Polish Author in Modern Chinese Literature and Translation', *Monumenta Serica*, Vol. 31, (1975), pp. 407–45. Esperantists were not lacking in China since the early years of the twentieth century, and the language continued to enjoy some popularity in the 1950s. See Honfan, 'Boom of Esperanto', *People's China*, 16 April 1957.
5. Yao Yi'en, Senior Research Fellow at the Shanghai Research Institute of Culture and History, has written a brief and incomplete description of Sholem Aleichem's works in Chinese. In the 1980s (that is, after the disaster of China's Cultural Revolution), several novels were translated. *Menachem Mendel* appeared in 1980 with 70,000 copies; *Tevye* was printed in 1983 in an edition of 42,000 copies; *The Adventures of Mottel* was reprinted from an earlier edition with 36,500 copies. Typewritten ms., 5 pp.
6. *Hu Shi wencun* (Collected works of Hu Shi), Taipei, 1953, Vol. 1, pp. 64, 67–70, 73.
7. Zhou Zuoren, 'Ren de wenxue' (Human literature), in *Kong dagu* (Empty drums), Shanghai, 1928. This essay first appeared in *Xin qingnian* (New youth), Vol. 5, no. 6 (December 1918), pp. 575–84.
8. Zhou Zuoren, *Yuwai xiaoshuo ji* (Collection of foreign short stories), Shanghai, 1920. First published in Japan in 1909.
9. Witold Jabonski, 'Mickiewicz w Chinach' (Mickiewicz in China), *Przeglad Orientalisticzny*, no. 20 (1956), pp. 497–503. Lu Xun (pen-name of Zhou Shuren, 1881–1936), elder brother of Zhou Zuoren, first discovered Mickiewicz in Georg Brandes, *Poland, A Study of Polish People and Literature*, London, 1903.
10. A. Galla, 'Bai Meng and Petoefi' (aus der Geschichte der Aufnahme der ungarischen Literatur in China), *Acta Orientalia*, Vol. 15 (1962), pp. 119–124.
11. Lu Xun, 'Molo shi li shuo' (On the power of Mara poetry), in *Lu Xun sanshi nianji* (Lu Xun thirty-year collection), *Fen* (The grave), *1907–1925*, 1937, pp. 53–100. In this essay, first published in *Henan zazhi* (1907), Lu Xun compares the search for a new culture in China with the desire to arouse the people to new life in Europe.
12. *Short Story Magazine* (henceforth *XSYB*), Vol. 12, no. 10 (October 1921), p. 2. A recent work dealing with the content analysis of the journal for 1910–13 is Denise Gimpel, *Lost Voices of Modernity: A Chinese Popular Magazine in Context*. Honolulu: University of Hawaii Press, 2001.

13. Apparently no translations were prepared from Hebrew language literature at this time. There were, however, two articles which discussed Hebrew poetry. One is Ye Qifang, 'Gu Xibailai shi yun yenjiu' (A study in ancient Hebrew verse rhymes), *Chenbao fugan*, November 1923. The other is a translation by Mao Dun (published under the pen name Chi Cheng), 'Xiandai de Xibailai shi' (Modern Hebrew poetry), *XSYB*, Vol. 14, no. 5 (May 1924), pp. 1–7. The article was originally written by T. Shipley.
14. Shen Yanbing (Mao Dun), 'Xin Youtai wenxue gaiguan' (Views on new Jewish [Yiddish] literature), *XSYB*, Vol. 12, no. 10 (October 1921), p. 61.
15. Ibid., pp. 65–6.
16. *Yiwen* (Translations), September 1957, p. 105, and Tang Zhen in *Translations*, July 1957, p. 88.
17. Chen Zhenguang, 'Tan Xiaolomu Alaihanmu he da de zuopin' (On Sholem Aleichem and his works), *Zhongshan daxue xuebao* (Journal of the Sun Yatsen University), nos. 1–2 (1959), p. 93.
18. Chiba Kameo, Han Jing (Mao Dun), trans., 'Youtai wenxue yu Binsiji' (Jewish literature and Pinski), *XSYB*, Vol. 12, no. 7 (July 1921), pp. 3, 7–8.
19. Hai Jing, 'Youtai wenxue yu Gaobalin' (Jewish literature and Kobrin), *XSYB*, Vol. 16, no. 12 (December 1925), p. 1; Shen Yanbing (Mao Dun), 'Youtai wenxue jia shinshi' (A Jewish writer about to die), *XSYB*, Vol. 13, no. 11 (November 1922), p. 3.
20. Shen Yanbing (Mao Dun) and Zheng Zhenduo, 'Xiandai shijie wenxue che luezhuan' (Brief biographies of present-day world authors), *XSYB*, Vol. 15, no. 3 (March 1924), p. 2, and 'Views on Yiddish literature', p. 68.
21. Mao Dun, 'Views on Yiddish literature', pp. 64–5.
22. Zhao Jingshen, 'Xin Youtai zuojia Nadier' (The Yiddish writer Nadir), *XSYB*, Vol. 21, no. 11 (November 1930), p. 1675.
23. Mao Dun, 'Views on Yiddish literature', p. 67. After reading my earlier essay, 'Yiddish Literature and the Literary Revolution in Modern China', *Judaism*, Vol. 16, no. 1 (Winter 1967), pp. 42–59, Jacob Glatstein commented, 'While a nation of hundreds of millions of people took the leading Yiddish writers as models and incentive for their own literary revolution, we, the Yiddish writers in the West, believed ourselves to be the loneliest writers in the world'. 'Yiddish and the Chinese Literary Revolution', *Midstream*, (August–September 1988), pp. 49–50.
24. This is in a translation of Isaac Goldberg, 'The Yiddish Drama', in *The Spirit of Yiddish Literature*, Girard, Kansas, 1925, pp. 50–7. The translation is by Yang Zhenhua, 'Xin Youtai de xiju' (Yiddish drama), *Shijie zazhi* (The world), no. 5 (May 1913), pp. 928–33.
25. Mao Dun, 'Views on Yiddish literature', p. 67.
26. See, for example, *Wanguo gongbao* (The Globe Magazine), Vol. 10 (1878), pp. 305b–6a; 418a–19b; Vol. 14, no. 11 (167) (December 1902), pp. 18a–18b; Vol. 17, no. 4 (196), (1905), pp. 21–2.
27. For example, Ge Suicheng, 'Youtai rengou de fenbu he ji minzu yundong de gaiguang', (The scattering of the Jewish people and their national movement), *Dongfang zazhi* (Eastern miscellany, henceforth *DFZZ*), Vol. 26, no. 20 (October 1929), pp. 113–23; Yu Songhua, 'Youtai ren yu Youtai fuxing yundong', (The Jews and their revival movement), *DFZZ*, Vol. 24, no. 17 (September 1927), pp. 21–8.
28. 'Youtai xuanmin' zai Zhijiago shang yangu ju' (The 'Chosen Jewish people' is performed in an old drama in Chicago), *Wenyi yuekan* (Literature and art monthly), Vol. 4, no. 5 (November 1933), p. 173; 'Yanjiu Yutai xin wenxue de san zhong xin chu Yingyiban' (Three newly published translations of Yiddish literature in English), *XSYB*, Vol. 12, no. 1 (January 1921), p. 2.
29. Mao Dun, 'Views on Yiddish literature', p. 60.
30. See the essay by Marián Gálik, 'Mythopoeic Warrior and Femme Fatale, Mao Dun's Version of Samson and Delilah', in I. Eber, S.K. Wan, K. Walf, with R. Malek, eds., *Bible in Modern China: The Literary and Intellectual Impact*. Sankt Augustin: Monumenta Serica Institute, 1999, pp. 301–320.
31. Shen Yanbing [Mao Dun], *Xueren*, Shanghai, 1928; *Xin Youtai xiaoshuo ji*, Shanghai, 1924.
32. Mao Dun, 'Modern Hebrew poetry', p. 5.
33. Marián Gálik, *Mao Tun and Modern Chinese Literary Criticism*. Wiesbaden: Harrassowitz, 1969, p. 80.
34. See ibid, pp. 70–82, for a discussion of the complexities of these terms.

35. Joseph R. Levenson, *Revolution and Cosmopolitanism*, Berkeley-Los Angeles-London, University of California, 1972, pp. 6–7.
36. The table is by no means complete and, as the years go by, stories continue to surface in often obscure journals. Also missing are one story each by Tajc and Rabinovitch whose identity as authors I am unable to determine. Stories marked with * were also included in Mao Dun, *Snowmen*. Stories marked with† were included in *Collection of Yiddish Fiction*. The stories are arranged by year of appearance. Where a Hebrew translation existed, I have given the translated title. Otherwise I have translated the Yiddish title. In some cases I was unable to trace the Yiddish original, in which case I have translated the Chinese title. Sholem Aleichem's stories are not always easily categorized, and some often fit into more than one category. Where the source language is uncertain, Russian originals were most likely used.
37. For a collection of essays on this topic, see Zhang Junmai, *Kexue yu rensheng guan* (Science and the view of life), Shanghai, 1925. The controversy is reviewed by Gad Yishai, 'The Philosophy of the View of Life in Modern Chinese Thought', Ph.D. Dissertation, The Hebrew University of Jerusalem, 2000.
38. I am not certain whether the story 'The Jew's Dance', published in 1931, is a translation. It may be a story created on a Jewish theme by a Chinese author, although it has the ring of an anonymous Jewish folk-tale.
39. Luyan, trans., *Youtai xiaoshuo ji* (Collection of Jewish fiction), Shanghai, n.d., and *Binsiqi ji* (Pinski collection), Shanghai, n.d. According to Zhang Jinglu, *Zhongguo xiandai chuban shiliao* (Materials on contemporary Chinese publishing), Beijing, 1957, Vol. I, p. 271, both books were published before 1929. According to Yao Yi'en (above, note 5), the first collection appeared in 1926.
40. 'A Pity for the Living' and 'Passover in a Village' are signed Nanming, obviously a penname. According to Austin C.W. Shu, comp., *Modern Chinese Authors: a List of Pseudonyms*, Michigan State University, Asian Studies Center, Occasional Papers, 1969, p. 44, Nanming is Zhou Zuoren's pseudonym. However, on p. 76, Shu attributes the pseudonym to his brother, Lu Xun.
41. Márian Gálik, 'The Names and Pseudonyms Used by Mao Tun', *Archiv Orientalni*, Vol. 31, no. 1 (1963), pp. 89–90.
42. Zhou Zuoren refers to this aspect in particular in his preface to *Collection of Foreign Short Stories*, p. 5.
43. Tang Zhen, tr., 'Yongsheng', *Yiwen*, (July 1957), pp. 67–83.
44. Xi Zi, tr., 'Qiancheng de miao', *Yiwen*, (September 1957), pp. 83–4; Tang Xuzhi, tr., *Fuchou shen*, Shanghai, 1936.
45. Li Nianpei, tr., 'Yige zhigong de luanai', *Yiwen*, (September 1957), pp. 92–105.
46. Chen Gu, tr., 'Yige ouren de gushi', *XSYB*, Vol. 16, no. 2 (February 1925), pp. 1–14.
47. Luyan, tr., 'He' ermusi yu Ahsimen,' *Ku ang biao*, no. 3 (24 October 1926), pp. 78–80.
48. Nanming [Zhou Zuoren], tr., 'Cibei' (Compassion), *Yusi* (Thread of talk), Vol. 5, no. 12 (May 1929), pp. 647–56.
49. Mao Dun, tr., 'Dong', *XSYB*, Vol. 12, no. 9 (September 1921), pp. 24–33. Also in Shen Yenbing [Mao Dun] and Shen Zimin, trs., *Xin Youtai xiaoshuo ji* (Collection of Yiddish fiction), Shanghai, n.d.
50. [Wang] Luyan, tr., 'Hexianolapo de qiji', *DFZZ*, Vol. 22, no. 15 (August 1925), pp. 115–22. Also in *Collection of Jewish Fiction*; Luyan, tr., 'Labaiyige', *DFZZ*, Vol. 21, no. 9 (May 1924), pp. 107–15. Also in *Collection of Jewish Fiction*; Luyan, tr., 'Puxing', in *Collection of Jewish Fiction*.
51. Chen Zhenguang, ed.,*Yichang huanxi yichang kong*, Beijing, 1959.
52. Xi Zhen [Mao Dun], tr., 'Bolan yijiu yijiu nian', *XSYB*, Vol. 12, no. 8 (August 1921), pp. 1–10.
53. Dong Fen [Mao Dun], tr., 'Mei ni', *XSYB*, Vol. 12, no. 8 (August 1921), pp. 21–8.
54. Hu Yuzhi, tr., 'Waijiao', in *Xiandai dumuo qu* (Contemporary one-act plays), Shanghai, 1924.
55. Nanming [Zhou Zuoren], tr., 'Cunli de yuyue jie', *Yusi*, Vol. 5, no. 13 (June 1929), pp. 677–93.
56. Blood libel refers to the widely held belief among the Christian population that Jews killed Christian children in order to use their blood for baking matzah. Violent excesses were often carried out against the Jewish population at the time of Passover.
57. Xi Zhen, tr., 'Labi Aqiba de yuhuo', *XSYB*, Vol. 13, no. 1 (January 1922), pp. 26–32.
58. Luyan, tr., 'Linghua', *DFZZ*, Vol. 21, no. 11 (June 1924), pp. 117–24. Also in *Collection of Jewish Fiction*.
59. Zhao Zhongqian, tr., 'Yeye', *Wenxue* (Literature), Vol. 2, no. 5 (May 1934), pp. 931–5.

60. Chen Zhenguang, 'Yake', in Chen, *Poor and Happy*.
61. Huang Yi, tr., 'Yuyue jie de keren', *Wenxue*, Vol. 2, no. 5 (May 1934), pp. 936–40.
62. In Chinese, various terms for the monotheistic concept of God can be used, and the problem of term is most suitable has been discussed among theologians, missionaries, and Chinese Christians since the nineteenth century. A review of the issues raised is Eber, 'The Interminable Term Question', in I. Eber, S.K.Wan, K. Walf, with R.Malek, *Bible in Modern China*, pp. 135–61.
63. Chen Gu, tr., 'Baofeng yuli', *XSYB*, Vol. 15, no. 3 (March 1924), pp. 1–4.
64. Zhou Zuoren, tr., 'Beixing wangque de renmen' (Forgotten by luck), *Xin qingnian* (New youth), Vol. 8, no. 3 (November 1920), pp. 427–38.
65. Tang Zhen, tr., 'Sange xiao tou'er', *Yiwen*, (July 1957), pp. 83–8.
66. I. Eber, 'Western Literature in Chinese Translation, 1949–79', *Asian and African Studies* (Bratislava), Vol. 3, no. 1 (1994), pp. 34–54.
67. Eber, 'Perceptions, Interpretations, Translations: Jews and Their Literature in China', in M. Gálik, ed., *Chinese Literature and European Context*, Bratislava: Institute of Asian and African Studies, Slovak Academy of Sciences, 1994, pp. 143–8.
68. Xu Xin, tr., 'Dahai shenchu', *Dangdai waiguo wenxue* (Contemporary foreign literature), 2 (April 1990), pp. 4-49.
69. Xu Xin, tr., *Xiandai Xibailai xiaoshuo xuan*. (Collection of contemporary Hebrew fiction), Guilin, 1992.

8

Martin Buber and Daoism

At various times during his life Martin Buber (1878–1965) had a considerable interest in Daoist thought.[1] In 1910 and 1911 this led to the publication of two small volumes of translations, the first, selections from the *Zhuang Zi* and the second, the following year, consisted of a number of stories from Pu Songling's *Liao Zhai Zhi yi* (Liao Zhai Tales).[2] In later years he occasionally commented in lectures or essays on Daoist ideas, specifically those of the *Dao de jing* (*DDJ*), and in 1942 he translated into Hebrew a number of the *DDJ*'s chapters.[3] In 1944 he translated once more several lines from chapters 12, 20, 52, 76, and 81 of the *DDJ* and selections from Confucius's *Lunyu* (Analects), and from the philosophical works of Zhuangzi and Mozi.[4] Throughout these decades Buber's interest was, however, confined to certain selected concepts, chosen in accordance with his philosophical concerns. This essay will not explore whether Daoism had a lasting impact on Buber's philosophical work.[5] Rather the object here is to outline the background that led Buber at various times to occupy himself with Daoist concepts and then inquire more specifically how he understood these and which concepts he considered significant to his philosophical enterprise.

THE BACKGROUND OF BUBER'S CONCERN WITH MATTERS CHINESE

Buber's initial concern with matters Chinese occurred against the background of a wider German interest in China which began in 1897 with Germany's occupation of Jiaozhou Bay and the port of Qingdao. But German interest in Chinese culture went well beyond purely practical matters of the military or trade. German writers after the turn of the century enviously eyed the accomplishments of English sinology and the work of translators such as James Legge.[6] But even if German scholars considered themselves initially to lag behind the British, modern Chinese studies, including Sino-German scholarly contacts, developed rapidly.

In the first decade of the twentieth century, the Berlin University's

Seminar for Oriental Languages grew in importance and its offerings included, in addition to language instruction, practical knowledge on Asia. After 1912, generous budgets leading to the substantial growth of its Chinese library holdings together with the presence of the outstanding Dutch scholar J. J. M. de Groot (d. 1921) established, furthermore, Berlin's Sinological Seminar as a leading academic centre for Chinese studies.[7] At the same time numerous Chinese students began to study at Western universities. Some also came to German institutions and, as a result, Chinese intellectuals as well began to show an interest in German thought and literature.

Buber's encounter with China took place against this larger background and it coincided with his preoccupation with Hasidic materials and his interest in questions of myths and culture. He may also have come across materials on China when he was a reader for the publisher Rütten and Loening in 1905 and later. With Rütten and Loening he published his own works as well as a series called 'Society' (between 1906–12) which consisted of socio-psychological monographs.[8] At about this time Buber became acquainted with Wang Jingtao, who in 1907 was a lecturer, or Chinese language instructor, at the Seminar for Oriental Languages.

Wang remained in Germany until 1911, but little is known about him. He translated several Chinese short stories into German (no doubt, to earn extra cash) and he introduced Buber to Pu Songling's stories.[9] But Wang's scholarly interests seem to have been more political than literary as is apparent from the one or two publications he has to his credit. After his return to China he held some kind of official position in the newly established Republican government.[10] Buber and Wang collaborated on the translation of a number of stories from the *Liao Zhai Zhi yi* collection, Buber translating from the English version by Herbert A. Giles and Wang translating several from the Chinese original. Most of the *Zhuang Zi* portions were also prepared from Giles' English version.[11] In the preface Buber acknowledged the aid of Chinese colleagues without, however, mentioning Wang or anyone else by name.

Enthusiastic reviews in the German language press greeted the appearance of both volumes. Buber was praised for making these works available to German readers and for thus furnishing evidence of the universality of ideas. The poetic content of the *Liao Zhai Zhi yi* was highly praised by Hermann Hesse.[12] Considering the paucity of translated works from Chinese in the early decades of the twentieth century, the widespread response is not surprising. Except for the *DDJ*, German-speaking readers had few translations from Chinese available to them and even fewer critical works. Confucius' *Lunyu* (Analects) could be read only in a very dated edition, and Chinese poetry translations, aside from the *Shijing* (Book of Songs), were still in the future.[13] Buber's collection of Pu Songling's stories was apparently only the second selection of Chinese fiction in German[14] and thus deserved the well-earned praise it received.

Although Buber published no further long translations from Chinese, his interest in Daoist ideas did not cease in 1911. In 1924 he subjected the *DDJ* to a fairly systematic study when asked to give a series of privately arranged lectures to a lay group. These lectures, not recorded by Buber himself but probably by one of the participants, were neither revised nor published, and exist today only as a typewritten manuscript entitled, 'Talks with Martin Buber in Ascona, August 1924 about Lao Tzu's Tao Te Ching.'[15]

In 1924 Buber was living in Heppenheim, coming regularly to the University of Frankfurt where he lectured on the history of religions. Although the majority of the courses which he offered between 1924 and 1933 were clearly on Jewish topics, some course titles suggest that he also included other subjects and that he probably discussed Daoist concepts as well.[16] In 1924, Richard Wilhelm (1873–1930) joined the faculty, beginning a distinguished albeit short-lived career in Chinese studies. Apparently the Wilhelm and Buber families also met informally on occasion.[17] Hermann Hesse (1877–1977) whose friendship with Buber was of some years standing, also visited the university and was there, for example, at the end of 1926 to read from his works. Wilhelm's close friendship with Hesse dated from 1897.[18] In addition, a rare personal relationship existed between Wilhelm and Carl Gustav Jung (1875–1961), who was brought into this charmed circle for a time due to Wilhelm and Jung's mutual interest in Chinese thought, especially Daoism and the *Yijing* (Book of changes).

Wilhelm had gone to Qingdao in 1899 as a missionary for the General Evangelical Protestant Missionary Association,[19] two years after Germany occupied the Shandong peninsula. His missionary career was soon diverted, however, into other channels. He acquired remarkable expertise in Chinese and Chinese classical literature, and from 1910 he published a series of outstanding translations and beautifully crafted books about China. In 1926, after he joined the philosophical faculty of the University of Frankfurt, he also founded the China-Institut, which became a focal point for a variety of China oriented cultural activities. The institute attracted visiting sinological luminaries from other

European universities, as well as major Chinese literary and religious figures, among them the ever popular Hu Shi (1891-1962).[20]

But Wilhelm's hopes for the institute transcended the mere staging of cultural activities: the institute was to be a beacon for the culture of the future when, he believed, east and west would at last meet. Both parts of the world had elements to contribute to this future culture, which like yin and yang, Wilhelm argued, complemented each other. The institute's function, said Wilhelm at its opening in 1924, is to promote this aim.[21] To what extent Buber subscribed to similar views is uncertain. Nor do we know how active a participant he was in the institute's many events. Did Buber, Wilhelm, Hesse, and Jung engage in discussions and did they share thoughts on Chinese philosophy? Unfortunately, concrete evidence for Buber's involvement in the institute's activities and in an ongoing dialogue is meagre. It seems Wilhelm kept Buber informed on matters of interest to him,[22] and Buber (together with Jung) participated as discussants in the institute's 1928 autumn lectures delivered by Wilhelm.[23]

Apparently, however, Buber still had other contacts. Between 1927 and 1931 Buber corresponded with Willy Tonn (d. 1957) about the latter's Chinese interests and work. Tonn pursued Chinese studies in Berlin in the late 1920s and early 1930s, but seems not to have earned a doctorate.[24] He was at the time translating a brief, esoteric Daoist text and the 1512 stele inscription of the Kaifeng Jews.[25]

Tonn, who in the 1950s assisted Buber with the *Zhuang Zi* revisions, had fled to Shanghai in 1938, shortly after *Kristallnacht* ('Night of shattered glass' when the Nazis instituted a pogrom against the Jewish population), where he devoted himself to educating his fellow refugees about China. His many publications in the refugee press of the 1940s include translations from Chinese prose and poetry as well as critical articles on a variety of Chinese subjects.[26] During that decade he also established an Asia Seminar where he lectured to the German-speaking refugees on Chinese history and culture. After Tonn came to Tel Aviv in 1948 or 1949, contact between the two men was resumed. But Tonn in Tel Aviv, like Buber in Jerusalem, found little interest then in China, her history, and civilization.

Buber continued a slight but steady interest in the *DDJ* in the 1940s while teaching at the Hebrew University in Jerusalem. Among his notes from those years, there are several translated chapters from the *DDJ*, notations on Chinese classical grammar, and several translated passages from the *Lunyu*, suggesting that he included materials on Chinese thought in his lectures[27]. In 1942 he published the translation of eight *DDJ* chapters and in 1944 he published the Hebrew translation of several additional excerpts, mentioned earlier, from the Chinese classics.[28] Finally, in the 1950s, he revised the *Zhuang Zi*, enlisting Tonn's help on points of transliteration and translation.[29] Still, for both men this must have been lonely work. Jerusalem's Hebrew University then had neither a department of East Asian Studies nor did its library boast even the most basic works on China and Chinese philosophy.

These, briefly, are the years and circumstances of Buber's interest in Daoist ideas. Clearly the *DDJ* occupied him more than the *Zhuang Zi* and, except for work on the *Zhuang Zi* revisions, he returned time and again to concepts expressed in that brief, enigmatic work. The two questions this raises are, which Daoist concepts did he consider significant, and how did he understand and use them. In what follows some answers will be attempted.

Buber recorded his initial reflections on Daoist thought in a brief essay which he later appended as an 'Afterword' to the 1910 translations from the *Zhuang Zi*.[30] Whereas the *Zhuang Zi* text was twice revised for the 1918 and the 1951 editions, the essay has remained in its original form. In later years Buber distanced himself from this essay, describing it as belonging '...to a stage that I had to pass through before I could enter into an independent relationship with being. One may call it the 'mystical' phase....'[31]

The essay discussed ideas found in both the *Zhuang Zi* and the *DDJ*, but relatively more space is devoted to the latter, thus only loosely connecting the 'Afterword' with the translated text. In this essay Buber regarded the *DDJ* as the fountainhead of Daoism following which no further original contributions were made. Indeed, he assigned to Zhuangzi the subordinate position of 'apostle', stating that 'Chuang Tzu was a poet... who did not "continue to develop" the teachings of Laozi (Lao Tzu) from the words in which they have come down to us, but he shaped them into poetry.'[32] According to Buber, therefore, Zhuangzi was not an independent philosopher, and he ignored or glossed over Zhuangzi's innovative and original contribution to Chinese thought as well as some of the important differences between the *Zhuang Zi* and the *DDJ*.

DAO, WU-WEI, YI, ZHI

The Daoist concepts that Buber sought to explain in this essay are the meaning of Dao and those which he considered associated with Dao: non-acting, *wu-wei*, the One (unity or oneness), *yi*, and knowledge (understanding), *zhi*. In Buber's view an inherent interrelationship exists between the four concepts. He recognized philosophical Daoism's claim that at the basis of genuine existence is an unknowable of which nothing can be predicated. Dao cannot be named and it cannot be investigated for it has no attributes. The presence of Dao in the phenomenal world, stated Buber, is as Oneness where it is neither recognized nor known; Dao is lived, Dao is acting; Dao manifests itself in the genuine existence of the sage. Knowledge consists in being, not in the knowledge of external matters or objects. But knowledge is also acting. It is the deed. Yet genuine acting is non-acting because it originates in 'a gathered unity', or Oneness. To experience Dao directly means being one with Dao and means also being unified within oneself:

> ...the unified [geeint] person is described as one who lives and experiences Dao directly. He perceives unity in the world. But that does not mean that the world is a closed thing outside himself, whose unity he penetrates. Rather, the unity of the world is only a reflection of his unity...

Dao in relationship to the human being is what interested Buber, not Dao as an abstract idea, and it is, no doubt, for this reason that he chose to discuss the interrelationship of these particular concepts.[33] For this reason he also apparently ignored the cosmogonic implications of the One, expressed, for example, in chapter 42 of the *DDJ*.

Knowledge and non-acting were assigned an important place in this essay because it is, after all, the living person who knows and acts. Acquiring and storing knowledge is, however, not the goal,[34] nor is it the 'emptying' stressed by the *DDJ*. Buber argued that knowledge acquired in non-acting – knowledge that is not in knowing but in being – leads to a different way of existing, the way of the 'perfected person'. Buber did not differentiate between the *DDJ* and the *Zhuang Zi's* ideas here. Both texts give different names and attributes to this kind of person. In the former, he is the sage, *shengren*, who still exercises his calling toward practical ends, although he is like the new-born child, unsullied by the dross and artificiality of civilization. In the latter, he is the genuine person, *zhenren*, to whom practical ends are a matter of indifference. He is someone who has shed all learned and acquired preconceptions, who regards his individual existence as having merged with everything there is, who is one with cosmic being.

That Buber did not sort out these differences was not due to his having misunderstood them. Rather, he was after something else, more concrete, on the one hand, but also more related to his own interpretations of mysticism, on the other. As pointed out by Benjamin Schwartz, common to all mysticism is the ineffable ground of reality which is accessible only to a higher kind of knowledge (*gnosis*), beyond commonly used language. Also commonly held is the assumption that only some human beings (perfected in their essence) can attain to oneness with the ultimate source.[35] Buber's concept of the *tzaddik*, developed in his works on Hasidism at that time, was thus not only the result of his reflections concerning mysticism, it was also indebted to how he interpreted the significance of the sage and the genuine person in Daoist thought. According to Hans Kohn, Europe's philosophical discourse was undergoing changes in the first decade of the twentieth century, precisely when Martin Buber had his fateful encounter with both Hasidism and Daoism. By means of Hasidism, writes Kohn, Buber found and developed his own teaching, while Daoism (Kohn does not specify which ideas of Daoism) left a lasting imprint on his theories.[36] Buber's study of Hasidism between 1904 and 1909, which resulted in two books, *Tales of Rabbi Nahman* (1906) and *The Legend of the Baal Shem* (1907) dealt with the men, the *tzaddikim*, the 'righteous' or 'proven', who exemplify the teaching in their own lives. Although called by different names, *tzaddik*, sage, or genuine person, the attributes by which they are known are essentially the same as far as Buber was concerned. Therefore, his description of the *tzaddik* does not differ greatly from that of the Chinese sage: for the *tzaddik* too, thinking (knowing) is being; outer and inner are one; he who has attained wisdom will not lose himself; evil is a lack rather than something in itself and is also worthy of love.[37]

Buber's interest in Pu Songling's stories at that time was similarly related to his preoccupation with Hasidism. In these stories Buber saw the meeting of the divine and the human in mundane existence, which he defined as the unity or Oneness (*Einheit*) obvious in Daoism as well as in Hasidism.[38] Although in his studies on Hasidism Buber dwelled on the religious motif and the nearness of God, he seems to have perceived something not altogether dissimilar in the easy co-existence of spirits and humans in the *Liao Zhai Zhi yi*. Today, critics are agreed that Pu Songling's deceptively simple stories possess a rare sophistication and, upon closer analysis, exhibit startling complexities. It is indeed remarkable that Buber, in his encounter with Chinese literature over a century ago and without the benefit of a critical apparatus to point the way, realized that these stories contain a philosophical substratum as well as important aspects of the Chinese world view.

Buber was apparently little concerned with the divergence of his and the Chinese idea of unity. In Chinese thought the idea of unity is that of an all-embracing order which encompasses this and the world beyond. The two spheres, the socio-political order and the order of spirits and gods, are not hermetically sealed off from one another. They interact in often strange and unexpected, although never chaotic, ways. Within this all-encompassing order, ancestor worship has a central function (as Buber was to point out in 1928) by assigning to ritual the continued maintenance of the human and cosmic order. But Buber's idea of unity developed from an entirely different basis and was motivated by his assumption of a dualism in Jewish existence. The Jew, he believed, forever vacillated between historical and existential contradictions. Therefore, the creative impulse of Judaism lies in the reconciliation of these contradictions and in the attempt to overcome the dualism and to achieve unity.[39] To Buber and a Chinese reader, Pu Songling's stories certainly suggested multiple and different messages on the nature of unity and order, yet both would have agreed on the importance of unity and order.

The ideas which Buber had first developed in connection with the *Zhuang Zi* and the *Liao Zhai Zhi yi* translations continued to recur in different contexts. He again raised the question of overcoming dualism in existence in a lecture some years later.[40] Entitled 'The Spirit of the Orient and Judaism', the lecture's message was that Judaism had closer affinities with Oriental (in his view, Indian, Near Eastern, and Chinese) thought and attitudes than with Occidental ones.[41] Especially remarkable for its day was Buber's assertion that men like the prophets, Laozi, and the Upanishadic thinkers (Buber neglected to include the Buddha) shared a common mission to restore, to regenerate, and to announce a renewal.

Humanity in the West, said Buber, is caught in a dichotomous state. Westerners objectify the world and thus draw a distinction between themselves and the objects of the external world. This dichotomization (*Entzweiung*) of the self with the self of the world can be remedied only by reunifying the human personality and by entering into what he calls genuine existence. None of the great religious teachings had their source in the Occident, said Buber. These originated in the Orient and were received and adapted in the Occident. But as receptor, the Occident has been unable to construct a view of a seamless world together with a supra-rational divine teaching. Lacking in the West, therefore, is 'the exclusiveness of the message about genuine existence'. In distinction to the West, the Orient considers genuine existence a fundamental metaphysical principle, conditioned by no other consideration.

By genuine existence Buber had in mind a non-bifurcated life, lived both in thought and in deed, in knowing and in acting. Once a person recognizes how the original Oneness was severed and distorted, it is incumbent upon him – and this is his mission – to return to the original unity. Oriental thought significantly insists that such knowledge, such a realization, is a matter of life lived. The Daoist, said Buber, recognizes the duality of existence, but he knows that this duality is rooted in the One, the Dao. Dao assumes reality in the life of the sage by his acting and non-acting which, in turn, permits the emergence of the real significance of the world.

In this lecture Buber did not intend to establish general east–west considerations; he was concerned once more with the condition of the Jew and how to remedy dichotomous Jewish existence. The Jew, Buber declared, was and has remained an Oriental in spite of using Western languages, in spite of martyrdom and oppression. Buber defined the Jew's affinity with the Orient as follows:[42]

> Action is more vital to him than experience, or, more accurately, his experience is his acting. He experiences the world's objects less in their separate, multiple, singular existence than in their relationships, their mutuality.... The Greek considers the concept as the conclusion, the Jew considers it the beginning. Stronger than others, the Jew possesses the Oriental's elementary drive to unity (*Einheitstrieb*)....

However, where the Chinese accepts the duality of existence by realizing its unity in Dao, the Jew consciously decides and engages in restoring unity and completeness. The Jewish belief that the deed's absolute value consists in the decision to act is, therefore, a distinguishing characteristic, according to Buber.

In this lecture Buber skilfully wove together strands of the *DDJ*'s ideas with his own reflections on how to give meaning and substance to Judaism. The ideas he had deemed important in his earlier encounter with Daoism, Oneness, and duality, acting and non-acting, were translated in this lecture into coherent views on the meaning of Jewish existence. A mystical Oneness continued to figure in his thought, but this unity was already more action-oriented and was combined with the conscious act of deciding. And decisions were based on knowing.

In 1928, Buber returned briefly to thoughts on Dao and non-acting.

By then the 'mystic phase', as he had called it, was behind him, and his preoccupation with the Bible, his concerns with God, the life of dialogue, and the world, led him to locate spiritual endeavours in the 'living reality of every-day'.[43] Dao, he wrote, 'affirms the whole reality of the world'. In the world's separateness is embodied the working of Dao.[44] His discussion on non-acting also differed significantly from the 1910 essay and the lecture some five years later. Commenting on Richard Wilhelm's suggestion in his China-Institute lecture that Confucianism had something to offer a Europe in crisis, Buber expressed considerable pessimism. Defining Chinese culture as Confucian culture, Buber doubted that the West would find in it much that was congenial. For one, said Buber, Chinese people have a fundamentally different relationship to their dead, neither abhorring nor dreading them. A Chinese continues to maintain contact with his ancestors through ancestor worship and, therefore, Chinese culture conceives of generational continuity in entirely different terms than the West. Secondly, the Chinese have a profound trust in a person's fundamental 'being'. This trust does not exist in the West.

For this reason Daoism, stated Buber, and specifically Daoist non-acting as non-interference, striving for success by non-aggressive means, has something to offer to the West. In a radical departure from his views of 16 years earlier, Buber's comments did not relate non-acting to either cognition or a special person; anyone can practice it, he implied, as long as the person realizes that short-term success in the historic here and now is illusory. Non-acting is genuine acting, it has imperceptible effects, is long lasting, becoming 'a part of the life of mankind'.[45] Non-acting in this sense is concrete and takes place in the world's arena. *Wei wuwei*, act by non-acting, which Buber apparently had in mind here, occurs twice in the *DDJ*, in chapters three and sixty-three. The latter especially recommends to the sage (*shengren*) a way of life in this world where goals must be achieved, but where the means for achieving them are supremely important and must be carefully chosen. Buber's intellectual concerns had changed and, perhaps as a result, he had reached a more profound understanding of some of the *DDJ*'s ideas.

BUBER'S ASCONA LECTURES ON THE *DAO DE JING*

Buber had already expressed similar views at greater length in 1924, when invited to give a series of talks on the *DDJ* in Ascona, Switzerland.[46] The talks consisted in a chapter-by-chapter exposition of the text, and he discussed altogether 33 of the book's 81 chapters. Broader religious and philosophical issues were also raised in conjunction with the text either by Buber or the participants. Buber's lectures are not preserved among his manuscripts (was there, in fact, a written text?), but their contents was recorded by one (or several) participant(s). It can be assumed that the typewritten manuscript conveys in abbreviated form the gist of his talks.[47]

Buber obviously was no longer interested in the *Zhuang Zi*. In part this may have been due by then to the *DDJ*'s popularity as one of the most widely translated works of Chinese philosophy. In German there were as many as half a dozen different translations by the second decade of the twentieth century, several of them in multiple editions. The *DDJ* appealed to scholars and laymen alike, whereas the *Zhuang Zi's* audience was much smaller. Unlike the *Zhuang Zi*, the *DDJ* was not burdened with unpronounceable Chinese names; in fact, not a single proper name occurs in its 81 chapters. To its often cryptic sayings many ascribed a universal sense, pregnant with meaning for all times and in all places. Hermann Hesse compared the book to the Bible, and C.G. Jung considered it a part of the world's literary heritage, a pillar in the '...bridge of the spirit which spans the morass of world history'.[48] Perhaps, to the serious-minded, Zhuangzi's humour seemed too frivolous; his strain of anarchism too daring in post-First World War Europe; his method of argumentation too pugnacious.

Buber's intellectual enterprise at the time was, no doubt, also important in how he interpreted the *DDJ*. His major work, *I and Thou*, with its emphasis on the meeting of the human and divine, was published in 1923 and the issues he had raised in the book continued to occupy him in subsequent years.[49] At that time, furthermore, Buber engaged in wider educational activities outside of the university, among these his lectures at the Frankfurt Freies Jüdisches Lehrhaus, founded by Franz Rosenzweig in 1920.[50] Thus the 1924 'Ascona Talks' reflected a significantly different approach to the *DDJ*'s ideas. Although caution is indicated, since the talks were probably not recorded by Buber himself, the lectures reveal a new understanding of the *DDJ*'s concepts. They also established a wider philosophical context for the text by comparing its ideas with Jewish, Christian, and Confucian thought. In these talks, Buber created for the *DDJ* a place in his philosophical and religious discourse, and his explanations of the various chapters, now far less mystically interpreted, can be considered an attempt at a commentary on the *DDJ*. Non-acting was no longer accorded a central position, and he was also not overly concerned with the role of the sage. On the other hand, issues related to society and the political state received more attention, and the Dao in the world (not as mystic Oneness) was exhaustively discussed.

For their *DDJ* text Buber and his small band of devotees used the translation by Viktor Friedrich von Strauss und Torney, *Lao-Tse's Tao Te King* (Leipzig, 1870).[51] That Buber preferred this translation to more recent ones (such as Wilhelm's translation, of 1910) can be attributed, no doubt, to finding Strauss's assumptions and most of his interpretations congenial to his own way of thinking. This will be obvious when we take a closer look at Strauss's introduction to the text. Strauss's introduction assumes that there was a time before time, an 'Urzeit', when all religions were one, out of which both Judaism and Daoism developed. In more historic times, but long before Laozi, there must have been a Daoist community (perhaps with participants in mystery rites) from which Laozi took the name Dao and the religious basis of his teaching. Thus the *DDJ* is a religious text. Laozi's basic ideas are theosophical, stated Strauss, and he belongs, therefore, to that group of thinkers whom we call mystics. For these theosophical mystics being (*Seyn*) was their vital source, from which they intuitively drew.[52] Men turn to theosophy not by choice or influence, but by religiously motivated individual inclinations. Theosophical thought does not discover divine truth, but needs the religious heritage to test divine truth. Now, China does not have a body of religious literature referring to the existence and activities of the Highest Being in His relationship to man and history. Nonetheless, Strauss believed, there are religious traditions, mentioned both in the *Shujing* (Book of history) and *Shijing* (Book of Songs) as well as in the *DDJ*. In the latter they appear as rhymed hymns and songs.[53] That so little of Daoist thought (or religious thought) remains in the *Shujing*, according to Strauss, is because Confucius edited the text. Strauss was not overly fond of the sage, describing him as an immodest, ambitious man with high-flown plans, who opposed everything sacred and otherworldly.[54]

After he established that the *DDJ* is a basically religious text which reflects ancient religious traditions, Strauss easily identified Dao with God. Laozi, stated Strauss, had a profound awareness of God (*Gottesbewusstsein*) comparable to the concept of revelation. Such an awareness existed only in China and among Israel at the time. Therefore, when referring to the Dao, Strauss consistently used the personal pronoun 'he', labelling Dao a being (*Wesen*). Other names in Chinese which can be translated as God, such as *di*, *Shangdi*, or *Tiandi*, did not worry Strauss and he argued that in antiquity, these together with Dao may have been simply different names for the One God. He concluded not surprisingly that the ancient Chinese were monotheists and not polytheists. Their worship of nature deities was not polytheism, but resembled the Catholic worship of saints and angels.[55]

If Daoism is in large part a religious system, what distinguishes it then from Western religious systems, according to Strauss? Chinese religion of antiquity, he explained, was a-historical. It was neither mythology nor revelation. This religion was transmitted without manuscripts, without teachers, heroes, or writings about the faith. Thus no possibility existed for constant renewals of religious consciousness as in the West. With Laozi religious consciousness reached its apogee, but thereafter declined and deteriorated.[56]

DAO AND GOD

The 'Ascona Talks' notes indicate that Buber accepted most of Strauss's notions, building his interpretations in many parts on these. Buber, too, viewed the *DDJ* as a religious text which, he apparently believed, must be interpreted in a religious spirit.[57] Although he never explicitly described Dao as synonymous with God, he attributed to Dao the quality of the divine (*das Goettliche*). Strauss's technical explanations – points of Chinese grammar, interpretations of Chinese characters according to the Kang Xi dictionary, or Strauss's frequent resort to Heshang Gong's[58] commentary to the *DDJ* – were, however, not repeated in the notes. Possibly, some of Buber's Chinese acquaintances advised him on interpretations of Chinese terms, since there are occasional explanations of terminology other than those given by Strauss.[59]

Buber's comments on chapters 1 and 19 ascribe an ontology to the *DDJ*. By stipulating both an eternal Dao and one that is manifested in the world, Laozi established an ontological fact (p. 1). Dao is, therefore, not a law of nature, not abstraction, but being or substance. Two indivisible parts of the divine exist; one transcendent and unknowable, the other immanent and personal. Because the human being interacts with the immanent part, it can be termed the personal aspect of the divine (p. 14). Buber argued that the ineffable, the transcendent Dao, is not the beginning of existence, stipulating a difference between origin (*Ursprung*) and cause (*Ursache*). The origin which makes possible creation is the transcendent Dao and the cause that sets the process in motion is the immanent Dao (p. 2). Buber's comments to chapter 7 stress two additional points. One, Laozi was not interested in other-worldliness, his ideas deal with reality itself, and two, Dao manifests itself in multiplicity. But the idea of Dao must not be taken to mean that the One is real and the many an illusion (p. 7). Possibly Buber aimed for consistency here for he did not comment on chapters 42 and 51, for example, where Dao is said to begin the process of creation.

In spite of stipulating transcendence and immanence, Buber did not want to suggest a dichotomizing of Dao. Hence his comments to chapters 10 and 22 reiterated once more the Dao's Oneness (pp. 7, 17). But Oneness that had been so important to him more than a decade earlier now had somewhat different implications. It was no longer only a mystic and difficult to explain concept. Oneness now signified to Buber completeness and he related it to the person who participates in the divine, who stands in proximity to God (p. 24), who exists in a higher sphere of undividedness (p. 7), or who has sought the divine and been united with it (p. 21). When such a person acts, the difference between acting in the name of man or in the name of God disappears. It is one and the same (p. 19).[60] Man is a religious being, he asserted in his comments to chapters 55 and 62. He possesses creative powers, spontaneously, without willing. He creates. Such a person is holy when he enters the sphere of completeness. Holiness is, therefore, not primarily an attribute of God alone (p. 24), but of the human being as well. For this reason, Buber apparently did not hesitate using Strauss's the 'holy one' for sage (*shengren*), to describe such a persons's wholeness and godliness.

But Buber obviously chose his vocabulary carefully. This can be seen in his references to God and the divine (*das Goettliche*). It can, furthermore, be seen in the uncertainty of precisely how to deal with Dao and the Tetragrammaton, a subject extensively discussed by Strauss in his comments to chapter 14.[61] According to Strauss, the issue of the Tetragrammaton was first raised in 1823 when the three characters, *yi*, *xi*, and *wei* in the following sentences of chapter 14 (my translation) were said to represent the Tetragrammaton:

> Looking at it, it is not seen; we call it by the name 'ordinary' (*yi*).
> Listening to it, it is not heard; we call it by the name 'sparse' (*xi*).
> Seizing it, it cannot be grasped; we call it by the name 'minute' (*wei*).

Strauss, basing himself on the Heshang Gong commentary, believed that *yi* means without color, *xi* means without sound, and *wei*, without form. In short, the three characters refer to the same ineffable

Being the Tetragrammaton refers to and who is no other than Dao.[62] *Yi, xi*, and *wei* were probably pronounced differently, argued Strauss, closer to the original Hebrew pronunciation. Laozi, no doubt, obtained his knowledge of YAHVE from Jews in China who claimed to have arrived as early as the Han dynasty (206 BCE–AD 220). (Strauss must have read the eighteenth-century Jesuit accounts about the Kaifeng Jews who, citing the 1512 stele inscription, assign the arrival of the Jews in the city to the Han dynasty.) He supported his argument further by stating that the Jews' reluctance to pronounce the Name occurs also in the *DDJ* and later generations therefore did not know that the three characters referred to God's name.

Buber did not dismiss out of hand the YAHVE–Dao identification. The three characters, according to Buber, express something esoteric, the manner of expression is different, the gist being that the attributes spoken of cannot be investigated except when someone experiences their effects and becomes conscious of them (p. 9). Although we cannot know for certain exactly what Buber said, the notes nonetheless indicate that even if he distanced himself from Strauss's argument he did not reject it.

Perhaps because he now interpreted the *DDJ* as a this-worldly rather than as a mystic text, he devoted considerable attention to those portions (altogether six chapters, chs. 29, 30, 57, 61, 78, and 53) which deal with society and the state. The state to him meant community (*Gemeinschaft*). But not community as the sum total of individuals, rather community as a spiritual joining and acting together. Such a community resists domination by any one person, for it is constituted by the relationship its members have to the person in the centre. Buber argued that Laozi considered the political state both a state of human beings and a state of God. 'To Laozi the state consists of the community and legitimate authority', by which he meant the lawful, religious rule of the person who is central to the community (pp. 25–7). Buber, however, did not develop the ideas of the political state and authority, or to what extent the sage (holy one) was the ruler. He pointed to messianism in chapter 49, stating that the *DDJ*'s messianism concerns the sage, but that all messianisms are, in the final analysis, the yearning for a king. His definition of the sage or the holy one in chapter 78 is more in keeping with his own views than the *DDJ*'s, when he assigns to him the position of intermediary between God and the world who assumes responsibilities as well as guilt, who steps into the gap that has been created between God and the world (p. 31).

In these chapters dealing with the state and society Buber did not resort to Strauss's commentary and he engaged in free and far-reaching discussions, including remarks on contemporary events. Strauss's comments to these chapters had referred to textual matters, and only once, in discussing chapter 61, did he also include some less than complimentary remarks on the Christianity of his day.[63] But Buber's purpose, 50-odd years later, was not to provide only a learned commentary to the *DDJ*. In addition, he seemed interested in these lectures to test the *DDJ*'s relevance and applicability to the world of his day. Thus, his discussion of this same chapter (61) also raised among other topics the problem of Russia, where he saw six years after the Revolution a process of dehumanization. A person, said Buber, is not seen in his relationship to others, or the life of the community, but as a cog in a vast, brutal, and senseless machine (p. 29). His remarks to chapter 30 take in the First World War, which he saw as having begun due to 'the fiction of a mutual threat'. Some people pretended to be pacifists, some made as if to devise plans, yet most people only did what seemed expedient at the moment (p. 28).

DAO DE JING AND *ZHUANG ZI*

Buber returned to several *DDJ* chapters in 1942 when he published a Hebrew translation of chapters 17, 29, 30, 31, 57, 58, 66, and 67.[64] It is not clear toward what end he prepared the translations. He may have translated them for use in his courses and then decided to publish them. Or he may have prepared the translations in accordance with his increasingly active interest in the future state and society in what was then Palestine. It may not be a coincidence that in the same year, 1942, and four years after his arrival in Jerusalem, he joined the Ihud (Union) Association, which consisted of a group of like-minded people. Except for a brief note on the *DDJ* and Laozi, no other comments are attached to the translated text, and the chapters he translated have a decidedly political content.[65]

He obviously did use Strauss's German text as the source for the Hebrew rendition, and a remarkable feature of Buber's Hebrew version is its closeness to the Chinese text.[66] Both the sentence structure and the wording – even, for example, the repetitions that frequently occur in the *DDJ* – are singularly felicitous to the original. Yet it is highly unlikely that he was able to translate from the Chinese on his own. Nor is it likely that anyone versed in classical Chinese resided then in Jerusalem. The content of the chapters, however, suggests that they were not chosen at random.

All eight have two themes in common, government and the condemnation of the use of force and instruments of war. Chapters 29, 30, and 31 reject armed force leading to devastation and sorrow. All-under-Heaven (*Tianxia*) can be obtained by abstaining from the use of force, according to chapter 57. In chapter 66 the sage (*shengren*) is above the people, but they do not feel his weight; he is in front, but does not harm the people, and chapter 67 warns not to be first in All-under-Heaven. In a similar vein, chapter 17 states that in antiquity the people merely knew of the ruler's existence, thus implying that they did not feel his rule. Faith between the ruler and the people, moreover, is a prerequisite in governing. Buber's choice of these and not other chapters may once again reflect his specific concerns at the time. His courses at the Hebrew University in the 1940s dealt with society and aspects of sociology, such as the sociology of culture or religion, and included materials on social dynamics and the relations between the group and institutions.[67] In Palestine, moreover, a new society and a new state were in the making. The foundation on which both would develop were an important consideration to Buber, and he saw himself as a participant in its construction. In articles which he published after 1938 he addressed the issue of fashioning a new society in various ways: questioning values of Zionism, suggesting the need for a transvaluation of values, proposing to construct the new society from the bottom up and not from the top down.

The concern with society and the state was not new. He had voiced views on this subject earlier, and he had included comments in the 'Ascona Talks'. In Jerusalem, however, he expressed it in a new context and there was an urgency to his proposals.[68] The translated chapters refer not only to the horrors of war, they also suggest the means by which such horrors can be avoided. These *DDJ* chapters about society and the state were in many ways then, as others had been earlier, in accord with ideas which preoccupied Buber.

Martin Buber's interest in the *DDJ* and his early encounter with the *Zhuang Zi* and the *Liao Zhai Zhi yi* did not apparently lead to a sustained exploration of Daoist ideas in these or other Daoist works. It must be assumed, therefore, that Buber selected and appropriated from the *DDJ* those ideas that at various times corresponded to his own, re-translating them into his philosophical discourse. In this essay the process of re-translation together with the impact on his philosophical works was not discussed, leaving this topic to future investigations.

The emphasis in this essay has been on Buber's contact with Daoist philosophical concepts, which ideas were important to him and how he understood these. Thus the *DDJ*'s struggle with the namelessness of

Dao, the Dao's reversal, or the notions of spontaneity and being and non-being (*you* and *wu*) did not interest Buber as much as did the ideas of Oneness, duality, and non-acting. Although Zhuangzi's mysticism, his rejection of dichotomies, and insistence on Oneness with Dao attracted Buber probably initially, the *DDJ*'s combination of a practical way of acting (or non-acting) combined with a near-mystic understanding of existence was ultimately more in accord with his own ideas. In the *DDJ*, especially in the Strauss translation (I would rather call it a 'mistranslation'), Buber found affirmation for ideas that he had been in the process of formulating. These were ideas of personal Oneness or completeness, Dao as both transcendent and immanent, and the personal aspect of the divine.

The *Zhuang Zi*'s rejection of political involvement of any kind may have struck Buber as too passive an attitude toward the world's affairs. The *DDJ*'s combination of mystical questioning with practical advice on how individuals manage in society and society manages in the political state, no doubt, appealed more to Buber. Thus the 1924 lectures on the *DDJ* took up topics concerned with society, the ruler, and government, and his 1928 comments on Richard Wilhelm's lecture were made in reference to practical issues in post-First World War Germany. Although we cannot be certain exactly when he translated the *DDJ* chapters which he published in 1942, their contents similarly indicate that Buber then was drawn to the *DDJ*'s condemnation of aggression and rule by force. Buber's interest in the philosophical ideas of Daoism may not be an isolated phenomenon in pre- and post-First World War Germany. Thus this interest is not significant because it is unique. It is unique, however, because he may have been the first among Jewish philosophers who appropriated ideas from Daoism and integrated these into a specifically Jewish philosophical discourse.

NOTES

1. This essay is based in part on my introduction in Martin Buber, Alex Page, trans., *Chinese Tales, Zhuangzi: Sayings and Parables and Chinese Ghost and Love Stories*. New Jersey-London: Humanities Press International, Inc., 1991, pp. ix–xxiii. I wish to thank the Humanities Press for permission to use portions of the introduction.
2. Martin Buber, *Reden und Gleichnisse des Tschuang Tse*. Leipzig: Insel Verlag, 1910, and *Chinesische Geister- und Liebesgeschichten*. Frankfurt/Main: Rütten und Loening, 1911. Both volumes were republished many times, most recently in Zürich, Manasse Verlag, 1948 and 1951 respectively, the *Zhuang Zi* in a revised version.
3. Martin Buber, 'Laozi al hashilton (Laozi on government)', *Hapo'el Hatsa'ir*, 35, nos. 31–2 (May 1942), pp. 6–8.
4. Martin Buber, 'Lekah meSin (Lesson from China)', *Hagalgal*, Vol. 1, no. 14 (20 January 1944), pp. 14–15.

5. See Maurice Friedman, 'Martin Buber and Asia', *Philosophy East and West*, 26, no. 4 (1976), pp. 411–26, who writes that Buber's '...Dialogues with Taoism remained of central importance to him throughout his life'. See also Hans Kohn, *Martin Buber, sein Werk und seine Zeit, ein Beitrag zur Geistesgeschichte Mitteleuropas, 1880–1930*. Cologne: Joseph Melzer Verlag, 1961, pp. 59, 67–8, 82–3, 86, 280.
6. Thassilo von Scheffer-Berlin, 'Literarische Wanderung', *Koenigsberger Allgemeine Zeitung*, 13 January 1913. Jewish National and University Library (hereafter JNUL), Arc. Ms. Var. 350/13-46. I wish to thank the JNUL's Buber Archive for making this and other materials available to me. I am especially grateful to Mrs Margaret Cohen, archivist, for her patient guidance through the archival collection.
7. Erich Haenisch, 'Die Sinologie an der Berliner Friedrich-Wilhelms-Universität in den Jahren 1898–1945', *Studium Berolinense*, edited by Hans Leussink, et al., Berlin: Walter de Gruyter Co., 1960, pp. 554–66. I am grateful to Dr Hartmut Walravens for setting me straight on the different functions of the Seminar for Oriental Languages and the Sinological Seminar.
8. *Hundertfünfzig Jahre Rütten und Loening 1844–1969, ein Almanach*. Berlin: Rütten und Loening, 1969, p. 58.
9. According to Buber's foreword in *Chinese Tales*, p. 111, Wang introduced him to the *Liao Zhai* stories. Pu Songling (1640–1715), an impoverished and unsuccessful scholar, completed the manuscript of his stories around 1679, but it was not printed and published until nearly 100 years later. The collection of almost 500 stories was enormously popular not only in the eighteenth century but later as well. See Zhunshu Zhang and Xuelun Zhang, 'Pu Songling and His "Liao-chai Chih-i" – Literary Imagination and Intellectual Consciousness in Early Ch'ing China', *Renditions*, no. 13 (1980), pp. 60–81.
10. I am indebted to Dr. Hartmut Walravens for most of the information on Wang Jingtao. I also wish to thank Dr. Jonathan Herman for bringing to my attention a book by Wang, *Confucius and China, Confucius' Idea of the State and Its Relation to the Constitutional Government*. Shanghai: Commercial Press, 1912. The preface is signed 'Nanking Bureau of Foreign Affairs'. The book, obviously the English translation of a German essay, also mentioned by Dr Walravens, which appeared in *Mitteilungen des Seminars für Orientalische Sprachen. Abt. 1: Ostasiatische Studien*, 16 (1913), pp. 1–49. *Minsheng zhuyi renkou wendi* (The problem of people's livelihood and population). Shanghai: 1927, was probably also authored by Wang.
11. Herbert A. Giles, *Strange Stories from a Chinese Studio*. London: Thomas de la Rue, 1880, 2 Vols. A second revised edition appeared in 1909, and Herbert A. Giles, *Chuang Tzu, Mystic, Moralist and Social Reformer*. London: B. Quaritch, 1889.
12. Alfred Frhr. von Mensio in *Allgemeine Zeitung*, Munich, 2 November 1911. JNUL, Arc. Ms. Var. 350/48, 13; 'Literarische Wanderung'; Hermann Hesse, 'Chinesische Geistergeschichten', *Neue Züricher Zeitung*, 25 March 1912. JNUL, Arc. Ms. Var. 350-46. Other reviews appeared in numerous newspapers, such as the *Frankfurter Zeitung, Schlesische Zeitung*, and *Breslauer Zeitung*.
13. The *Lun Yu* (Analects) was translated by Wilhelm Schott, *Werke des tschinesischen Weisen Kung-Fu-dsu und seiner Schüler*. Halle, 1826, first part; Berlin, 1832, second part. Two early translations of the *Shi jing* were one by Friedrich Rueckert, *Shih-king, chinesisches Liederbuch, gesammelt von Konfuzius*. Altona: J.F. Hammerisch, 1833, the other by Viktor von Strauss und Torney, *Shih-king. Das kanonische Liederbuch der Chinesen*. Heidelberg: C. Winter, 1880. The latter was in dreadful rhyme.
14. Hartmut Walravens, 'Martin Buber und Willy Tonn und ihre Beiträge zur Kenntnis der chinesischen Literatur', *Monumenta Serica*, 42 (1994), pp. 465–81 mentions what is probably the earliest translation of a selection of Chinese fiction from the *Jinqu qiguan*: Eduard Grisebach, *Kin-ku Ki-kuan, Neue und alte Novellen der chinesischen 1001 Nacht*. Stuttgart, 1880.
15. JNUL, Arc. Ms. Var. 350/45-bet. I am grateful to Professor Paul Mendes-Flohr for pointing out that the manuscript is most likely a stenographic record of Buber's talks. Even so, it no doubt reflects his ideas quite accurately.
16. Rita van der Sandt, *Martin Buber's bildnerische Tätigkeit zwischen den beiden Weltkriegen*. Stuttgart: Ernst Klett Verlag, 1977, pp. 91–4 lists the courses from the summer semester 1924 to the summer semester 1933.
17. Schriftlicher Nachlass Richard Wilhelm in Bayrische Akademie der Wissenschaften, München, diaries of Salome Wilhelm. I thank Ursula Ballin for making these entries available to me.
18. Salome Wilhelm, *Richard Wilhelm, der geistige Mittler zwischen China und Europa*. Düsseldorf:

Eugen Diederichs, 1956, p. 346. After 1924, Buber, Hesse, and Wilhelm were apparently in close contact.
19. The German name is Allgemeine evangelisch-protestantische Missionsverein. For a brief history of this mission and Wilhelm's early years in Qingdao, see Lydia Gerber, *Von Voskamps 'heidnischen Treiben' und Wilhelms 'höheren China', die Berichterstattung deutscher protestantischer Missionäre aus dem deutschen Pachtgebiet Kiautschau 1898–1914*, Hamburg: Hamburger Sinologische Gesellschaft, 2002, pp. 74–88.
20. Ibid., pp. 352, 356. See also Hu Songping, *Hushizhi xiansheng nianpu zhangbian chugao* (Draft chronological biography of Mr. Hu Shi). Taibei: Lianjing chuban shi, 1984, Vol. 2, p. 658. Hu gave a lecture at the China-Institut in October 1926.
21. Salome Wilhelm, *Richard Wilhelm*, pp. 330–9.
22. See JNUL, Arc. Ms. Var. 350/902.
23. Salome Wilhelm, *Richard Wilhelm*, p.363. Wilhelm's three lectures were constructed around the *yin* concept in Chinese culture. His lecture is printed as 'Sitte in China', *Chinesisch-Deutscher Almanach für das Jahr Gi Si 1929–30*. Buber's response appears in the same volume, pp. 40–3. The English translation is 'China and Us', in Maurice S. Friedman, *Martin Buber, A Believing Humanism, Gleanings*, New York: Simon and Schuster, 1967, pp. 186–90 and in *Pointing the Way – Collected Essays*, New York: Harper, 1957, and New York: Schocken, 1974, pp. 121–25.
24. This according to a communication from Dr. H. Walravens, 21 December 1991.
25. I wish to thank the Leo Baeck Institute, New York, for making these letters available to me. Dr. Walravens has compiled a useful bibliography of Tonn's work, which he kindly made available to me. According to it, the Daoist text referred to in Buber's letter is probably the translation of *Chang qing jing jing*, published in German as 'Das Buch von der ewigen Reinheit und Ruhe', *Weisse Fahne* (December 1929), pp. 212–5. *The Combined Indices to the Authors and Titles of Books in two Collections of Taoist Literature*, Harvard-Yenching Institute Sinological Index Series, no. 25, p. 51, lists various annotated editions from different periods, generally entitled *Taishang Laojun shuo chang qing jing jing zhu* (Explanations of the most high master Lao's sayings on eternal purity and tranquility). The English translation was published in the *China Journal* (September 1939), pp. 112–7. On Chinese Jews, Tonn published, 'Eine jüdische Inschrift der Synagoge in K'aifeng fu aus dem Jahre 1512', *Gemeindeblatt der Jüdischen Gemeinde zu Berlin*, (20 ? 1930), pp. 360–4. Buber expressed an interest in both the translations and in the work on Chinese Jews in two letters to Tonn, dated repectively 7 March 1927 and 31 January 1931.
26. For the bibliography of Tonn's works, see Walravens, 'Martin Buber und Willy Tonn', pp. 475–78.
27. JNUL, Arc. Ms. Var. 350/B45 and 350/B50b. The notes which Buber actually used for his lectures are apparently not in the archive.
28. See above, p. 148.
29. Unfortunately not all of Tonn's letters which discuss these points are dated, and those which are, omit the year. I assume that they were written in 1950, and I count one from 5 July another from 22?, and a third undated. Courtesy of the Leo Baeck Institute, New York.
30. The essay appeared in Martin Buber, *Die Rede, die Lehre und das Lied*. Leipzig: Insel Verlag, 1920, 2nd ed., pp. 35–94; also in *Werke*. Munich: Kosel Velag, 1962, Vol. I, pp. 1021–51. The English translation, 'The Teaching of the Tao', is in Maurice S. Friedman, ed., *Pointing the Way, Collected Essays by Martin Buber*. New York: Schocken Books, 1974, pp. 31–60.
31. Friedman, *Pointing the Way*, p. ix. 'Buber's Foreword' to the 1957 collection.
32. Buber, *Chinese Tales*, p. 103.
33. The above was summarized from Buber, 'Afterword', *Chinese Tales*, pp. 81–103.
34. Ibid., pp. 97–100.
35. Benjamin I. Schwartz, *The World of Thought in Ancient China*. Cambridge: Harvard University Press, 1985, p. 193.
36. Kohn, *Martin Buber*, pp. 59, 67–8, 82–3, 86, 280.
37. Martin Buber, *Die Geschichten des Rabbi Nachman*. Frankfurt/Main: Fischer Bücherei, 1955, pp. 18–9.
38. Buber, 'Foreword', *Chinese Tales*, pp. 111–13.
39. Kohn, *Martin Buber*, pp. 77, 87, 100.
40. Van de Sandt, *Buber's Bildnerische Tätigkeit*, pp. 20–1.
41. The lecture summarized here is reprinted in Martin Buber, *Der Jude und sein Judentum, gesammelte*

Aufsätze und Reden, introduction by Robert Weltsch. Cologne: Joseph Melzer Verlag, 1963, pp. 46–65. It was probably delivered in 1915, and was first printed in *Der Neue Merkur*, 2. No. 3 (June 1915), pp. 353–7.
42. Ibid., p. 53.
43. Kohn, *Martin Buber*, p. 263.
44. JNUL, Arc. Ms. Var. 350/45 a-b. Undated notes on Dao. From the content I surmise that they were made in conjunction with preparing his discussion at the China-Institut.
45. Martin Buber in *Chinesisch-Deutscher Almanach*, pp. 40–3. Typewritten and corrected ms., entitled 'China und Wir', JNUL, Arc. Ms. Var. 350/2-50a. See also Maurice Friedman, *Martin Buber's Life and Work, the Middle Years 1923–1945*. New York: E.P. Dutton, Inc., 1983, Vol. 2, p. 88.
46. The Ascona lectures were privately arranged by a lay group interested in Chinese philosophy. The meetings were held 10–31 August 1924. JNUL, Arc. Ms. Var. 350/627.
47. JNUL, Arc. Ms. Var. 350/45-bet. 'Besprechungen mit Martin Buber in Ascona August 1924 über Lao-tse's Tao-te-king'. The religious questions are recorded in the appendix. See also note 15, above.
48. Adrian Hsia, *Hermann Hesse und China, Darstellungen, Materialien und Interpretationen*. Frankfurt/Main: Suhrkamp, 1974, pp. 99, 270, and Gerhard Adler, ed., *C.G. Jung Letters*. Princeton: Princeton University Press, 1973, Vol. 95, no. 1 in the Bollingen Series. Letter to Max Rychner, 28 February 1932, pp. 88–9.
49. According to Maurice Friedman, *Martin Buber's Life and Work, The Early Years 1878–1923*. New York: E.P. Dutton, 1981, Vol. 1, p. 212, Buber 'imported' the idea of *wuwei* into the second part of *I and Thou*.
50. Van der Sandt, *Martin Buber's bildnerische Tätigkeit*, pp. 24–5, 75–84.
51. Strauss (1809–99) was known as a poet and author. Active in politics for the greater part of his life, he withdrew from public affairs in 1866 to devote himself to writing and study. He apparently had no formal training in Chinese language or Chinese thought. In addition to his translation of the *DDJ* and the *Shi jing*, he also published in 1885 a study entitled *Ancient Chinese Monotheism*.
52. Viktor Friedrich von Strauss und Torney, *Lao-Tse's Tao Te King*. Leipzig: Friedrich Fleischer, 1870, pp. xxvii, xliii.
53. Ibid., pp. xxx–xxxi.
54. Ibid., pp. lx, lxiv–lxv.
55. Ibid., pp. xxxv, xl, xliii. Strauss seems to echo here Protestant arguments raging at the time about whether the Chinese were mono- or polytheists.
56. Ibid., pp. lxxix, lxxx.
57. In a letter to Franz Rosenzweig, dated 24 August 1922, Buber commented on the Chinese *'Gottesverschwiegenheit'* and he asserted that to him Daoists were not pagan. See Grete Schaeder, ed., *Martin Buber Briefwechsel aus sieben Jahrzenten*. Heidelberg: Verlag Lambert Schneider, 1973, Vol. 2, pp. 119–20.
58. Heshang Gong is a problematic figure. He may have lived at the end of the Warring States period, or in the earlier Han dynasty. Yen Lingfeng, *Zhou, Qin, Han, Wei zhizi zhijian shumu*. Taipei: Zhengzhong shuju, 1975, pp. 3–4, assigns his commentary, *Laozi zhangjiu*, to 195 BCE, during Han Wendi's reign. Heshang Gong's work would, therefore, predate Wang Bi's (226–49) commentary. Arianne Rump and Wing-tsit Chan, trans., *Commentary on the Lao Tzu by Wang Bi*. Honolulu: The University Press of Hawaii, 1979, pp. xxiv–xxvii, argue for a post-Wang Bi dating, and assign the commentary to the Wei-Jin period. Strauss did not use Wang Bi's commentary. See also Livia Kohn, *Early Chinese Mysticism, Philosophy and Soteriology in the Taoist Tradition*. Princeton: Princeton University Press, 1992, who writes that the Heshang Gong commentary developed the Daoist mystical tradition from a 'vague philosophy of the Tao', p. 69.
59. In the following I cite from the 'Ascona Talks', JNUL, Arc. Ms. Var. 350/45b. The ms. consists of 42 typewritten pages; pp. 1–35 are the notes to the *DDJ* chapters; pp. 36–42 are on related topics not specifically concerned with Chinese thought.
60. He made a similar point with somewhat different implications in the appendix (p. 33). Life, he stated, is God and men acting together. For belief to be real, the reality of the self must be taken for granted.
61. Strauss, *Tao Te King*, pp. 61–79.
62. Ibid., pp. 65–6, 68.

63. Ibid, p. 276.
64. Buber, 'Laozi al hashilton'.
65. Buber's translation appeared in a popular magazine and was, I believe, only the second translation into Hebrew. An earlier translation of the complete text, probably from Richard Wilhelm's German, is A.Z. Aescoly, trans., *Sefer haderekh ve'orah me'yesharim* (Book of the way and way of honesty), Jerusalem: Reuven Mas, 1937. Buber did not refer to this book anywhere and he may not have known about it.
66. Using a more classical (and by now rather old-fashioned) Hebrew, Buber's text, despite the extensive use of pronouns, which are, of course, not in the Chinese text, strikes one as remarkably authentic. Buber's seven chapters compare very favourably with those in a Hebrew translation by Dan Daor and Yoav Ariel, *Lao Tzu. Sefer ha'dereh ve'hasegula*. Israel: Universities Publications, 1981.
67. JNUL, Arc. Ms. Var. 350/17a. There are course titles, but not descriptions of courses.
68. Buber, 'Sie und Wir', and 'Hebräischer Humanismus', for example, in Weltsch, *Der Jude*, pp. 648–54, 732–44.

Transliteration of Names and Terms

Airen	愛人
An San	俺三
Baihua	白話
Baojia	保家
Baojuan	寶卷
Bendi	本地
Bishu	比疏
Boshi	博士
Bu Wangbian	補網編
Cao mushen	草木神
Chen Dayong	陳大鏞
Chen Gu	陳䩺
Chen Yuan	陳垣
Chen Zhenguang	陳珍廣
Cheng	成
Cheng Shen	成神
Dao	道

Dao De Jing	道德經
Daomei jiahuo	到楣傢伙
Datong shijie	大同世界
Dayuan chu yutian	大原出於天
Dian	殿
Difang	地方
Dingda zhi liqi	頂大之力氣
Dudai	杜代
Emala	俄摩拉
Fa	法
Feizi	榧子
Fenfu	吩咐
Foshen	佛神
Fuhuo	復活
Fujia	父家
Fu Ming	復明
Geli	割禮
Guanhua	官話
Guishen	鬼神
Guo	國

Guoyu	國語
Hao	號
He Shang Gong	河上公
Hu Shi	胡適
Hu Yuzhi	胡愈之
Huang Pinsan	黃品三
Huang Zhuohan	黃倬漢
Hui Tang	會堂
Huntun	混沌
Jia	家
Jian Wuxun	件五旬
Jiao	教
Jiao Zhu	教主
Jiaochong	教眾
Jiaojingjiao	教經教
Jiaoren	教人
Jiaotang	教堂
Jiaoyi	教義
Jiapu	家譜
Jin Xiaojing	金校靜
Jing	經

Jing	敬
Jing Xia	經匣
Junwang	君王
Kaipi	開辟
Kao Zhenzi	考真子
Kewu	恪物
Kexue yu renshang juan	科學與人生觀
Labi	拉比
Lanmao Huihui	籃帽回回
Lao Tianye	老天爺
Leibai	累佰
Libai tang	禮拜堂
Li Rongfang	李榮芳
Lian Yinghuang	連英煌
Liangshi	糧食
Linghun	靈魂
Liyue	立約
Luan	亂
Lunyu	論語
Mao Dun	茅盾
Mao Jie	茅節

Miejue	滅絕
Minzi	民族
Ming	名
Mogui	魔鬼
Nanming	南明
Nianre	年日
Pan Gu	盤沽
Puxi	譜系
Pu Songling	蒲松齡
Qi	氣
Qinxi	秦西
Qinzu	親族
Qipian	七騙
Qixing	秦西
Quan nengde Tianzhu	全能的天主
Rendao zhuyi	人道主義
Rende wenxue	人的文學
Renmin	人民
Rong	容
Ruoxiao minzu	弱小民族
Shang Di	上帝

Shang zhang	膳長
Shang Zhu	上主
Shanghai Tebie Shi Shehui	上海特別市社會
Shen	神
Shen Yanbing	沈雁冰
Shen Zhemin	沈澤民
Shen ming	神命
Shengjing sunhua	聖經訓話
Shengren	聖人
Shifa	師法
Shijing	時經
Shiqian daogao	食前禱告
Shujing	書經
Shushi	術士
Sishu	四書
Shizimu	始祖母
Soujiao	搜剿
Tang xuzhi	湯旭之
Tang Zhen	湯真
Tian Dao	天道
Tian Di	天帝

Tianxia	天下
Tianxin	天心
Tianqi	天氣
Tianxuanzhi min	天選之民
Tian Zhu	天主
Tiao jin jiao	挑筋教
Tula	土拉
Tusha	屠殺
Wanguo gongbao	萬國公報
Wang Jingtao	王警濤
Wang Luyan	王魯彥
Wang Yisha	王一沙
Wanzu	萬族
Wei	微
Weiwuwei	為無為
Weitian ming	畏天命
Wenxue geming	文學革命
Wenxue yanjiu hui	文學研究會
Wenyan	文言
Wujing	五經
Wuwei	無爲

Transliteration of Names and Terms

Xi	希
Xiaoshuo yuebao	小說月報
Xiawa	夏娃
Xi Zhen	夏娃
Xila	細拉
Xin	心
Xin wenzi	新文字
Xin Youtai xiaoshuo ji	新猶太小說記
Xin Qingnian	新青年
Xing	形
Xun	郇
Xueren	雪人
Ya	郇
Yadang	亞當
Yehehua yongsheng Tian Zhu	耶和華永生天主
Yi	義
Yi	夷
Yijing	易經
You	有
Youtai fashi	猶太法師

Youtai guo	猶太國
Youtai jiaohui	猶太教會
Youtai mushi	猶太牧師
Youtairen	猶太人
Yuxin	慾心
Yuwang	玉王
Yue	約
Zan meishi	讚美詩
Zhangjiao	掌教
Zhang Lubei	張露蓓
Zhao Yingcheng	趙映承
Zhao Zhongqian	趙仲謙
Zhi	知
Zhongmin	眾民
Zhouli	周禮
Zhou Zuoren	周作人
Zhu Zai	主宰
Zhu Xi	朱熹
Zhuangzi	莊子
Ziran erran	自然而然
Zu	祖

Transliteration of Names and Terms

Zun	尊
Zushi	祖師

Select Bibliography

Blodget, Henry, *The Use of T'ien Chu for God in Chinese* (Shanghai: American Presbyterian Mission Press, 1893)
Broomhall, Marshall, *The Bible in China* (London: The China Inland Mission, 1934)
Buber, Martin, Alex Page, trans., *Chinese Tales, Zhuangzi: Sayings and Parables and Chinese Ghost and Love Stories* (New Jersey-London: Humanities Press, 1991)
Eber, Irene, *Voices from Afar: Modern Chinese Writers on Oppressed Peoples and their Literature* (Ann Arbor: University of Michigan, 1980)
Eber, Irene, *The Jewish Bishop and the Chinese Bible, Samuel Isaac Joseph Schereschewsky 1831–1906* (Leiden: Brill, 1999)
Eber, I., Wan S.K., Walf K., eds., *Bible in Modern China: The Literary and Intellectual Impact* (Sankt Augustin: Monumenta Serica Institute, 1999)
Gálik, Marián, *Influence, Translation, and Parallels, Selected Studies on the Bible in China* (Sankt Augustin: Monumenta Serica Institute, 2004)
Gao Bolin, *Shengjing yu wenxue yanjiu* (Bible and literature studies) (Commercial Press, 1940)
Goldstein, Jonathan, ed., *The Jews of China, Historical and Comparative Perspectives* (Armonk-London: M.E. Sharpe, 1991 and 2000)
Heppner, Ernest G., *Shanghai Refuge, A Memoir of the World War II Jewish Ghetto* (Lincoln-London: University of Nebraska Press, 1994)
Kranzler, David, *Japanese, Nazis, and Jews, The Jewish Refugee Community of Shanghai, 1937–45* (New York: Yeshiva University Press, 1976)
Legge, James, *The Notion of the Chinese Concerning God and Spirits: With an Examination of the Defence of an Essay, on the Proper Rendering of the Word Elohim and Theos, into the Chinese Language, by William J. Boone, D.D.* (Printed at the 'Hongkong Register' Office, 1832)
Leslie, Donald D., *The Chinese-Hebrew Memorial Book of the Jewish Community of K'aifeng* (Belconnen: Canberra College of Advanced Education, 1984)
Leslie, Donald D., *The Survival of the Chinese Jews, The Jewish Community of K'aifeng* (Leiden: Brill, 1972)

Malek, Roman, ed., *Jews in China, from Kaifeng... to Shanghai* (Sankt Augustin: Monumenta Serica Institute, 2000)

Maynard, Isabelle, *China Dreams, Growing Up Jewish in Tientsin* (Iowa City: University of Iowa Press, 1996)

Meyer, Maisie J., *From the Rivers of Babylon to the Whangpoo – A Century of Sephardi Jewish Life in Shanghai* (New York: University Press of America, 2002)

Muller, James A., *Apostle of China, Samuel Isaac Joseph Schereschewsky, 1831–1906* (New York: Morehouse Publishing Co., 1937)

Pollak, Michael, *Mandarins, Jews, and Missionaries, The Jewish Experience in the Chinese Empire* (Philadelphia: Jewish Publication Society of America, 1980)

Pollak, Michael, *The Torah Scrolls of the Chinese Jews, the History, Significance and Present Whereabouts of the Sifrei Torah of the Defunct Jewish Community of Kaifeng* (Bridwell Library, Southern Methodist University, 1975)

Schereschewsky, Samuel Isaac Joseph, *Jiuyue quanshu* (The Old Testament in the Mandarin colloquial) (American Bible Society at the Press of the A.B.C.F.M., 1875)

Schwarcz, Vera, *Bridge Across Broken Time, Chinese and Jewish Cultural Memory* (Yale University Press, 1998)

Staunton, Sir George Thomas, *An Inquiry into the Proper Mode of Rendering the Word 'God' in Translating the Sacred Scriptures into the Chinese Language* (London: Lionel Booth, 1849)

Wasserstein, Bernard, *Secret War in Shanghai, Treachery, Subversion and Collaboration in the Second World War* (London: Profile Books, 1999)

Zhou Xun, *Chinese Perceptions of the 'Jews' and Judaism, A History of the Youtai* (Richmond: Curzon, 2001)

Index

Abraham, D. E. J. 7
Abronheim, Heinz 54
Agnon, S. Y. 143
　In the Heart of the Sea 143
Ai Tian 25
Almi, A. (pen name for Sheps,
　Elihu–Haiim) xiii
　Di Chinesishe Filozofje un Poesje xiii
Alter, Robert 97, 99
American Joint Distribution Committee
　10, 18
Amichai, Yehuda 144
An San 26
Anschluss 17, 39, 41, 43
Asahi Shimbun 48
Asch, Sholem xi, 128, 129, 132, 136–7
　'God of Vengeance' 132, 136–7
　'Winter' 132, 138, 141
Axenfeld, Israel 127

B

Baller, Frederick W. 103
Barnstone, Willis 76
　The Poetics of Translation 76
Bellow, Saul 143
Berman, Hannah 135
　*Jewish Children From the Yiddish of
　Sholem Aleichem* 135
Birman, Meir 50–2, 54–5, 57–8
Birnboim, M. xii–xiii
Blodget, Henry 71–2, 75, 103
Bolshevik Revolution 3, 8, 13, 163
Boone, Bishop William J. 90
Braun, David 54, 57–8
Bridgman, E. C. 81–2, 94, 97, 101, 102,
　106, 110
Bu Wangbian 114–5

Buber, Martin xii, xvi, 148–65
　I and Thou 158
　Tales of Rabbi Nahman 154
　The Legend of the Baal Shem 154
Buchenwald concentration camp 10, 43
Buddhism xii, 29, 109, 155
Burns, William C. 91

C

Chen Dayong 113
Chen Gu 132
Chen Shouyi, Professor xiv, xv–xvi
Chen Yuan 22
Chen Yuanliang 22
Chen Zhenguang 133
Chiang Kai-shek 16, 18
'China fashion' xii
Chinese Cultural Revolution 131, 143
Chinese literary revolution 124–6
Chinese Recorder, The 73
Chuang Tzu *see* Zhuangzi
Cohen, Siegfried 42
Committee for the Assistance of
　European Jewish Refugees in
　Shanghai (CAEJRS) 47, 52–3
Confucius xii–xiii, 148, 159
　Confucian religion xii, 28, 29, 35, 112,
　158
　Lunyu (Analects) 74, 148, 150, 151
　Shijing (Book of Songs) 74, 116, 150,
　159
　Shujing (Book of Documents) 74, 116,
　159
　Yijing (Book of Changes) 74, 116,
　150
Culbertson, M. S. 81–2, 94, 97, 101, 102,
　106, 110

Index

D

Dachau concentration camp 10, 42
Daoism xii, xvi, 29, 148–165
de Groot, J. J. M. 149
de Wette, Wilhelm M. L. 101, 102
   Commentar über die Psalmen 101, 102
Deman, Grete 42, 59–60
Deman, Wilhelm 42, 59–60
Deutsch, Hugo 55
Deutschkron, Inge 41
Dienesohn, Jacob 128
Domenge, Jean 23, 28–9
Dreyfuss, Alfred 43
Dubsky, Hugo 42

E

Edkins, Joseph 91
Eichmann, Adolf 41, 43, 59
Eight Trigrams Uprising 30
Eisfelder, H. (Peter) 41–2, 43, 59
Évian Conference 41
Evreiskaya Zhizn 13
Ezra, Nissim Ezra Benjamin 7
Fairbank, Professor John 72
Fen Dong *see* Mao Dun
Fleishman, Akiba xii
Foreign Missionary, The 91
Frank, Dr. Herbert 53
Frank, Helena 135
   Yiddish Tales 135
   Stories and Pictures by Isaac Loeb Peretz 135
Frischman, David 127
Frug, Simeon 128, 130

G

Gadegel 13
Gálik, Marián 89, 91, 118
Gao Bolin 97
German–Soviet Pact (1939) 49
Gershevich, Lev I. 15
Gesenius, Wilhelm 101
Giles, Herbert A. 149
Glantz, Aaron *see* Leyless, A.
Goldberg, Isaac 135

'Jewish Life' Anthology, 1946–1956 135
Temptations: a Book of Short Stories by David Pinski 135
Ten Plays by David Pinski 135
Gozani, Jean–Paul 23, 29
Graves, Frederick R. 73
Guguo (The Old Country) 143
Gützlaff, Karl F. A. 101

H

Haas, Heinrich 55
Hagen, Herbert 40–2, 43
Han dynasty 34, 162
Harbin xi, 12–15, 55–6
   Jewish community 12–15, 17, 18, 19
Hardoon family 7, 18
Hardoon, Silas A. 7–8
Hayim, Ellis 48
Heppner, Ernest 44
Heshang Gong 160, 161
Hesse, Herbert 149, 150–1, 158
Heydrich, Reinhard 39, 40, 42–3, 48
Hitler, Adolf 40
Hong Kong 7, 11–12
   Jewish community 11–12, 18
Hongkong and Shanghai Banking Corporation 7
Hongkou xi, 8, 10, 17, 40, 53
Honkew *see* Hongkou
Horal, Phyllis 27
Hu Shi 125, 151
Hu Yuzhi 132–3, 134, 140
Huang Yi 133, 141
Huang Zuohan 133

I

Inuzuka Koreshige, Captain 53
Ishiguro, Consul 53
Israel's Messenger 7

J

Jiang Jieshi *see* Chiang Kai–shek
Jiaohui Xinbao (The Church News) 73
Jin Xiaojing 32
John of Montecorvino, 109

Jung, Carl Gustav 150–1, 158
Jurchen (Jin) dynasty 4, 24

K

Kadoorie family 7
Kadoorie, Sir Elly 12
Kaifeng xi, xiv, 4–6, 19
   Jewish community xiv, 4–6, 19, 22–36, 151, 161
Kameo, Chiba 127
Kangxi dictionary 74, 160
Kann, Eduard 48, 52, 54
Kassel, D. xii–xiii
Kaufman, Dr. Abraham I. 14
King James I 70
Kobrin, Leo 127–8, 130
Kohn, Hans 154
Kristallnacht 10, 39, 41–2, 43, 45, 59, 151

L

Lao Tzu *see* Laozi
Laozi xii, 150, 152, 155, 159–62, 163
   Dao de jing (DDJ) 148, 149–50, 151–2, 153, 156–65
Lardner, Ring 143
Legge, James 74, 148
Lerner, Yosel xiii
   Bajm offenem Fenster xiii
Leslie, Donald D. 22
Levenson, Joseph 131
Levin, Howard (Horst) 42, 52, 60
Levin, Mendel 127
Leyless, A. 128
Li Enshou 26
Li Nianpei 127, 132
Li Yongfang 116
Lian Yinghuang 91, 106
Liang Gong 89, 118
Liang Yunshong 72
Libin 132
   'Picnic' 132, 141
Linetzki, Joel 128
Lischka, Kurt 43, 46
Literary Research Society 125–6
Liu Changxing 112
Lu Xun (pen name for Zhou Shuren) 134

Luo Jialing 7–8
Luther, Martin 70

M

Malamud, Bernard 143
   The Assistant 143
   The Fixer 143
Manchukuo 14, 54, 55–7, 59
Manchuria 8, 13–16, 18, 54
   Japanese invasion 10, 14
Mao Dun (pen name for Sheng Yanping) 125, 127–8, 129–30, 132–3, 134, 140
Mao Zedong 18, 137
Mateer, Calvin W. 103
Mencius xii
Mendele Mocher Sforim (pen name for Abramowitch, Shalom Jacob) 127
Mickiewicz, Adam 126
Mikra'ot Hagedolot (Rabbinical Bible) 101
Milne, William 101, 102
Ming dynasty 4–5
Mongol (Yuan) dynasty 4, 29, 109
Morgenstern, Dr. J. 51
Morrison, Robert 101, 102, 106, 110
Mote, F. W. 30–1
Mozi 148
Mucnik, Salem–Alehem 135
   Perec, Hebraj Rakontoj 135
Müller, Heinrich 39
Municipal Gazette 49

N

Nadir, Moishe 128
Nanming 132–3
Naquin, Susan 30
Nasha Zhizn 9, 16–17
Nazi persecution xiii, xiv, 3, 10, 14, 39–60
Neuman, Dr. J. *see* Neuman, Dr. S.
Neuman, Dr. S. 69
New Testament (N.T.) 67, 68–9, 73, 75, 76, 89, 101
Ningbo 4, 24, 67
   Jewish community 4
Ningxia 4

Jewish community 4
Nobel, Genia 43, 49
Nobel, Günter 43, 49
Nomberg 132
   'Zerach and Bulani' 132
Nomonhan Incident 49, 56–7
Northern Song dynasty 4, 24

O

Old Testament (O.T.) xi, xiv–xv, 67–85, 89, 90, 91, 101–2, 110–18, 129
   Aaron 98
   Abraham 29, 32–3, 34, 35, 77–8, 79–80, 114
   Adam 32–3, 34, 79, 82, 113
   Benjamin 81
   Book of Exodus 111
   Book of Genesis 32–3, 76–85, 113–5, 116
   Book of Joshua 114
   Book of Judges 114, 115
   Book of Kings 115
   Book of Leviticus 115
   Book of Numbers 115
   Book of Samuel 114, 115
   Cain 82, 83
   Esau 78
   Eve 76, 79, 82, 83, 113
   Ezra 33, 94
   Isaac 77–8
   Ismael 78
   Jacob 77–8, 81, 82–3
   Joseph 80–1, 83
   King David 94
   King Josiah 115
   King Nebuchadnezzar 94
   King Solomon 94
   Laban 82–3
   Lamentations 96–7
   Lemech 82
   Lot 114
   Moses 33, 34, 111–2, 115–6
   Nehemiah 94
   Noah 32, 83
   Psalms xv, 89–106, 127
   Rebecca 78
   Reuben 83
   Samson 129
   Songs of Solomon 96–7
   Ten Commandments 111–2
   Tubal–Cain 82
Opium Wars 6
Oz, Amos 144

P

Pacific War 8, 11, 39, 51–2
Pan Gu 32–3
Pearl Harbor 9, 11
Pell, Robert T. 45
Peretz, Isaac Loeb xi, 127, 129, 130, 132, 135, 136–8
   'A Weaver's Love' 132, 137–8, 140, 141
   'Bontshe the Silent' 132
   'Ormuzd and Ahriman' 132, 138
   'Pidjon Shwuim' 132
   'Seven Years of Plenty' 132
   'The Devout Cat' 132, 136
   'The Fast' 132
   'The Messenger' 132
   'What is the Soul?' 132, 140
Petöfi, A. 126
Pinski, David 127, 128, 129, 130, 132, 135, 137, 139
   'Diplomacy' 133, 139, 140
   'Down with the Burden' 132
   'Forgotten Souls' 132, 141
   'In the Storm' 132, 141
   'Poland 1919' 133, 139, 140
   'Rabbi Akiba's Temptation' 132, 140
   'Tale of a Hungry Man' 132, 137
   'The Beautiful Nun' 133, 139
   'The Cripples' 132
Plaks, Andrew 35, 97
Polo, Maffeo 109
Polo, Marco 109
Polo, Niccolo 109
Prickett, Stephen 89
Pu Songling 148, 149–50, 154, 155
   Liao Zhai Zhi yi (Liao Zhai Tales) 148, 149–50, 154, 155, 164

Q

Qin dynasty 75
Qing dynasty 12, 13

R

Rashi 80, 81, 82, 83, 101–2
Ravitch, Meylekh (pen name for Bergner, Zaharia–Chone) xiii
  Kontinentn un Okeanen xiii
Reiss, Isaac *see* Nadir, Moishe
Ricci, Matteo 25
Rosenfield, Morris Jacob 128
  Songs of the Ghetto 128
Rosenmüller, E. F. K. 101
Rosenzweig, Franz 158
Roth, Philip 143
Russo–Japanese War 13

S

Sachsenhausen concentration camp 42
Sanneh, Lamin 70
Sassoon family 6–7
Sassoon, Sir Jacob 7, 12
Schereschewsky, Samuel I. J. xv, 67–85, 89–106, 110
Schereschewsky, Susan 71, 72
Schiffrin, Professor H. Z. xiii–xiv
Schlie, Heinrich 43–4, 59
Schrangenheim, Erich 54
Schwartz, Benjamin 154
Seligsohn, Dr. Julius 44
Shang dynasty 116
Shanghai Municipal Council (SMC) 40, 47–8, 49–50, 51, 52–3, 57, 58, 59
Shanghai xi, 6–11, 14, 15, 17, 39–60, 67, 70, 72, 73, 90, 143, 151
  International Settlement 8, 11, 47, 49, 60
  Jewish community xiv, 6–11, 16, 18, 19
Shen Chemin 132
Shen Yanping *see* Mao Dun
Shi Zhongyu 6, 27, 31
Sholem Aleichem (pen name for Rabinovich, Shalom) xi, 127, 129, 131, 132–3, 134, 135, 136, 138–9, 142, 143
  'A Pity for the Living' 132, 138, 141
  'Bad Luck' 133, 139
  'Eternal Life' 132, 136, 140, 141
  'Gymnazya' 132
  'If I Were Rothschild' 133
  'Joseph' 133
  'Menachem Mendel, Agent' 133
  'Methusela' 133, 139
  'Miracle of Hashana Raba' 133, 139
  'Passover in a Village' 133, 139, 140
  'Poor and Happy' 133, 139
  'Rabchik' 133, 139
  'Song of Songs' 133, 134, 139, 141
  'The Passover Guest' 133, 141
  'The Person from Buenos Aires' 133
  'Three Little Heads' 132, 141
  'Treasure' 132
Shuck, J. Lewis 112
Si Xiansong 72
Silk Road 3–4
Sima Qian 75
Singer, Isaac Bashevis 143
  Enemies, A Love Story 143
  The Manor 143
Sino–Japanese War 8–10, 16, 40, 46–7
Southern Song dynasty 4, 24
Speelman, Michel 47–8, 53
Spitzer, Dr. Franz 51–2
Spitzer, Judith 51–2
Spitzer, Louise 51–2
Spitzer, Michael 51–2
Staunton, George 74
Steinbeck, John 143
Sydenstricker, Absalom 103

T

Tang dynasty 3–4, 109
Tang Xuzhi 132
The Jew's Dance 132
Tianjin xi, 13, 14, 15–16, 18, 71
  Jewish community 13, 15–16, 17, 18–19
Tonn, Willy 151–2
Tsar Nicholas I 69
Twain, Mark 127, 143

V

von Neurath, Constantin Freiherr 45
von Ribbentrop, Joachim 41, 45
von Strauss, Viktor Friedrich 159–63, 165

W

Waiguo wenxue (Foreign Literature) 143
Walsh, Jerome 96
Wang Guowei 8
Wang Heng *see* Wang Luyan
Wang Jingtao 149
Wang Jingwei 54
Wang Luyan 132–3, 140, 142
Wang Yisha 26
Wanguo gongbao (Globe Magazine) 116, 117
Wendroff, Z. 129, 132
  'In the Mountains' 132
Wenwei 133
Werblowsky, R. J. Zwi 24
White Lotus sects 30
White, Bishop 27
White, William Charles 22
Wilhelm, Richard 150–1, 159, 165
Williamson, Alexander 115, 116
Witting, Annie 44
Wright, Arthur 85

X

Xi Zhen *see* Mao Dun
Xia dynasty 114
Xiaoshuo yuebao (Short Story Magazine) 125–6, 129
Xin qingnian (New Youth) 125
Xin Youtai xiaoshuo ji (Collection of Yiddish Fiction) 129
Xu Xin 143–4
Xueren (Snowmen) 129
Yangzhou 4, 16, 24
  Jewish community 4

Y

Yao Keming 54
Yehoshua, A.B. 144
Yin Yan 132
Yitzhaki ben Isaac, Solomon *see* Rashi
Yu Baosheng 91

Z

Zetzsche, Jost 89, 103
Zhang Binglin 8
Zhang Jiezhi 91
Zhang Luobei 133
Zhang Zhenduo 125
Zhao Yingchen 28
Zhao Yingdou 28
Zhao Zhongqian 132
Zhou period 32, 34
Zhou Zuoren 125, 129, 132–3, 134, 140, 141
Zhu Xi 117
Zhuangzi 148, 152, 158, 165
  Zhuang Zi 148, 149, 151, 152, 153, 155, 158, 164–5
Zi Xi 132
Zionism 7, 9, 14, 15, 129, 143, 164